CANADA AFTER THE WAR

STUDIES IN POLITICAL, SOCIAL AND ECONOMIC POLICIES FOR POST-WAR CANADA

The Canadian Institute of International Affairs is an unofficial and non-political body founded in 1928 to promote "an understanding of international questions and problems, particularly in so far as these may relate to Canada and the British Empire, and . . . an understanding of questions and problems which affect the relations of the United Kingdom with any other of His Majesty's Dominions or of these Dominions with one another."

The Institute, as such, is precluded by its constitution from expressing an opinion on any aspect of British Commonwealth relations or of domestic or international affairs. The views expressed in this book are, therefore, purely individual.

CANADA AFTER THE WAR

STUDIES IN POLITICAL, SOCIAL AND ECONOMIC POLICIES FOR POST-WAR CANADA

Edited by

ALEXANDER BRADY
Professor of Political Economy, University of Toronto

and

F. R. SCOTT
Professor of Civil Law, McGill University

Issued under the auspices of
The Canadian Institute of International Affairs

TORONTO
THE MACMILLAN COMPANY
OF CANADA LIMITED
1943

Printed in Canada by
The Hunter-Rose Co. Limited

FOREWORD

The problems which Canada will face in the post-war world are so various, and so liable to change as the war itself continues, that any book attempting to analyse them is likely to impress the reader as much by its omissions as by its positive contributions. This difficulty is increased by the unavoidable delays which now occur between writing and publication, which make it impossible to bring the latest developments under review.[1] The editors are conscious that the present volume somewhat suffers from these weaknesses. It has gaps. There is no study of the problem of monopoly in the post-war world, and of the effect of war upon the growth of Canadian monopolies. There is no analysis of the new developments in the far North, which is so rapidly becoming an area of great strategic and economic importance. The social and technical problems involved in the change over of war industries to peacetime production are scarcely touched upon. Limits of space and inability to find authors at once competent and able to spare time for such studies have prevented their inclusion. Nevertheless, it is hoped that the cardinal features of some of our major post-war problems are here usefully presented, and that from the various chapters will emerge valuable guides to policy. The contributors to this volume have not been

[1]In most cases the chapters were completed early in 1943, but in certain instances the authors were unable, because of the pressure of other work, to bring their facts up to date. In no case, however, is this a matter of much importance.

chosen because of any agreement in social philosophy, but solely because it was considered that they had something significant to say. The book is not planned as an integrated programme, like that which a pressure group or political party might presumably offer. Each article in itself is intended to submit ideas and information to further the discussion of an important issue, and freedom was left to the individual contributor in the development of his subject. A select bibliography provides the reader with a guide to further study.

The editors wish to thank the contributors for their ready collaboration, and to acknowledge a debt to Miss Margaret Avison of the Institute staff who ably assisted in preparing the bibliography and to Mrs. S. N. Ward who saw the whole manuscript through the press.

A.B.
F.R.S.

CONTENTS

Section I

Political and Social Policies

CHAPTER — PAGE

I. National Policy 1
B. S. Keirstead

II. Parliamentary Democracy 31
A. Brady

III. The Constitution and the Post-War World . 60
F. R. Scott

IV. The Reconstruction of the Social Services . . 88
Charlotte Whitton

V. Canada and the World 122
F. H. Soward

Section II

Economic Policies

VI. The Project of Full Employment and Its Implications 161
D. C. MacGregor

VII. Problems of International Economic Reconstruction 199
J. F. Parkinson

VIII. Exchange Control—During and After the War . 234
F. A. Knox

IX. Canadian Agriculture in the Post-War World . 264
W. M. Drummond

X. A Long-Term Policy for Canadian Industry . 297
Francis Hankin

Select Bibliography 325

Index 337

C.I.I.A. Publications 343

LIST OF CONTRIBUTORS

BRADY, ALEXANDER, B.A. Oxon., M.A., Ph.D., F.R.S.C., Professor of Political Economy, University of Toronto.

DRUMMOND, W. M., M.A., Professor of Agricultural Economics, and late Head of that Department, Ontario Agricultural College.

HANKIN, F., Montreal industrialist.

KEIRSTEAD, B. S., B.A. Oxon., Professor of Economics, McGill University.

KNOX, F. A., B.A., Professor of Economics, Queen's University.

MACGREGOR, D. C., B.A., Assistant Professor of Political Economy, University of Toronto.

PARKINSON, J. F., B.Com. Lond., Assistant Professor of Political Economy, University of Toronto.

SCOTT, F. R., B.A. Bishops and Oxon., B.Litt. Oxon., B.C.L., Professor of Civil Law, McGill University.

SOWARD, F. H., B.A., B.Litt. Oxon., Professor of History, University of British Columbia.

WHITTON, CHARLOTTE, M.A., C.B.E., distinguished social worker.

SECTION I

POLITICAL AND SOCIAL POLICIES

Chapter I

NATIONAL POLICY

B. S. Keirstead

The editors of this book have asked me to write a sort of prolegomena to a study of Canadian post-war national policy, special aspects of which are to be considered in later chapters. Of the many questions which might properly be considered in this chapter I have made an arbitrary selection, and have concerned myself primarily with two problems: (a) the way the development of national policy in the past—and present—must limit and influence our decisions as to the future, and (b) the extent to which we may think of unified national policy in the sense of a real community of interest at all. I have here, for reasons indicated in the text, limited discussion to the economic conditions of a national policy. These questions are taken up conjointly rather than consecutively, for the argument as it developed seemed to indicate that they must be answered together.

We are frequently told these days that "after the war" life is going to be different, that Canada is going to be a better place to live in, that there will be security, justice, and plenty. So the Israelites were told during the forty years of strife, hardship, and insecurity in the wilderness, and if they did find an easier and better life in the Promised Land it was partly that in the hard and testing years they set themselves a definite goal and accepted a rigorous code of social and personal ethics. Always, in time of war and crisis, a people hold before themselves the promise of a better life to come, often in terms of material ease, of a "land flowing with milk and honey". But sometimes, realizing that their present ills flow at least in part from their own mistakes, they think rather in terms of greater social wisdom or a higher and more sensitive code of social ethics. However, as the record of human frustration shows, not only are these aspirations never realized fully and perfectly, they are not attained even partially and imperfectly if they are left in the form of vague aspirations and never thought of as the concrete policies which their achievement must require, never given precise definition, never planned in terms of the various social institutions necessary to serve and maintain them. Thus, to hope for social justice after the war is not in itself enough to establish adequate social institutions such as old age pensions and health, hospitalization, and unemployment insurance, or to set up the sort of economic controls necessary to prevent another depression. We are all familiar with the type of social hypocrite who favours "reform", "social justice", "fair play", and so forth, but who invariably finds reasons why he is opposed to unemployment or health insurance or raising the school-leaving age or prohibiting child employment.

Today, in the midst of the disaster which the well-intentioned blunders of ourselves and our fellows in England, France, and America have brought on us, we should be on guard against these reactionaries and their comfortable belief that after the war all is going to be well, if only we will leave the "details" of post-war policy to them. Clearly, if we are not now to take thought for the future we can expect nothing but backsliding to the bad old ways of the inter-war period. As to the claim that thinking of the post-war future slackens the war effort, nothing could be more paltry. People are bound to think of the future. Only the promise of better things to come sustains us in war. If this promise is not to be frustrated and our high hopes disappointed, we must be prepared to discuss now in a realistic manner the modifications of our institutions necessary to fulfil man's aspirations for a "better world".

In what way the social scientist may help to provoke such discussion is a controversial point. Some social scientists, with a natural and proper desire to remain objective and impartial, believe that their rôle is simply to analyse the functioning of our social institutions, to explain how the machinery operates, but not to advance opinions about social goals, and not to try to repair the machinery. They say that they are concerned with means, not with ends. We should hesitate to be impatient with this view, for it has been the traditional defence behind which the social sciences have matured free from the dangers of political advocacy and have built up a solid and significant body of social analysis. But we may well believe that social science can if necessary be used *now*, without losing its impartial and scientific nature. Means cannot be disassociated from ends as these arguments suggest. If we want full employment in a free democratic society, if that is a goal or complex of ends, the very complexity of such ends rules out certain means (such as Hitler used, for instance, to achieve full employment in Germany), and conversely the choice of means determines the nature of the ends. When, for example, we set up a central banking authority in Canada, we did more than establish an institution that would act as a means of credit control; we modified certain of our basic social principles, notably the tradition of "rugged individualism". So today scientific analysis, while it ought not to advocate *political opinions*, can throw much light on our current social aspirations and show us what freedom of choice we have to elect certain social ends—for you cannot plan a new society adequately unless your plans take into account the country's tradition, its geography, and the existing economic and social institutions. Again, it can show us what means are implicit in our social ends, how far they are practicable and mutually compatible, and what institutional changes are required to attain them. As I understand it, the purpose of this book is to discuss in that provocative but still objective manner some of the institutional problems involved in the post-war social aspirations of Canadians. In this first chapter we have the task of asking in a more general way what those aspirations appear to be, how they may be defined in specific political and economic terms, and what light is thrown on them by our past experience.

It is probably fair to say that all Canadians want peace and security: peace both in the sense of absence of war and also in the sense of good relations with their fellows; security from foreign attack and security also as individuals in their employment and in the daily pursuits of their lives. The problem of peace abroad—security from attack—is foreign to the discussion of this chapter. The question of security in domestic life is thus the chief concern of the present writer. To most Canadians this security means primarily, regular employment at good wages, but it means more than this. Security, so used, is a negative term; it belongs to the defensive Maginot-line phase of social thought. We wish to be free of the anxieties—and realities—of unemployment, inadequate wages, poor living conditions. There is, however, a positive or offensive significance. We want to be free of those evils so as to achieve in our individual and social lives certain positive values. These will not be the same for all of us, but there are certain of them we share.

Out of our community life we want on the one hand the sense that the community protects, fosters, and guarantees our right and our security to live our individual lives to the fullest, and on the other hand we want the sense of sharing in and contributing to the social functioning of the community as a group, of helping to achieve those social objectives which we share, which are group interests, so that we feel both that the group supports, protects, and enriches us as individuals and that we in our turn also sustain and maintain the group with which we identify ourselves and in whose proper functioning we participate. It is this complex of feeling ourselves a part of a group in whose sum of welfare we share and of contributing to a common effort which in turn furthers our interests as individuals, that we mean by the phrase "community of interest". Now, a community of interest ought not to look to purely material things. Common interest cannot be defined, as some economists have tried to define it, as a standard of living. The Québecois, for example, thinks of community of interest in terms of his own culture, language, and religion. He insists that no national policy can be conceived as embodying his interest if it does not guarantee cultural autonomy to his people. At the same time common language, common culture, or a sympathy of cultures—if one may coin the phrase—are not enough to give a common national interest if there is a division of economic interest. If economic policies are being pursued, for example, which enrich one region or one class or one industrial group to the impoverishment of others, no community of interest can emerge. Thus, though the economic concept does not exhaust the notion of community of interest, a common sharing of material welfare is one condition of national purpose, just as economic security in employment at good wages is one condition of a full and happy individual life. Hence, in what follows, we must betray a preoccupation with the economic conditions of community of interest and with the economic limitations on a true harmony of national interest in Canada.

Canada became a nation at a time when it was generally held that the unfettered pursuit by enlightened businessmen of their own self-interest would make for the attainment of the highest general good. Each businessman, pursuing his own interest would have to make the most efficient possible use of the productive resources at his disposal. Competition in the products market would lead to maintaining quality and keeping cost to a minimum, and competition by employers for labour and capital would give to the agents of production a reward commensurate with their contributions to the national income. The national interest was the harmony, a beneficent provision of

Providence it almost seemed, that emerged from this relentless but enlightened pursuit of private advantage. Confederation, in Canada, enshrined this principle, though with a difference. It was true that Confederation was based on the appreciation of the potentialities of the Canadian West which were expected to develop following the westward extension of the American frontier. Confederation was further expected to offer, both in the Maritimes and in Quebec and Ontario, a sound basis for a rich and profitable manufacturing industry,[1] but the Conservative Party was quick to see the need for a modification of the *laissez-faire* thesis in the direction of protection against imports and a developmental rather than a "neutral" fiscal policy. Canada, the two provinces, that is, before Confederation, had already achieved under Galt some measure of protection for manufacturing industry, and it was conceived that the raw produce of the West would pay for capital imports incurred in railway development. If these two items balanced or nearly balanced the foreign trade sheet, Canada could afford to protect her own manufactures against English and American competition. The National Policy of 1879 was a conscious formulation of this philosophy and the speeches of that session of the House show clearly how confident the representatives both of the Maritimes and of Ontario

[1]This is not meant to stand as a purely economic interpretation of the move to union. In the Maritimes there were from the first sceptics of the material advantages that would accrue to the smaller provinces, and the argument that weighed was the need of union for defence, an argument that the American Civil War and the Fenian raids had underlined. In Quebec, Confederation was seen as a move towards French autonomy. But the concept of an east-west trade with railway development, the notion of a growing market, was one that had greatest appeal to far-sighted manufacturers.

were, that the new policy was to the advantage of all the regions as of all the classes of Canadians.

As to the adequacy of the philosophy of Confederation and the new national policy we cannot here speak. It clearly did not disappoint its proponents of the manufacturing classes in Ontario and Montreal; it did create a great manufacturing industry that has proven its value in two wars; it did lead to a development of communications and the opening of the western provinces; it made of the British North American colonies a single state with something gradually approaching a national consciousness and a sense of unity. Like many social ideas it played a unifying part in its day. But its day was a limited one. Very early in post-Confederation history came disappointment and disillusion which served to lend support to the groups in Quebec and the Maritimes who had opposed Confederation from the first. In the Maritimes, technical developments from the days of the disappearance of the wooden ships through the period of capitalistic integration and concentration worked to the disadvantage of the small manufacturers, and there was a tendency to find political reasons for this and to seek for a scapegoat in the form of the "Upper Canadian" politicians who had forced Confederation on the Maritime provinces. This movement was largely one of the small-scale entrepreneurs feeling the pressure of the technical trend, who asked to be bought off by increased subsidies in the form of either direct payment to the provincial governments or special concessions to the Maritime ports and special freight rates. But, in the later periods when special depressions brought on by the natural movements of the world economy and by the special circumstances surrounding the too-often uneconomic exploitation of resources began to hit the Maritime workers of the lumber camps and the fisheries and coal mines, their attention tended to focus on the regional rather than the economic and social divisions in the Canadian community. In Quebec, Confederation had won support chiefly because it seemed to offer what, for religious and racial reasons, was generally desired—a greater autonomy than was enjoyed under the 1841 union. The drive towards closer national union which the Conservative fathers of the National Policy naturally desired, brought disappointment. Accordingly, Quebec manifested growing and steady resistance towards increasing the central authority at Ottawa, a resistance which stood in the way of the realization of the sort of national union which was required for the successful development of the modern capitalist state. Montreal Island gained in strength and wealth from the new capitalism and the opening of the West, but rural Quebec with its unique sense of identity, was not interested in migration, in railway development, the opening of the West, or national expansion. These were meaningless phrases to the *habitant*. Moreover, the integration of industry to which we have already referred meant that the new large-scale industrial economy was concentrated under English control. Though much of it centred in Montreal it was a foreign development to the French and they were excluded from it. The small-town French-Canadian entrepreneur remained the typical small-scale competing entrepreneur of the classical tradition, and he had to watch the encroachments of the trusts which either damaged him directly if they competed with him, or indirectly in the sense that they accumulated to themselves the most profitable enterprises and the great weight of economic and political power. Thus the chief focus of a national community of interest, the common economic advantage, was, so to speak, shut out of the Quebec range of vision, and so failed to bring into the balance against racial and religious division any compensating force. The western provinces themselves soon felt that the national policy was conceived for the East—as it was—and that the tariff weighed heavily against them, while bringing them no advantages. They disregarded the railway development which was the condition of their community existence, and saw themselves as the party which was exploited to pay for the advantages that eastern Canada was gaining. Inasmuch as they were socially and economically much more a homogeneous group, the protest of the West gave birth to the first radical opposition which really challenged the fundamental faith of Confederation.

Though criticism and opposition thus made an early appearance the interesting thing is that the national policy was never seriously challenged politically. Liberals as well as Conservatives pursued much the same ends; their fundamental faith was essentially the same faith. Protests from West and East never reached proportions that could not be met by increased subsidies, small tariff changes on individual articles, revised railway freight rates. Until the First World War, in spite of the great development of the Canadian economy and the revolutionary changes in her position abroad, particularly *vis-à-vis* England, there was no significant change in the economic policy or in the philosophy or social tradition which was supposed to justify and sustain it. Yet even by 1914 the system was revealing that it had outworn its time. Technical changes in industry which make for decreasing costs result in unstable competition, the formation of larger productive units, the disappearance of the small firm, and the concentration of industry and of ownership. This process, which some writers have called "trustification", has profound results. It leads in the first place to geographic concentrations as well as ownership concentration, and this results in the destruction of the smaller and outlying communities dependent on small industries. Thus, while in all Canada between 1871 and 1931 the number of manufacturing firms decreased by about 45 per cent. and output increased by about 1,000 per cent., in Nova Scotia the decline in the number of firms was more than 80 per cent. and the increase in output only some 300 per cent. That meant the technical trend concentrated industry elsewhere than in Nova Scotia, and that relatively speaking manufacturing declined there. In the second place, the instability of competition and the appearance of the trust gave the businessman an interest which was definitely contrary to that of the community as a whole. Whatever may be said of the *mores* of competitive enterprise of the *laissez-faire* tradition, it was true that price competition led to the maximization of output—the effort to achieve the greatest possible total production consistent with normal profits and all costs of production. But when competition breaks down and a monopolist or near-monopolist is left controlling the market it is to his interest to restrict production to the maximum profit point, a point that is reached far short of the point of competitive equilibrium. Monopolistic restriction without reducing social costs does reduce the national income and thus works contrary to the first requirement of a high level of material welfare. At the same time, and in the third place, it redistributes the national income in favour of the fewer and fewer controlling families and to the detriment of the masses. Thus in still another way it militates against the realization of the maximization of material welfare, introduces a conflict of interest, and prevents a national harmony of purpose. It is true that the technical process which sets in motion this institutional development is a beneficial one, but through the institutions of unrestricted domestic *laissez-faire*, particularly when that is qualified by protection against foreign competition, it distributes those benefits so unevenly that it fails to win, as under different institutions it ought to win, a common interest and a sense of mutual progress.

The First World War and its aftermath, with Quebec sullen from the mishandling of conscription, shook Canadian faith in the accepted tenets of national policy, but it led to cynicism and indifference rather than reforming and revolutionary zeal. Soldiers were put on the land with some capital but no sustaining subsidies and little experience and supervision, and post-war recovery and the re-adaptation of industry were left to private initiative. There was an unhealthy boom paralleling that of the United States in certain industries, while others even in the boom period were left crippled and permanently depressed. While pulp and paper, automobiles, light metals, and electrical power boomed, coal, lumber, shipbuilding, and heavy steel slumped cruelly. The boom was in those industries which were able to find new demands, to make rapid technical progress, and to establish price agreements. Some of the older established industries, frequently though not always highly competitive, which had over-expanded during the war, never enjoyed the boom at all. The very nature of the industrial expansion, making the Canadian economy increasingly tributary to the United States and leaving Canada as ever in reliance on a few export staples, prepared the way for the peculiar severity of the depression when it came. Small-scale, already depressed, marginal industries in the Maritimes, over-capitalized, trustified, price-rigging industries like pulp and paper, industries like wheat, depending on a high demand abroad, all suffered, if not to the same degree, from the great trade recession. Canadian fiscal tradition, with ten non-co-operative authorities, was unprepared to attempt anything but the most timid and inadequate measures. Because of divided constitutional authority Canada lacked even those ameliorative devices of social insurance which in most western countries robbed widespread unemployment of its most terrible physical effects. This latter consideration seemed to block our vision of the need for more positive action to control the economy, so that in Canada the depression led not to a "New Deal" challenge to the accepted *laissez-faire* social philosophy but rather to a nineteenth-century humanitarian demand for unemployment insurance and other social legislation which would, so to speak, leave the economic system untouched but would cushion the impact of depression on the working class. When Mr. Bennett's social legislation was held by the Judicial Committee of the Privy Council to be *ultra vires*, the incoming Liberal administration determined to examine the whole question of the fiscal competence of, and the division of authority between, the Dominion and the provinces. To this purpose it named a Royal Commission whose Report, returned at the very outbreak of war, has been the subject of wide discussion and, important as it is, has crowded out of the public attention the perhaps equally important Report of the Royal Commission on Price Spreads which appeared five years earlier.

The Report of the Rowell-Sirois Commission was naturally concerned chiefly with the problem which had led to its creation, that is, the fiscal inability of the provinces to maintain the services demanded of them, particularly the relief services made necessary by the depression. It was thus indirectly concerned also with the problem of economic depression and economic controls. Its recommendations try to compromise between regional and cultural demands for autonomy and the need for central national economic controls. Thus it recommends that fiscal power, control over public borrowing, be concentrated along with the central monetary authority in the national administration, but it would otherwise maintain the powers of the provinces, bolstering them, even, by subsidization on an increased scale so as to level out regional differences in standards. The writers of the Report seemed to see the chief divisions of economic interest in Canada as regional and to have attempted to outline a policy for a common interest almost purely in terms of overcoming the regional rivalries and the uneven sharing of welfare among the regions. With this approach the Royal

Commission accomplished much. It is true that our Canadian provinces have different levels of welfare, that they have progressed unevenly, that they do not have equality in natural resources and hence have benefited most unevenly from the national development. It is also true that some of our regions like the prairies, Quebec, and the Maritimes are distinct cultural groups—Quebec has an independent culture—and naturally these areas look on any accretion of powers by the Dominion with jealousy and suspicion. They fear that their interests as special groups will suffer, though they are not sure just how. But they presumably imagine that both in economic and cultural affairs they will be sacrificed to the larger group. Quebec people fear that economic policy will be directed towards the enrichment of the "English" in Ontario and that the impoverishment of rural Quebec will be accomplished. They fear further—and more acutely—the corruption of the rural Quebec community, the migration of rural labour to the towns, the decadence of village and family life, the decline of the influence of the Church and the gradual assimilation of the distinctly French-Canadian culture by Anglo-American urbanism. Now, the Commissioners recognized these fears and attempted to allay them, maintaining, in their recommendations, provincial autonomy and control over education, welfare, and justice, providing, too, for a greater equality of welfare throughout the Dominion. But the provincial rivalries are such that this very force to which the Report pays such respect was its undoing. For the richer and stronger provinces, notably Ontario and British Columbia, were not prepared to make the sacrifice envisaged by the

Report. They did not see why they should share with provinces they may have regarded as both less provident and less aggressive, the wealth which nature and the industry and trained intelligence of their people enabled them to enjoy. The way to a sense of national interest does not lie through efforts to achieve a common defence against the worst evils of depression and to protect all Canadians in some common minimum standards of living. Such policy is defensive only. It fails to unite all citizens in any positive common undertaking. It is not sound economically, because it fixes attention (a) on regional divisions which are largely physical and natural, not institutional, and (b) on purely remedial action, not to make the economy work better, but to prevent people being too badly hurt when it does not work well. It is not sound politically because it tries to win the acceptance of all Canadians by appealing to the stronger regions on the grounds that they should help the weaker ones and to the weaker ones on the grounds that they may retain the right to misgovern and under-educate themselves all they wish, and still be assured of aid from their more progressive fellow-citizens. Thus, politically, the Report met with opposition, particularly in Ontario, and it failed to present to Canadians a sense of unifying purpose in common achievement.[2]

[2]This is harsh treatment of a really great document. The Report of the Rowell-Sirois Commission was a scholarly and comprehensive achievement, which has tremendously influenced Canadian thinking. It was unfortunate in its publication at a time when the evolution of Canadian life and the development of the economic problem were suddenly hurled forward, so to speak, by war. It is easy now to see in the Canadian scene developments and problems which at the time the historical process had scarcely made apparent.

The Report of the Commission on Price Spreads of 1935, a sort of nine days' wonder which precipitated a first-class cabinet crisis and was the subject of some purely temporary and sensational publicity, seemed to attract much less permanent and thoughtful public attention. Yet in some ways it was a more significant document, probing more profoundly the real causes of our social discontents, our maladjustments, and our lack of a sense of national interest and community of purpose. This Report showed the extent of monopolistic practices in the Canadian economy and described some of the institutional devices of monopolistic control.

We must provide here, in a short digression, against misunderstanding on two heads. In the first place, we do not mean to urge that there are no regional problems in Canada, that the only real division of interest is that of economic class against economic class. Of course there are regional problems. But the regional problems are of three sorts. They arise from (a) cultural differences, (b) inequality of natural resources and (c) industrial specialization in certain regions, e.g., wheat in the prairies. The cultural differences need lead to no real national discord if there is both a real mutual tolerance for different ways of thought and religion and also no coincidence of economic exploitation of a cultural group. Thus, Quebec cannot maintain its cultural values intact by attempting to maintain a separate economy and distinct political entity, for the provincial area is inadequate for proper economic controls and the Quebec economy would continue to reflect the exploitation and instability of the national economy. Even if Quebec were an independent state the process of exploitation of the French worker, the gradual denudation of the country-side, the gradual undermining of the small-town, small-scale French-Canadian entrepreneur would continue with the consequent corruption of French-Canadian culture. The only salvation for Quebec as a cultural entity, we hope to show, must be in a common effort with all Canadians to resolve economic conflict and establish economic stability on a national scale.

Inequality of natural resources is, if you will, unfortunate; but it is something, unlike economic institutions, that we have to accept. It is no good complaining about it, making it the focus of attention of our political thinking, and making the worst of it by subsidizing the uneconomic use of sub-marginal resources. Much better, surely, to accept the economist's view that the mobile factors of labour and capital be moved, by state-aided schemes if necessary, to work on those resources which will yield more profitable returns.

Industrial specialization makes for a healthy economy and the maximization of income. Unhappily, in Canada there has been in all probability over-specialization in certain regions and those regions may have a legitimate claim for special consideration *as regions*, but only for temporary sustenance while they adjust themselves to the actual requirements of the market.

The other misunderstanding is one to which we alluded earlier. National consciousness, unity of purpose, community of interest, are states of being, not economic policies, and of course are not to be attained by economic action. We shall attain them, if at all, with the growth of a national tradition and culture or complex of cultures, by doing things together, entering one with another into the fruits of our common efforts. But the condition which will permit this national unity is a real or actual sharing of welfare, a real community of economic interest, real in the sense that out of common effort and economic progress we all share in the benefits; out of our economic policies, our conscious, directed development of natural resources, our technical progress, we all enjoy material gains, are enabled to live fuller lives as individuals and to discern more clearly the way in which these goods have flowed from the common pool. Hence the analysis of the following paragraphs is primarily economic, not because the possession of material wealth constitutes individual or national well-being, but because no people can become a nation if divided in groups conflicting with and exploiting one another in the economic field.

Canadian experience of the development of modern industry is by no means unique. The capitalist system of production has led to a concentration which has injured small manufacturers everywhere. The concentration of industry which adversely affected the Maritime provinces similarly affected Maine, New Hampshire, and Vermont, and the small manufacturers of Ontario. The effects of the technical process have sometimes been interpreted as regional, but the cause lies in the nature of the capitalist system and its technical development. Similarly the resultant trustification of the economy has led to a division of interest between the monopolistic producer and the consumer, and the processor and prime producer. Whereas under a system of free competition business tends to put on the market the fullest output that will enable enterprisers to cover their costs, in a monopolistic market the enterpriser maximizes his profits by restricting production and raising price. The interest of the consumer and of the producer conflict and policy directed towards the protection of the producer and towards greater price stability, as, for example, the newsprint policies of the Quebec and Ontario Governments in 1929-35, are in the interest of only a section—and a very small section—of the national community. The advantages of technical progress are unevenly distributed, and the social gain from the development of industrial science is less than it might be.

Again, the trustification of the economy and the disappearance of the moving frontier has intensified the conflict between labour and ownership. There is no doubt that what is called a monopsonist buyer—for example, a big trust—is able to buy labour at terms that are exploitative in the sense of being less than the labour is worth to the firm. The only possible protection for labour against this type of exploitation is trade-union organization, and even that is an inadequate protection. Moreover, whereas skilled labour is able through higher wages to get its share of a technological advance, unskilled labour is unlikely to receive any appreciable share of the benefits. There is thus a conflict of interest as between labour and management and between one class of labour and another.

Finally the economic system is subject to the movements of the business cycle. No doubt all classes of society regard the depression period of the cycle as an unmixed evil and all would regard themselves as having a common interest in having the cycle controlled. But all have not the same sort of interest in control. Whereas the worker has everything to lose from the depression—livelihood, skill, morale, independence, health, and hope for the future—the entrepreneur is less seriously affected. But the worker bears little if any of the cost of cycle control schemes, whereas these require of the businessman the sacrifice of some of his freedom of action and perhaps of his rate of profit. Though he would welcome the elimination of the cycle he may not always be willing to pay the cost of adequate control schemes. We must conclude, then, that our present economic institutions are such as to preclude the possibility of any harmony of interest in the nation as a whole. The notion of a common national interest, and thus the notion of national policy conceived for the benefit of the great mass of Canadians will require structural changes in our economic institutions. These changes are essential before we can begin to talk of a "national" policy after the war, essential for security either of our individual lives, of our regional cultures or of our nationhood.

Some such changes are now taking place in the very midst of the war itself. We should realize that these changes will set the limits of our freedom of choice and determine the shape of the economic and political problem we shall have to face when the war is over. We may say, in brief, that the wartime changes are (1) an accentuation of the trustification of the economy through the increasing concentration and integration of industry and the growth of the international unions, (2) the acceptance of government control over private industry by monetary and fiscal means and by direct intervention, (3) a shift in the balance of the economy as between extractive and manufacturing industry in favour of the latter, and (4) a change from a debtor to a creditor status in the balance of our foreign indebtedness *vis-à-vis* our chief overseas market, Great Britain. Social modifications do not come abruptly, new institutions cannot be built up *de novo* without relation to the previous institutional structure, and men are only capable of reacting to new situations and problems within the framework of their accepted ways of knowing and through established and understood social institutions. Thus the limits of free social choice are set by the operative dynamic economic forces and the pattern of established interpretation. The wartime economic and social developments which are now in process are determining the general course of the stream of social history for the next generation; our established tradition of institutions are determining how we react to the process of change; and, to maintain the metaphor, what we have freely to decide is the manner in which we shall use and modify our established institutions to make the stream in its new course serve our people and their needs. We cannot reverse the trend towards the larger productive unit nor the trend towards the union of governmental agency and trustified business management. We cannot reverse the trend towards labour organization and employers' associations; we cannot now change back without enormous dislocation and capital loss the structure of our economy to a balance of extractive over processing industry, nor can we alter the fact that our chief market is become a debtor rather than a creditor country, a country, that is, which will be unable to buy from us in accustomed quantities unless we alter the barter terms of trade in her favour. We must equally accept the determination of our people to share more equably the material goods our productive system is capable of producing, their desire for stability, security in employment, their anger and dismay at the thought that after the war restrictions of output and under employment should be our continuing lot.

We must try to approach these questions now a little more closely, try to restate them in more concrete form. A truly national policy in Canada can be successfully pursued only if these questions can be given concrete form and the possible answers to them set out precisely and simply so that the politically practicable courses are clear to the Canadian people who ultimately will have to adopt them.

The national interest as such can only be served, we have argued, by an economy that unites the interest of producers and consumers and the interests of labour and capital. This implies that the system of privately owned and freely operating trusts must be modified and brought under social control. The objectives of this control are to eliminate the familiar cycle movements and the artificial restriction of output which reduces the level of real income so as to create exceptional profits. Two groups of practical questions at once emerge. The first has to do with the political machinery of control. What agencies are to regulate industry? What are to be the relations between control boards and political authority? How are we to maintain popular sovereignty and at the same time achieve a business-like management free from petty political interferences? The second group of questions has to do with the principles of control. How is economic control to be exercised? Do we wish to go the whole way and set up public corporations, state-owned and managed? Do we wish to leave ownership and operation in private hands on a lease system with the basic capital owned by the state and leased to private operators on terms which leave a veto type of control in public hands? Do we wish to rely largely on anti-trust legislation and attempt to achieve something like the *laissez-faire* ideal of "perfect competition"? Do we wish to rely principally on fiscal and monetary methods of indirect control? Do we want to work out a system of corporate controls whereby each industry with a delegated sovereignty makes rules for itself governing fair practices and fair prices?

Then, on contemplation of our federal institutions, further questions appear. Are we prepared to make suitable transfers of authority to the Dominion Government to enable it to effect adequate control? Are we prepared to accept the necessary limitations of provincial authority? If this centralization comes about are the richer provinces prepared to pay the price of socially managed and financed population transfers? Are they prepared to subsidize the welfare and educational services of the poorer provinces, to maintain a national minimum standard of welfare? Are the poorer provinces willing to see population and capital centred on the most productive resources, regardless of their provincial interests? Finally, with respect to our trading position, are we ready to accept the proposition that a control policy within Canada will not work, cannot achieve full employment, without probably revolutionary changes in our economic relations with other states? Are we prepared to accept capital losses in certain manufacturing industries which have capacity in excess of the domestic market and which cannot sell abroad if we are to export foods and minerals to Britain and to receive British manufactured produce in payment? Are we prepared to assist the mobility of our productive factors and reduce tariffs? If we cannot make satisfactory decisions on these matters we shall find our aspirations for a better economic and social order are inconsistent with the hard drive of events.

It is not the business of the social scientist to answer these questions. All he can do is make clear some of the implications of possible answers to the questions. But they must be answered by the people of Canada, and in this connection one general proposition of some importance may be stated as a truism. No one can escape the responsibility of making a decision on these problems. A negative attitude—"I don't know enough about it; let someone else worry", is a positive answer, a decision in favour of going on as we have been; it is a definite, positive vote in favour of the unregulated trust, the unconfined swings of the business cycle, depression, unemployment, waste and want, division of interest, class conflict, and regional strife, a divided, frustrated, unhappy nation. No man can say positively what method of control is best, but one can say positively that a refusal to try to think out the issues involved and to take a decision is the act of an unworthy citizen.

It is clear that if we believe that corporations should govern themselves, should have a certain limited sovereignty devolved upon them, we must then accept the implication that the machinery of control shall be a board of nominees from the industry itself, with its authority in relation to government defined by the terms of association. This would be to concentrate economic and political power in the hands of a few interested persons, that is, persons with certain special interests of their own as distinct from the interests of Canada as a whole. This is the economic pattern of the Fascist state, and however humane and Christian the philosophy with which it may be dressed up, however good the men who undertake to wield this concentration of power, the brutal historical fact remains that such a concentration of power would rapidly rot away the basis of parliamentary power and thus would threaten our political democracy. It should be observed that wartime controls have frequently been of this nature and that, in consequence, if this type of control is not wanted, public opinion must be alert to see that under the disguise of social control a system is not developed in which industry will come to control the state, not the state industry.

If we decide we do not want to run the risks of great changes in the machinery of government involved in setting up direct controls we might choose a combination of fiscal and monetary indirect control, supplemented by long-term public works schemes—a policy suggested by the Swedish and Keynesian economics. We have here the advantage of working by indirection, of not attempting revolutionary changes in the institution of private property and the corporation as the unit of enterprise. But though this type of control might succeed in reducing the fluctuations of the cycle it is unlikely to change the fundamental conflict of interest between monopolist and consumer. It might be possible to devise a scheme of monopolistic taxation which would force the monopolistic firm to produce to the point of minimum or "normal" profit, but such a tax scheme is difficult and complicated in formula and it assumes an easy yielding on the part of big corporations of their present possession of great political influence. Nevertheless, in spite of grave objections on the grounds of complications and imperfections, this policy has the merits of requiring no great expansion of bureaucratic power, and of raising no difficult questions of changes in the machinery of government.

Outright ownership of decreasing cost industries, industries in which monopoly has developed or will develop, has the merit of great simplicity with an objective test or criterion for socialization. It would clearly give all the required control authority to the state. It would give the condition of industrial policy without conflict of interest. It is naturally attractive to many minds. Probably on economic grounds it has most to commend it, though there are grave problems to be worked out if capital is to be properly allocated between industries in the absence of a "free" capital market. These problems are probably not insoluble; in a sense the private capitalist state has worked out a technique in connection with that sector of the economy already dominated by public investment in roads, other public works, and defensive armaments. But the more the public sector is enlarged the more difficult the problem becomes. Proponents of outright nationalization must also bear in mind the possible complications from the political side. The state corporations must be run efficiently from the outset or a successful reaction will occur. To be run efficiently they must be separated from political interference, in the sense of being freed from political patronage and consequent inefficiency. Yet we cannot risk setting up an independent economic bureaucracy, a rival sovereign to parliament. We must be clear that adequate machinery of control exists so that ultimate authority for the broad lines of policy continues to rest with the people through their elected representatives, while technical decisions and the details of policy are determined by the technical experts without amateurish and often interested interference from the "local member".

The "lease" scheme as advocated by Mr. N. E. H. Davenport[3] has two merits. It gets around the question of the machinery of control very neatly: it could be adapted, by the terms of the lease, so as to leave the monopolist no motive to restrict production. Moreover, it would grow fairly naturally in Canada out of the lease system already operative in certain of the war industries, and familiar also in industrial use of certain timber and coal resources. I cannot see that by itself, however, it offers or attempts to offer any method of business cycle control. Advocates of a return to competition and competitive equilibrium by means of anti-trust legislation cannot be taken seriously. You cannot legislate a natural process out of existence. You might as well legislate against gravitation. You can control gravitation, but that is by understanding the physical laws and principles of which it is one. You can control monopoly by some of the means we have discussed. You cannot abolish it by decree.

Others will discuss our federal problems. Here it is

[3]N. E. H. Davenport, *Vested Interest or Common Pool?* (London, 1942).

only important to indicate the truth that in a federal community we cannot develop a national policy in the national interest without necessarily (because it is based on the economic principle of maximizing income by the most economic use of resources) requiring a lower level of welfare in some of the poorer regions than in the nation as a whole; we cannot get such a programme accepted if we are not prepared to pay out of the increased social income some equalization grant to the poorer communities who make sacrifices in the interest of the whole. Federalism requires the recognition of the principle that national interest cannot be won by pauperizing the less fortunate regions. Yet this protection of the poorer regions cannot come or ought not to come by an industrial policy which puts regional interest and a dead level of industrial activity throughout the country ahead of economic principles of comparative advantage and the most economic use of the factors.

A unity of interest in Canada should be achieved by our post-war policy. This unity of interest can be attained only by an economic policy directed towards the maximization of income and to a certain extent its redistribution so as to give all a common interest in production. In turn, this requires controls aimed at eliminating the business cycle and monopolistic exploitation of consumer and worker. Internal controls can be successful only if our external trading position is rendered consistent with domestic policy. Federalism also requires a deliberate correction of those disadvantages suffered by certain regions in the interest of national economic progress. Various control schemes are possible, but they carry important political and social implications. Canadians, who must ultimately decide, should be sure that control of one sort or another is inevitable. The important thing is to decide what method is the wisest, the most free of complication and contradiction; what would bring the greatest harmony of interest, most honestly establish a common sharing of welfare, a true national community; what would give us the nearest approximation of that vision of a democratic society which today sustains men in the midst of war.

Chapter II

PARLIAMENTARY DEMOCRACY

A. Brady

The institutional issues of Canadian democracy after the war will not be new; they will be very old issues intensively sharpened by new circumstances, concerned with the central problem of parliamentary government since its beginning: how to make the holders of power responsible to the people and how best to further harmoniously within the state the interests of its principal social groups.

Obvious and significant among the new circumstances will be the multiplied tasks to which government has been committed by the harsh facts of war and by the social exigencies of the transition from war to peace. During years of struggle, the Canadian economy has been mobilized by the national government in a manner with no precedent in the country's history. Large and fresh battalions of officials supervise every sector of the economic front; new departments are organized for the same purpose; public corporations, partially free from immediate parliamentary control, direct the volume of new products; the administrative discretion granted to officials overshadows in amplitude anything in the previous records of Canada; in brief, a massive totalitarian regime for prosecuting the war exists, and the primary political problem of reconstruction will be the adjustment or transformation of this totalitarianism into an order capable of serving the ends of a democratic society at peace. The assumption underlying this remark and the subsequent analysis is that Canada will desire to retain its democratic institutions, living by the competition of individual and group opinions which is the core of democracy.

What kind of peaceful order may be expected? Its character will be determined by the social and economic developments which have gone before, by general world forces at the time, for Canada will respond quickly to such forces, and by the subtle yet drastic influence of the struggle upon the attitudes of mind and the social valuations prevalent in Canada. "War," said Thucydides, "is a violent teacher." The precise effect of these forces is at present unpredictable, but it may be accepted as axiomatic that under their impact the Canadian State at peace will undertake vastly enlarged economic and social functions, made inevitable by the whole course of present development, by the magnitude of the change into a state-administered economy, and by formal decisions of the Canadian Government regarding social services from which retreat would be difficult. Illustrating this last point are the plans for civil re-establishment of soldiers, extending beyond anything attempted after 1918, embracing not merely the usual pensioning and hospitalization of the disabled, but various services for the physically fit, such as post-discharge allowances, vocational training, transitional re-establishment benefits, grants to assist in resumption of interrupted education, allowances while awaiting returns from private enterprise, and assisted settlement on the land. Here, for post-war administration, is a solid phalanx of obligations which will grow larger the longer the war lasts and the greater the proportion of Canadian manpower passing through the armed forces.

The development of social services for the general public has also been stimulated since 1939, their increase being properly enough regarded as a method of strengthening national morale. Unemployment insurance owed its swift enactment to the financial and other exigencies of a war year. Under similar pressures health insurance may be achieved, or, if it is not established during the war, it is likely to be enacted during the subsequent peace.

But admittedly the more difficult tasks of the new state collectivism will pertain to the management of the economy, the shift of production from war commodities to peace commodities, the stabilizing of employment, the guidance of agriculture in its needed adjustments, the control of the price mechanism to prevent inflation, and the linking of national to international commodity controls. With the ending of hostilities, strong pressures will be exerted to relax the rigid restraints affecting consumer goods, labour, and enterprise. A primary responsibility of those in political office will be that of assessing the aggressive arguments for control and decontrol; deciding where to yield, where to stand firm. Herein will ensue a violent pull and tug of militant interests, more intense and desperate than that experienced when the war economy was being mobilized, for the emotional drive which made revolutionary war controls feasible will be relaxed or totally absent, and the relatively simple goals of belligerent effort will be removed. Crucial matters for the existence of national democracy then and afterwards will be the capacity and imagination of leadership, the effectiveness and flexibility of parliament, and the responsibility and competence of the public service. On each of these matters a few reflections may be ventured.

The provision of what is included under the much abused word "leadership" is essentially a task for the political parties, which must offer alternative national programmes and guiding ideas, not merely at elections, but whenever significant issues come under public debate. Also they must direct and channel the changing tides of public feeling, for this is the higher and rarer type of leadership. Their performance of these tasks determines the quality of parliamentary democracy. Hitherto the two major Canadian parties have reflected reasonably well the peculiar federalism which fathered them. Composite groups, they have recognized and sought to express the different interests of the regional, racial, and religious cleavages within the country, and in the main they have endeavoured to extract a following from all. Their programmes and policies have inevitably been a tissue of compromises, for to the best of their lights they have tried to establish national unity by balancing off the excessive claims of regional and racial groups. This they do, not merely in the national interest, but because it furthers the party interests, since the wider its electoral appeal, the better is the chance that the party can secure office. The importance of this unifying influence has naturally depended upon the insight, skill, and imagination of contemporary party leadership. Admittedly at times unity seems to be promoted by obscuring issues rather than by sharply defining them. But such obscuration, carried too far, defeats its own end. Sooner or later hard facts catch up with the politician who tries to govern Canada without making the different interests face up to their differences.

At the conclusion of the war, the parties must continue to shoulder the chief responsibility of reconciling in policy the divergent interests mentioned. The magnitude of the task will not be lessened. To maximize unity will remain the major strategy of national policy, which for the parties implies that they must still seek to be component parts of a whole. If in this attempt the two older parties are to be successful, Quebec must be pried loose from an almost exclusive attachment to the Liberals. Quebec indeed will increasingly play the pivotal rôle in the alignments of political power because, thanks to the dwindling immigration to Canada since the last war, the proportion of its people to the population of the whole is advancing, and after each electoral redistribution its relative weight in the parliament at Ottawa will be enhanced, although its membership remains at the statutory sixty-five. Significantly, if a redistribution of seats had been carried out in keeping with the results of the 1941 census, the English-speaking provinces would have lost seven members in the House of Commons. That circumstance, the leaders of the Conservative Party particularly, do well to ponder. If the Co-operative Commonwealth Federation should become a serious challenge to the older parties in urban Canada by its appeals to labour and the lower middle class in the towns, the Conservative Party is likely to face the fact that gaining support in Quebec is the condition of its survival, since its primary support in English Canada has hitherto come from the towns.

Not merely, as in the past, must the parties be composite in order to further national unity; they must also exhibit, as never before, a flexible capacity to analyse and cope with intricate economic and social issues, as these infringe on both national and international interests. In brief, they are arriving at the stage reached by British parties prior to the last war. Hitherto, except perhaps in the lean and grim years of the early thirties, they were under no compulsion to create within themselves social laboratories. And the plain lessons of the thirties were not learned. The playing off of region against region and race against race, or for example, the construction of a railway, was carried through by an easy-going empiricism, slightly leavened at intervals by appeals to such general principles as those of free trade and provincial autonomy. But the collectivist era into which Canada has been moving since the early thirties—now speeded by war—makes other and more rigorous demands on party leadership. Scope for the dramatic aptitude, the dexterous use of political symbols, and the generous play of the conciliatory spirit still remains. More scope and encouragement, however, need to be given to the critical and analysing mind that will periodically clarify the merits of this or that scheme of social security, the strength or weakness of a marketing policy, the implications of a monetary manoeuvre, the case for or against a specific entrepreneurial activity by the state, or the merits and defects of a certain international wheat agreement. Economic vicissitudes turn up a perennial crop of problems that are never simple, never easy to solve. Hence, into the professionalism of the politician must go more science if not less art, otherwise he will invariably be beaten by the preacher of economic nostrums.

It is well to remember with Thomas Hobbes that "the passions of men are commonly more potent than their Reason". In politics the populace respond to many influences other than intellectual analysis: the temperamental attitude towards change of any kind, personal or class interest, and a variety of non-rational inferences of which the political and social psychologists have abundantly written. But a representative state wherein the leaders of the political parties, when in opposition as well as in power, do not take seriously the informed and rational analysis of economic and social problems, will fare badly in a world of controlled economics. Not merely will such party leaders fail to give intelligent leadership to the electorate; even perhaps more unfortunate they will be incompetent to supervise intelligently or work adequately with the public service. In much of the current debate on representative government there is the facile assumption that the element of expertise and the application of technical knowledge must be left to the permanent public servant, while the politicians proceed with the traditional arts of electoral manipulation, personal cajoling, and the periodic stoking-up of excitement at elections. This is a false and dangerous assumption. Collectivism in democratic terms means that party leadership must be related to what the state attempts and does, or otherwise all real power will slip into the hands of bureaucrats. Discussion in party councils cannot run in antique grooves, unrelated to the more meticulous analysis of experts in government bureaus. Politicians cannot go through an idle pantomime of their own, especially if they have little or no patronage to distribute, without revealing the stark hollowness of their position and undermining respect for the institutions whereby they live. In many countries democracy has been shaken to its foundations by such circumstances.

Fortunately, in the English-speaking world some developments indicate a current flowing against this situation. The pace of such developments in Canada needs to be immensely quickened, for in this country political leadership has too frequently lacked the qualities which I am emphasizing. The Co-operative Commonwealth Federation in its programme-making, which characterized it from the outset and in which each year it enthusiastically indulges, represents a significant trend related to the new collectivism. The practice of periodic and formal discussion impels party leaders to attempt at least to relate their policies to economic and social facts, to focus attention on definable goals, and to alter policies as the facts appear to dictate. It cannot entirely protect against the use of meaningless shibboleths in political talk, but it helps to introduce more than shibboleths. A meeting of Conservatives at Port Hope in September, 1942, reflected a similar appreciation of the necessity for discussing and formulating for the party a consistent line of attack upon primary economic and social problems. Can the Canadian national parties, with their fissiparous composition, successfully build a general staff to deal more seriously with socio-economic problems? I believe that they can, mainly for the cogent reason that they will have to. It is part of the price that they will pay for survival as democratic parties.

In addition, Canadian parties need more roots of a perennial kind; not simply the roots which wither and are inactive in the intervals between elections. In this as in other matters, the Co-operative Commonwealth Federation is endeavouring to effect innovations with its local organizations and its internal democratic structure. If it makes substantial and successful progress in the next decade it will force its political opponents to follow, as its counterpart in Australia, the Labour Party, influenced other groups in the Commonwealth by its organizing techniques.

Equally important with the re-fashioning of party methods is the adapting of parliament to the larger economic and social demands upon it, and especially the devising of sage collaboration with an extensive public service. Within the past three years there has been no satisfactory adjustment in Canada of parliamentary rule to the wider and more complicated administration mainly for the plain reason that parliament has entered a partial eclipse. In the first eight critical months of war, parliament sat for only six business days. Then and afterwards crucial policies were often adopted and enforced without any form of parliamentary debate, and in the final analysis the debating of policy is the minimum requirement of parliamentary government. A typical instance, much resented by many members of the Government and Opposition parties, was the announcement of the Prime Minister of the price and wage controls on the eve of a session without even delaying to make the statement before the House. To some members, at the time, it seemed merely to add insult to injury for the Prime Minister, in announcing the policy, to claim that it was "an experiment hitherto untried on this continent, and perhaps having regard to its breadth and variety, hitherto untried by the will and consent of any free people anywhere."[1]

Orders-in-Council introducing extensive innovations became a steady stream, and by 1943 numbered over twenty-five thousand. This method of law-making has been defended as inevitable while the country is in the throes of a harsh struggle. It is argued that when a man's house is on fire it is no time for him to engage in prolonged talk. Ministers contend that being absorbed in the details of administration they should not be disturbed by the debating demands of the chamber. More difficult to meet is the argument that the circumstances of war allow scant opportunity for the ordinary peaceful arts of parliamentary government, which operate slowly through conciliation and compromise. In war, as Mr. Churchill has said, "clear leadership, violent action, rigid decisions one way or the other, form the only path, not only of victory, but of safety and even of mercy."

Nevertheless, the long-run effect for democracy of reducing parliament to impotence is too evident to need argument. To neglect the basic representative institutions in war is to invite their neglect in peace. Orders-in-Council have of course an invaluable place in the methods of modern governments, but in peace or war when they embody vital policies parliament

[1]See speech of W. H. Moore, *Canada, House of Commons Debates*, Feb. 9, 1942.

should have the opportunity to discuss these policies. Among the public an ominous apathy prevails towards the question of parliamentary rule. The apathy rests partly in a tendency of the public to take parliamentary institutions for granted and partly in a cynical indifference towards them. At any rate the parliamentary tradition in Canada is weaker than that, say, of England where parliament has continued to meet and to debate even when bombs have reduced its main chamber to rubble, its speaker's chair to matchwood, and where, faced by immediate perils of war, it may still force a government to redress grievances and to reshape policy.[2] Indeed, the modern anaemic tradition of parliament in Canada, rather than singular perversity on the part of Mr. King, explains the facts previously cited. Regionalism, provincialism, racial sentiment, and cultural cleavages in a federal union of vast area undermine any intense interest of the public in the national House of Commons. Parliament is weak because the sense of national cohesion is weak. Federalism everywhere tends to break up and dissipate public opinion, such dissipation being accentuated in Canada by the many other forces which disrupt national unity. Constituents are often preoccupied in local politics in so far as they are preoccupied in any politics, and the preoccupation is fostered by local or provincial politicians with a mastery of the not too delicate art of making themselves attractive. Ordinary members of parliament dislike being absent from their local areas for long periods, partly because their business or professional interests may suffer (in

[2]For instances of the influence of the British parliament on war policy see *Round Table*, June, 1942, p. 361.

Ottawa they may be a thousand miles from their homes), and partly because they lose intimate contact with their constituents. Hence long or frequent sessions of parliament, like those in England, are generally resented. In three years of war, parliament sat for 42 weeks, whereas the British parliament sat for 127 weeks. Admittedly the comparison is not entirely fair, since parliamentary members in London are not separated so sharply from their home constituencies, like most of those in Ottawa. More of them make politics a profession, and the legislative labours of an empire are much larger than those of a Dominion. But whatever the extenuating circumstances, the contrast is still significant. Since parliament in Canada is not expected to do a full-time job, public opinion accommodates itself to the fact. The sense of an indispensable parliament is not as deeply rooted as in England, and the grim pressures of war have further weakened it.[3] Hence a revitalizing of parliamentary institutions will be a post-war problem of major importance, and one unpleasantly fears that it may be a neglected problem. Above it has been mentioned that parliament is weak because the sense of national cohesion is weak. But the effect may also be a cause. At least a weak and ill-organized parliament will do little to further national unity; a strong and effective parliament may exercise a unifying influence of much importance and make democracy more competent.

Is a revitalizing of parliamentary democracy feasible under modern conditions? Obviously it is quite feasible if the parties resolve to carry it through, and

[3]Even in England there is wide opinion that parliament has greatly declined in importance.

that assumes a public pressure on them to do so. Much, for example, could be done in making the two chambers more vital by overhauling their internal functioning, an overhaul long overdue, for the present methods reduce their maximum efficiency. Nowhere is the lack of freshness in Canadian political thinking more depressingly evident than in the working and procedure of the House of Commons. No extensive change in its methods has been undertaken in the past twenty-five years to adapt it to increased tasks. Urgent specially is a reform in the committees of the House. "A committee," says the anonymous cynic, "is a gathering of important people, who, singly, can do nothing, but together decide that nothing can be done." It is, however, only in well-organized committees that a large representative chamber can function with effect, and their character will determine the quality of work in the chamber. In the Canadian House of Commons, committees to deal with specific subjects likely to become the object of legislation or government policy should be used more frequently and more effectively. Too commonly now they are not established until the latter part of a session, when their work is hurried and unsatisfactory, and when the energies and interest of members are flagging. This delay in their appointment indicates how little importance has been attached to them. Furthermore, the methods of constituting them ordinarily reduce their efficiency, especially the general practice of apportioning members in accordance with the strength of parties in the House, and in keeping with the principle of providing representation for the chief provinces. With inevitable frequency such procedure fails to obtain on committees, men best qualified by knowledge or experience to deal with the specific matters. Thus badly constituted they stumble along, expending needless time over the obvious, for like convoys in marine warfare they cannot move faster than their slowest members. Geographic representation on committees is not in itself bad, but it should not be permitted to weaken greatly the competence of a committee. Particularly open to criticism is the appointment of chairmen only from the party dominant in the House instead of solely on the ground of ability. The chairman makes or mars the work of a committee, and his main qualifications should be skill and breadth of view.

The weakness of the existing organization is particularly evident in finance. The House acting as a committee of the whole scrutinizes and passes the estimates, but, however useful this parliamentary action may be—it has some merits—it does not in itself provide an adequate financial control, and the Canadian parliament has really no mechanism for such control. A Public Accounts Committee of the British type does not exist. There is such a committee in name, in keeping with our fashion of adopting British nomenclature, but years may intervene between its meetings, and in any case it is too defectively constituted to perform its tasks well. Its large membership, ranging sometimes in the past as high as eighty, makes it unwieldy, and like many other committees it is too slavishly dominated by the party in power. Not since 1908 does it seem to have made any useful suggestions regarding the accounting system of the Dominion. By contrast, the British Public Accounts Committee of fifteen members is appointed annually, at the beginning of a session, with a distinguished member of the Opposition as chairman, and submits to meticulous scrutiny the public accounts, dealing out relentless criticism of waste and inefficiency. But that critical and valuable rôle has been absent from the Canadian committee, and its reports have commanded no respect.[4]

The heavy expenditures in the war period resulted early in 1941 in the appointment of a special committee on war expenditures, resembling that in the British parliament. It consisted of twenty-four members, eighteen of whom belonged to the Liberal Party, in contrast to the fact that in the parallel British committee the Opposition and the government were equally represented except that the chairman belonged to the government party. Although the Canadian committee has done some useful work, almost inevitably it has been accused of partisanship because of its composition and the anxiety of Liberal members to defend the political virtue of the government. Yet a committee of this kind, properly constituted with clearly defined functions, would be valuable not merely in war but in peace.

Some reform of the committee system is therefore imperative to strengthen the general work of parliament, to defeat the sense of frustration experienced by many private members who have now little creative function in the House, and, among other ends, to give a stimulus to efficient administration. Reform becomes more urgent with the widening activity of government. A public accounts committee, for example, with able personnel and regular meetings in each session, would

[4]See remarks of M. J. Coldwell, *Canada, House of Commons Debates*, Feb. 19, 1941.

enhance the rôle of the auditor-general and would insure more effective parliamentary management of finances. Select committees of the House, appointed to explore policy before it reaches the bill stage, should be reasonably small, not exceeding perhaps fifteen members, these members being appointed solely because of their competence and knowledge in the given instance, and should meet earlier in the session instead of two months after its commencement. Before such committees evidence might be drawn from the higher public servants and from members of the public competent to provide it. A skilled and expert secretariat would frequently add to the value of the work done.

In committees and in the general sessions of the House, there is need for greater control over speech, which too often in the Canadian parliament hampers genuine deliberation by dreary repetition and prolixity. Rambling oratory is particularly evident in the general debates, such as those on the Address From The Throne or on the budget, where speakers range as widely as their casual interest dictates, with little or no correlation between most of the speeches. Mr. Brooke Claxton forcibly contended in the session of 1943 that the time had come for the Canadian House to follow the practice of the British and to "direct the government to assume the responsibility of allocating time to the debate, day by day, and indicating precisely what subjects will be discussed and how long will be spent on them. Such a practice requires no change in the rules of the House. It requires acquiescence on the part of members of the House; it requires that they should discipline themselves and co-operate with the government in seeing how best we can do the work of this House, to make it the most effective instrument for carrying out the national will."[5] In the same speech Mr. Claxton wisely advocated a question period like that at Westminster, where, unlike the information-begging queries in Ottawa, questions are commonly designed to present a point of view, to publicize a grievance, or to make the executive defend its administration.

In the senate also committees might be used oftener and more effectively, and that chamber in general, reformed in a few important details, could be made to play a more significant part in law-making and government by discussion. At present the life tenure of senators makes their office a reward rather than a job, and hampers the work they could perform. Superannuation of men over, say, seventy is accepted as a rule necessary to insure efficiency in ordinary modern institutions, and should no less apply to a second chamber in parliament, if that body is to command the public respect essential for its function. Finally, it may be admitted that the more adequate use of committees in both Houses almost inevitably implies the appointment of parliamentary under-secretaries to relieve the pressure of work on ministers. Under-secretaries, indeed, have much else to commend them, not least that their presence would involve an earlier placing of responsibility upon younger members in the House of Commons and thus encourage such men to enter public life.

With the expanding activities of the state, the problem of making parliament more effective is closely related to that of making the public service, or ruling

[5]*Canada, House of Commons Debates*, Feb. 9, 1943.

officialdom, more responsible and competent. In Canada the issue resembles essentially that in all modern parliamentary democracies. For a generation the hurried development of social services and economic controls, under the pressures of industrialism, has shifted extensive power to permanent administrators, and the war immensely quickened this trend. At the end of three years of struggle, the federal service of Canada had more than doubled, and on the working of the economy and the fortunes of the people its influence had greatly increased. An agglomeration of varied administrative organs came to exist, difficult to steer, difficult to control. An unavoidable aftermath of war, even after partial demobilization of the economy, will be a large, unwieldy bureaucracy, containing the directive brain of state policy. To make this brain responsible and highly competent and to give it scope to function flexibly within the giant body will be a central issue of government.

It is absurdly easy to emphasize that a public service can be made responsible, simply by insisting that it learn to curb the appetite for power (natural among those given a taste of it), consider public sentiments and attitudes rather than merely its own prejudices and convenience, and use suasion in its procedures rather than regimentation, conforming to the dictum of Walt Whitman that "the secretaries act in their bureaus for you, not you here for them." Similarly, it is easy to emphasize that the kindred efficiency may be attained by making the service an aristocracy of talent, fostering within it through various expedients mental alertness, and preventing officials from hiding incompetence behind formidable entanglements of red tape. But it is *not* easy to achieve the measures necessary to attain these ends, for unfortunately in political democracy there are often powerful pressures which defeat the purpose of democracy. At most times, it is highly difficult to obtain a sufficiently enlightened and sufficiently strong public opinion to force administrative reform and to watch vigilantly over the responsibility and competence of public servants. Like other inventions, administrative invention comes from the few, not from the herd. Elections can rarely be fought and won on the finer points of administrative technique. Electors are not aroused by such undramatic matters. One may say this despite the fact that Canadian politics affords examples of heated electoral discussion over customs scandals and departmental inefficiencies. These debates were usually incited by abnormal episodes, useful to the Opposition in belabouring the party in office by publicizing its alleged vices, but usually they missed altogether some of the more fundamental issues of administrative efficiency. In the highly controlled economy after the war, it will not prove less difficult than in the past to concentrate public opinion on the significant features of administration, and, to the degree of the difficulty, governments will be tardy in action.

But granted that some enlightened opinion can be brought to bear upon administrative issues, the general measures which it should support in order to make the bureaucracy responsible and efficient are well enough known and often enough discussed in the English-speaking world; such as, the competitive recruitment of men with capacity and character, the early elimination of the unfit and the encouragement of the best, the provision of special educational stimulus for the younger public servants in order to insure that departments become laboratories of animated thought rather than sheltered bureaus of stagnant attitudes,[6] the maintenance of sage promotional methods to provide incentives and wholesome emulation, the attainment of co-ordination in the work of departments, and finally the insurance within the state of an ample opportunity to criticize the mistakes of public servants.

Easy thus to summarize, these conditions are not easy to achieve in democracy, for their achievement depends upon delicate collaboration; upon the initiative of men in the Civil Service itself, of politicians, of learned institutions, of leading publicists, and of ordinary citizens who know enough about government to value the rôle of the public servant. One or two of these conditions I might briefly examine further, beginning with the last.

Parliament should take the lead in assessing, criticizing, or approving as the case may be the methods of public departments, a task which it can best perform in energetic committees properly organized for the purpose. In small committees the responsible chiefs in the service can meet parliamentarians to explain, or, if need be, to defend their administrative procedures. Lord Balfour once remarked that he had the greatest respect for experts, but never came across one who was not the better for twenty minutes cross-examination by

[6]In Ottawa there is an urgent need for in-service education, a need difficult to meet because of the absence in the capital of a richly established English-speaking university or even an institute of public administration. The need perhaps can be most readily and economically met by organizing an institute of administration, linked with the universities of the country.

a layman. It is essential to add that the wholesome functioning of parliamentary committees depends upon suitable attitudes of mind in their membership and of delicate techniques fashioned solely by wise men. Their purpose is not to harass government departments with harsh yet petty complaints, but to exercise a friendly vigilance and scrutiny; to co-operate in the administrative task rather than to throw sand in the machine. The perfecting of this system is obviously difficult because the personnel of parliaments in Canada rapidly change, and sound committee procedures develop only with time.

Criticism of administration, whether disapproving or appreciative, will not and cannot be confined to parliament. It will and should occur in the press and other media of opinion. Hitherto, referring to the last two decades, continuous and penetrating discussion of the public service has been provided by only a few Canadian newspapers and journals, beyond those in Ottawa. The reason for this fact has already been referred to, namely, the whole weight of electoral emphasis has been placed upon other and apparently more immediate goals, or dissipated upon regional ambitions. Institutes of government research, especially an institute of public administration, might give some useful lead to discussion, as such bodies have done in Europe and the United States. Admittedly public criticism, especially when flippant and ill-informed, may sometimes produce a devitalizing timidity and an administrative neuroticism in the ranks. The public servant may become so anxious to escape disapproving criticism that whenever possible he dodges responsibility, loses forthrightness, and nurses caution as a secret vice. For these ills there is little remedy, except to insure through recruitment in the upper grades of the service men of moral courage, unbending responsibility, and high capacity.

It is an administrative truism that public departments should work, not at cross-purposes, but in such a manner as to co-ordinate their efforts for a common end. Today co-ordination is a "blessed word", and, while one has a twinge in using it, there is no escape. An endemic feature of modern large-scale government is the existence of many different agencies which operate with respect to conflicting objectives, and frustrate any unity of purpose in policy and administration. Such rigid compartmentalization might with little difficulty be illustrated in the organization of Canada's war effort, particularly as it affects the manpower, wage, price, and financial controls combined with the planning of the military effort. Throughout, with the quick proliferation of offices and authorities, the essential co-ordination has not been adequately achieved, and is likely also to be deficient after the war, unless exceptional efforts are made to give it pride of place.

Nothing is easier and more tempting than to devise, on paper, co-ordinating machinery. In theory such machinery might seem complete enough now, since constitutionally the cabinet is the master co-ordinator, the fountain and origin of a unified will in parliamentary rule. But constitutional theory aside, a complete over-all co-ordination by the cabinet is in practice impossible because the multiplicity of tasks necessitates devolution to permanent departments or bureaus, within which co-ordination breaks down. In Ottawa, during the war, one method of harmonizing policies has been the appointment of able and key public officials to many important committees and boards on the plausible premise that, in the individual brains of such men, a unity of purpose can best be formulated. Unfortunately, the amount of committee work which even the ablest public servant can efficiently perform is limited because there is a limit to the number of problems which he can think through at one time. When he exceeds the proper amount of committee work, he becomes virtually useless on such bodies even if he does not become a positive bottle-neck, hampering their operations. Obviously it is difficult for an outsider to say how far this form of co-ordination in Ottawa has been successful. The general evidence is not encouraging, but, compared with Washington, Ottawa is doubtless a co-ordination paradise.

It is a commonplace that the power of an office depends upon the personality occupying it. The imaginative, self-confident, and aggressive public servant or political chief will always stretch the authority in his office beyond the conception of the government instituting it, and hence bring its action into conflict with other public jurisdictions. Sometimes this is done because of the hunger of the individual for power and wide territory of control; sometimes the motive is more gracious and ethically respectable, but the result is the same. Conversely, the unimaginative and timid public official will not fully utilize the potentialities of his office, for his primary concern is to avoid extra trouble. Inevitably he contributes no more to useful co-ordination than the other type.

For these administrative diseases there are no easy, palatable remedies, except to insure within the service as much well-devised co-ordinative machinery as possible, particularly inspection from the outside, and to provide abundantly for parliamentary discussion. Obviously the co-ordination cannot be performed by Civil Servants already heavily over-burdened with departmental tasks, and the parliamentary discussion is useful only in committees of the kind formerly mentioned, of which unfortunately in Ottawa we have few.

During the last generation efforts have been made in Canada to recruit and to promote a public service by merit. Such efforts have not been without some success, especially in the inter-war period. Political patronage in its more undesirable and flagrant features had lessened, although the new methods of insuring ability as the principal test for office still left much to be desired. In the post-war period, the task of recruitment by merit will be complicated by the fact that during the years of war the ordinary procedures of the Civil Service Commission have been impaired by the expansion of purely war departments wherein the peacetime modes of recruitment are in abeyance. Most of the new employees are on the temporary list, and hence do not enter government offices by the usual method of competition. The Commission, however, has assisted the war departments in creating the civilian staffs, scrutinizing the needs for new assistants, regulating rates of pay, and improving the organizations. Nevertheless, in recruitment and in organization the actual administrators have been left with wide discretion. While under the circumstances this practice was inevitable, indeed desirable, it obviously at times has the usual abuses of personal patronage. Officials recruited from the business world will be inclined to give positions, not so much to their political as to their business friends, on the simple ground that they know their capacities and are reluctant to rely upon strangers. Yet, on the whole, men of considerable ability have been introduced to the service of Canada.

At the conclusion of war large numbers of public servants will be on the temporary list, and not subject to the same treatment as the permanent employees. From the purely war departments many will be released, but some agencies created under pressure of war will survive as controlling agencies in peace. In such cases some of the top-ranking administrators drawn from outside the service will probably remain within it provided that they are given adequate salaries. In any case, the Civil Service Commission will face the difficult task of maintaining suitable categories, adjusting salary schedules, especially as between temporary and permanent employees, providing for promotions in non-war departments where promotion had been delayed, and generally reducing order out of administrative chaos. This last task particularly it will be poorly equipped to perform, and it will likely make little progress without a sturdy opinion supporting it, expressed in parliament, the press, and institutions of social research. Unless the tasks of the Commission are competently performed, efficiency and morale throughout the service will lamentably deteriorate, and the quality of federal administration will be damaged at a time when it is crucial for the success of post-war policies.

The preceding paragraphs pertain only to the principal machinery and mechanisms of democracy, and even in this matter the gaps are many and wide.

Federalism, for example (to refer to a mechanism not hitherto discussed), is the product of a grand strategy to achieve a democratic devolution and to facilitate economic and political experiment under the urge of a local opinion that does not have to wait for the whole nation to adopt its hopes and beliefs. In the present generation the federal mechanisms have operated none too well, thanks to the manner in which the rapid pace of economic and social development has made obsolete the rigid distribution of power inherited from 1867. In other words, the impact of industrialism has restricted the sphere within which certain forms of local democracy can satisfactorily function, especially with respect to the major economic controls and social security, and the adaptation of federalism to this fact seems imperative. The adaptation need not imply unifying all the functions of government in the new matters reserved for the Dominion, but rather centralizing in legislation and decentralizing in administration.

There are obviously many other factors at least as significant in the working of Canadian democracy as political institutions, important as these may be. Everything in the nation is indeed significant that affects the volume and quality of social thought and discussion, notably universities, other institutions of learning, institutes for social research and popular education, churches, the daily press, the radio, the activity of voluntary associations, and the national habits of debate. In the life of its free associations the nature of Canadian democracy is determined. With advancing industrialism, trade unionism and every type of occupational organization are likely to extend widely within the next decade, and such development will strengthen rather than weaken democratic society provided that the essential methods of discussion and compromise, the readiness to accept the verdict of debate, are secured. In the final analysis the quality of democracy rests upon states of mind. Radio and educational institutions are now the principal means under the state to further democratic attitudes.

Radio in Canada is a public utility which to a great extent is brought under the direction of a commission, following partially at least the example of Great Britain. But we have not yet mastered the proper techniques of administering this new engine of the mind in order to make it contribute most to profitable discussion of public problems and to the furtherance of public education. The achievement of these necessary techniques will test severely political ingenuity, for a radio under democracy must guarantee a discussion that will, at one and the same time, preserve the unity of the state as well as further its experimentation. It must be made to draw together skilfully the population in what Ernest Barker calls a "common mental effort". This description of the desired end, in terms of democratic logic, makes evident its difficulty. It implies breaking down popular apathy and ignorance through an enlightened radio bureaucracy, guided in part by a council or councils representing the public. If it is difficult to insure responsibility and efficiency in a public servant dealing with the plain affairs of finance and labour, the difficulty is intensified in securing such qualities, or even accurately defining them, in a man given authority over the delicate web of opinion and thought. Yet the achievement of such responsibility will be an imperative objective for post-war representative institutions.

"Education for democracy" is the contemporary slogan. It is manifest that such education is needed if it means arousing men to the character of their national and international environment, enlightening them as to the essence of the democratic method itself, making them critical of the antics of colourful but irresponsible politicians, and cultivating certain old-fashioned moral qualities without which democracy could never be anything but lunacy. The exponent of "education for democracy" is eager to emphasize that it must be education, not merely for the young, but also for the adult, a claim that may be accepted. Canada has been lavish in building schools for the young. In this respect its record compares favourably with that of any nation. But, except perhaps occasionally on the bleak frontier or in isolated instances in the towns, it has not yet really made these schools significant centres of adult neighbourhood life, an achievement which along with other social services discussed in another chapter of this book is essential to make democracy more dynamic and real.

The difficulty in achieving this education for democracy rests paradoxically in the fact that the electorate is not educated for democracy. Where can the circle be broken? The minority which may be deemed to be already so educated is commonly too absorbed in its own interests and feels too weak and faint-hearted to press vigorously forward with such adventures—faint-hearted, that is, in face of the heavy inertia of organized society. "We have," wrote Shelley in his *Defence of Poetry*, "more moral, political, and historical wisdom than we know how to reduce into practice." There are, however, the short, intense historical periods, created by the social disruption of violent events, when the guiding minority in society is readier to venture more, and hence accomplish more. That, perhaps, is the principal justification for discussing problems of reconstruction, for after the naked grimness of the present war the incentive to bring the state and society under more sage control will be stimulated.

Chapter III

THE CONSTITUTION AND THE POST-WAR WORLD

F. R. Scott

Wartime Centralization

The outbreak of war in 1939 changed the constitutional relationships within Canada more rapidly than it changed political or economic conditions. Owing to the experience of the First World War the Dominion statute-book and the federal administrative agencies were prepared for an immediate centralizing of emergency powers in Ottawa. The War Measures Act, first adopted in 1914, had never been repealed as were the Defence of the Realm Acts in England, and merely needed to be proclaimed by the Governor-General-in-Council in order to vest in the Dominion executive almost unlimited power over every matter deemed "necessary or advisable for the security, defence, peace, order, and welfare of Canada." Besides the War Measures Act, additional authority over the armed forces, including the power to conscript men for overseas service, lay ready for use in the Militia Act. The consent of parliament was thus not a legal prerequisite for any part of Canada's war effort at the start, except in so far as public monies had to be voted for war purposes. Hence the special session of parliament in September, 1939, adopted very little new legislation. The fact of war, and the proclamation of the War

Measures Act on September 1, 1939, brought about a drastic change in the balance of power as between the Dominion and the provinces and as between parliament and the executive, removing at once any constitutional barrier to federal war plans.

This swift settlement of constitutional difficulties stands in sharp contrast to the preceding decade of legal battle over legislative powers. At every turn during the 1930's when large numbers of the Canadian people were in dire need, the B.N.A. Act stood in the way of social reform. Problems of mass unemployment, industrial decline, and agricultural disorganization seemed incapable of solution because of insufficient Dominion authority. Three years of careful study were spent by the Rowell-Sirois Commission in analysing the problem, and various changes in the constitution were suggested, when the war emergency removed the immediate necessity for a decision. As so often happens in Canada, we did not make up our mind—events made it up for us. The ease with which we found new Dominion power for war purposes is comparable to the ease with which we found new money for the same purposes.

How was it that this sudden shift from federal impotence to federal omnipotence occurred? How is it that Canada has one constitution for war and another radically different one for peace? Did the Fathers of Confederation intend us to be united for war purposes only? The answers to these questions would lead us far afield, but it is clear that both the constitution itself, and the manner in which it has recently been interpreted by the courts, have contributed to the strange result. In the text of the Act the power to legislate upon the subjects of militia and defence belongs to the Dominion parliament. This field expands at once in time of war, particularly as the concept of "total war" brings out the idea of "total defence". But apart from this special authority, the Dominion increases its jurisdiction in wartime because the residuary clause of the constitution then comes to life. The power to make general laws in relation to the "peace, order, and good government of Canada", which the Privy Council has whittled down in peacetime till it is almost valueless to support any Dominion legislation, in time of war becomes restored to the place which in the opinion of most students it was originally intended to occupy, and is available as a basis for legislation designed to promote the national security and welfare. Whatever we may think of the oddity of the prevailing interpretation, which disunites us in peace while unifying us in war, at least it makes us a single nation in face of external danger. There can be no doubt that under the constitution adopted in 1867 the first loyalty of the Canadian citizen is to the country called Canada and not to any province.[1]

The War Measures Act is an enabling statute, not a precise plan for a war effort. It does not order things to be done, but simply authorizes the Dominion executive to issue regulations having the force of law. Its coming into force, therefore, opens the door to govern-

[1]So far the War Measures Act has withstood all attacks made upon it in the courts. One serious defect in its structure, namely, its failure to confer an express power of sub-delegation such as can be found in the British Emergency Powers (Defence) Act of 1939, has been overcome by the Supreme Court in a judgment that leans heavily in favour of the executive authority. See *Reference re Regulations re Chemicals*, 1943, Supreme Court Reports, 1.

ment by Order-in-Council on an unprecedented scale. The extent to which this power is used, instead of the more usual process of legislation, depends on policy rather than on legal considerations. There is nothing done by Order-in-Council in wartime that could not lawfully, though perhaps less expeditiously, be done by statute; and the National Resources Mobilization Act is proof that even parliament can act quickly. The Order-in-Council is secret, rapid, and authoritarian, and for many war purposes must obviously be employed. Democracy must acquire a vigour and flexibility to meet the challenge of dictatorship. But not all matters, even in time of war, have to be decided overnight. A country that can afford, for example, six months to debate the need for conscription might perhaps have spared a week or two to discuss the implications and dangers of wage-freezing.

The weakness of the Order-in-Council is that it excludes the Senate and the House of Commons from any active participation in the formation of policy. It makes the war effort more remote from the common people, and in matters where time is not of the essence a loss of morale may easily be the price of extra speed. It has been a characteristic of Canada's war effort since 1939 that the great majority of government controls have rested in Orders-in-Council issued under the War Measures Act rather than in special statutes adopted as new needs arose. There is a marked contrast between the introduction of overall wage and price controls in the United States, where special legislation by Congress preceded executive action, and their introduction in Canada, where this drastic control was announced by radio without consulting parliament.

Since the war began two further statutes have been passed containing a wide delegation of power from parliament to the executive. The most extensive is the National Resources Mobilization Act,[2] which became law after the fall of France. As a gesture of solidarity in a moment of crisis the Act may have had merit, but it added little, despite its broad terms, to the existing concentration of executive power. Inasmuch as it wrote into the statute law for the first time in Canadian history a limitation on the use of manpower for overseas service it suggested, though it did not perhaps in fact achieve, a restriction on governmental action that had not previously obtained.[3] There is no reason to suppose that anything done since the adoption of the Act could not have been done without it, and in fact it has rarely been mentioned in any Orders-in-Council, most of which continue as before to be based on the War Measures Act. The wage-freezing order, for example, was issued under the authority of the latter Act exclusively, though later in time than the National Resources Mobilization Act. The Order establishing Selective Service, issued on August 26, 1942, was based on the two Acts but it could undoubtedly have been rested on the War Measures Act alone.

The other important delegating statute is the Department of Munitions and Supply Act.[4] This confers on the Minister of Munitions and Supply very wide

[2] 1940, Chapter 13.

[3] The Prime Minister was of the opinion that the restriction did not fetter the government's power to send men overseas under the Militia Act, yet it was felt necessary to remove it after the plebiscite vote. See *Statutes of Canada*, 1942-43, Chapter 29.

[4] 1939, 2nd session, Chapter 3; 1940, Chapter 31; amended by Bill 7, assented to April 21st, 1943.

powers over war production and war materials. The authority thus delegated, indeed, duplicates in large part the more general powers that are contained in the War Measures Act, albeit providing more specific reference. The Order-in-Council containing the Plan for Priorities, issued on February 27, 1941, is based on this new Act and on the War Measures Act, though the latter would probably have been sufficient authority in itself.

It is under the War Measures Act, therefore, with but slight assistance from other wartime statutes like the National Resources Mobilization Act, that almost all Canada's war controls have been created. The taxation measures contained in the annual budget are the most notable exception. Such major regulations as wage-freezing, the cost-of-living bonus, the salary ceiling, commodity price controls, priorities, rationing, rent restriction, and selective service, depend entirely on these Acts. From them also is derived the authority of the chief new agencies of Dominion control such as the Wartime Prices and Trade Board, the Foreign Exchange Control Board, and the National War Labour Board.

This makes the vast control system now existing in Canada a purely wartime structure, resting very largely upon emergency statutes. For it is a common characteristic of the War Measures Act and The National Resources Mobilization Act that they are of limited duration. The War Measures Act carries the idea of emergency in its very title. It will lapse when His Majesty or the Governor-General-in-Council issues a proclamation declaring that the state of "war, insurrection or invasion, real or apprehended" has ceased to exist. It is at least arguable, as will be shown later, that it would lapse even without any declaration by the Governor-General-in-Council, either as a result of a British proclamation of peace, or simply because in fact the war emergency had passed. The National Resources Mobilization Act is declared to be in force "during the state of war now existing". It must end with the state of war to which it refers. The Department of Munitions and Supply Act was at first also limited in its duration, but by an amendment adopted on April 21st, 1943, the limitation was removed. This statute, therefore, alone of the three mentioned, will continue after the war until parliament decides to repeal it. However, as its validity as a piece of Dominion legislation in peacetime might be very doubtful, and as it is almost exclusively concerned with war production and munitions contracts, it would not seem to be a base on which post-war economic control could properly rest.

Legal Effects of Termination of the War

With this understanding of the legal basis of existing controls, we may attempt to analyse the situation that will probably face us at the end of the war. The experience of the last war provides interesting lessons which may still be valuable. The War Measures Act first became law on August 22, 1914. The armistice occurred on November 11, 1918. The mere cessation of hostilities did not terminate the Act. But early in 1919 the Canadian Government apparently became concerned lest the signing of the Treaty of Versailles might result in a British proclamation of peace that would make the Act inoperative in Canada. Accordingly Mr. Meighen introduced into parliament on

April 14, 1919, a bill to extend the operation of the orders and regulations passed under the War Measures Act in case an Imperial proclamation should be issued. He pointed out that either a proclamation by His Majesty *or* by the Governor-General-in-Council was sufficient to terminate the Act, and since in those days Canada was not conceived as having an independent right to belligerency any more than she had an independent right to neutrality, it did not seem possible for the war to continue in Canada after it had ended in England. Canadian regulations could thus be destroyed by British action. "It is presumed that the war will be declared to be at an end by an Imperial Proclamation," Mr. Meighen said, adding this opinion: "That proclamation will end the war so far as Canada is concerned, and the operation of the War Measures Act will cease."[5] However, as it soon appeared that there would be some delay in signing the treaties and ending the technical state of war, the bill was later withdrawn. Its legality in any event would have been dubious. The Treaty of Versailles was actually signed on June 28, 1919, but did not come into force until the exchange of ratifications on January 10, 1920. That was the official date of the termination of the war with Germany. War with the other enemy powers, however, still continued, so that "peace" was not yet restored.

Meanwhile on December 20, 1919, a Canadian Order-in-Council repealed all the regulations based on the War Measures Act except certain ones which were to continue until the end of the then current session of parliament. Thus a Canadian decision terminated all

[5]Hansard, 1919; p. 2148.

the war controls set up under the Act. But the Act itself through some oversight seems never to have been deproclaimed in Canada. The war with Austria ended on July 16, 1920, and with Bulgaria on August 9, 1920. On June 3, 1921, Mr. Doherty, speaking to a bill to amend the Patent Act, pointed out that "the expression 'the end of the war' has been interpreted as meaning that the end of the war comes when peace has been made with all of the powers with whom we have been at war."[6] Peace with Hungary did not come till July 26, 1921, and with Turkey not till August 6, 1924. During all this time, therefore, Canada was still at war.

Had any regulations under the War Measures Act remained, a nice question might have arisen as to their continued validity during a period of technical war but actual peace. There is some casual language of Lord Haldane's in the Fort Frances case which seems to imply that the courts in such a situation might overrule "the decision of the government that exceptional measures were still requisite",[7] and might terminate the Act at the request of a private suitor even though peace was not declared. The question never arose in concrete form. And although there was no separate Canadian proclamation declaring that the War Measures Act had ceased to be in force, there was an Imperial Proclamation of August 12, 1924, declaring that the war with Turkey ended on August 6 of that year, so this date presumably must be taken as the time when the Act ceased to operate in Canada, since it marked the termination of the war with Turkey,

[6] Hansard 1921, p. 4459.

[7] *Fort Frances Pulp and Power Co. v. Manitoba Free Press*, 1923 Appeal Cases 695, at p. 706.

Canada's last belligerent. Just as Canada made peace with Turkey entirely through the action of British officials, so her own emergency legislation seems to have been brought to an end by the same action. In so far as foreign affairs were concerned, the status of colonial dependency had by no means ceased at that time.

Several conclusions may be drawn from this period of our history. The first is that the War Measures Act contains a relic of colonialism that may cause confusion when this war ends. The alternative method of declaring the Act inoperative, through an Imperial proclamation not requiring any Canadian approval, should disappear. His Majesty, of course, should not now act with respect to Canada except on the advice of his Canadian ministers, but this was not the rule when the War Measures Act was adopted, and we cannot rely on a court to give us this interpretation today. The Act should terminate by a proclamation of the Canadian Governor-General-in-Council only. Any automatic ending without Canadian participation might not only upset Canadian plans after the war, but is a violation of the principle of equal status, and belies Canada's claim to an independent control over her foreign policy. The right to neutrality, made clear by our separate declaration of war against Germany on September 10, 1939, must surely imply a right to belligerency for as long as we wish to maintain it.

Another conclusion to be drawn is that, although where there are several belligerents, peace does not technically prevail until made with them all, nevertheless a condition of actual peace may prevail which would be sufficient to justify the courts in saying that the war emergency, if not the war itself, had passed. Canada's war controls might thus be upset by a private litigant, as implied by Lord Haldane, even before the peace treaty with the last belligerent was in force. Whether this be a true view of the law or not, it is indisputable that once war is finally disposed of by treaty the War Measures Act should by proclamation be declared no longer applicable. It has no place save in a state of "war, insurrection, or invasion", and any undue prolongation would be unconstitutional in spirit if not in law. It is no substitute for ordinary constitutional processes in time of peace, and the fact that the Dominion has done certain things under the Act is no evidence that those same things can continue to be done when the Act is in abeyance.

Some suggestions have been made by students of international affairs that at the end of this war there should be a "cooling-off" period between the armistice and the peace treaty, in order to allow for a calmer and more gradual approach to the problems involved in a permanent settlement. Such a policy, if put into effect, would bring about for Canada a state of actual peace but technical war. At once the problem which has been referred to would arise, of deciding whether there was still an emergency in existence sufficiently real to justify the continuation of the war controls under the War Measures Act. The courts might legitimately justify certain things done in that interval as being merely the completion of the war measures. This was permitted with the newsprint controls of the last war which came before the courts in the Fort Frances Case[8] and which were considered legal although

[8]See footnote (7) above.

they continued into 1920. On the other hand, an element of doubt would exist as to how long this process could go on, and no government would feel safe in trying to continue issuing Orders-in-Council based on the War Measures Act for very long after actual war had ended. The setting aside by the Privy Council of the Board of Commerce Act of 1919,[9] which was a statute passed to control profiteering while Canada was still technically at war, stands as a warning of what might happen to any attempt to transfer a wartime regulation of business to a permanent basis even before peace has legally been declared.

Thus it is clear that the end of the war, after allowing some indefinite but reasonable time for demobilization and de-control, must constitutionally bring to an end the War Measures Act, the National Resources Mobilization Act, and everything based upon them. The Canadian economy, which by that time will be more centrally regulated than ever before in our history, must at once cease to depend for its stability upon the particular controls developed during the war period, *unless these can be given a new and permanent constitutional base instead of the former emergency one.* We shall examine in a moment what this alternative base might be with respect to different kinds of control. No post-war plans of an economic kind will be of much use unless the nature and extent of this legal change is recognized. Canada can slip back into the constitutional morass as quickly as she pulled herself out of it. We shall have to plan for this contingency in advance as thoroughly as we plan any other phases of reconstruction, if we are to avoid unreliable makeshifts

[9] *In re The Board of Commerce Act, 1919*, 1922, I Appeal Cases, 191.

and false starts if not actual chaos. Even the unplanned, unco-ordinated Canadian economy of the 1930's had brought us face to face with the need for the extensive constitutional changes suggested by the Sirois Commission. How much more will the war economy, with its greater degree of inter-dependence and correlation, force us to bring the constitution into line with new ideas of national, continental, and, we may hope, world collaboration on economic matters?

The Weakness in Canada's Treaty-Making Power

Quite apart from the problems created by the cessation of the War Measures Act, however, there is another constitutional difficulty Canadians may have to deal with at the end of the war. This is the problem of the enforcement of the peace treaty itself. Ever since the disastrous holding by the Privy Council in 1937 that the Dominion parliament had no power to give effect to international agreements (other than "Empire treaties") such as the I.L.O. conventions, if their subject-matter would otherwise fall within provincial jurisdiction, Canada's international personality has been divided into two parts. Canadian plenipotentiaries may negotiate and sign a convention or treaty, but there is no absolute assurance that Canada can give it effect without the aid of her nine provincial legislatures. Whatever in any Canadian treaty falls within section 92 of the B.N.A. Act seems to require provincial implementation. Parts of any peace treaty would certainly be within Dominion competence, but other parts might well not be, and only the courts can say which part is of federal and which of provincial concern. This weakness in our international dealings is permanently with us and has no connection with the War Measures Act. The Sirois Commission recommended that the constitution should be amended to give full power to the Dominion to implement the I.L.O. conventions. Even this is not enough to remove the doubts regarding ordinary treaties; a national power to negotiate with foreign states on any matter is required. There seems no reason to postpone the change till the end of the war. Canada as a small power will have little enough influence at the peace conference anyway without having her representatives handicapped by uncertainty as to their constitutional authority.

New Constitutional Bases for National Controls

The question as to how much economic and social planning Canadians will want to perpetuate after the war is not, of course, a legal but a political one. If we wish to return to the pre-war economy or something closely resembling it, to hand back full freedom to private enterprise, and to take our chances once more with the system as we knew it in the thirties, then the constitutional problem is theoretically very simple. Time and the B.N.A. Act will bring back the *status quo* once the war is ended, without the need for any action. If we let things slide constitutionally they will slide back to their old position. The only change we have made in our constitution since the war is the adding of unemployment insurance to the Dominion powers, and this does not enable the Dominion Government to prevent unemployment but merely to pay out certain forms of relief when unemployment comes. The agreements made with the provinces by which income and corporation taxes are now collected by the Dominion will continue for the duration of the war only, lapsing automatically at the end.[10] We shall enter the post-war world with a pre-war constitution unless we prepare for change. Those Canadians who urge the abolition of all wartime controls have the existing law on their side. No legal problems arise for discussion on this hypothesis.

Because all the present controls based on emergency powers must end with the war, it does not follow that none of these controls could be continued by the Dominion Government in some other legal form in time of peace. A considerable number of them could be maintained if the Dominion parliament were to replace Orders-in-Council based on the War Measures Act with permanent statutes based on the Dominion's existing legislative powers. These powers, though reduced by judicial interpretation, are still extensive. Fiscal and monetary policy, for example, is clearly within Dominion jurisdiction. The knowledge of how to use this policy to produce the desired results on the internal economy has been greatly increased by the war experience. All the commercial banks derive their privileges and rights from Ottawa, and the legal power to regulate their functions or to nationalize them exists. The Dominion taxing powers are virtually unlimited, but they are not exclusive, and should the exclusive right to levy income and corporation taxes be considered an integral part of fiscal policy then the provinces will have to abandon these fields permanently

[10]These agreements contain a novel idea for fixing the termination date. It will be calculated from the "cessation of hostilities, complete or substantial." The Dominion may specify this date; but if it does not, a province may ask for the calling of a Dominion-Provincial conference for the determination of the date. In any event the date cannot be later than that of the proclamation ending the War Measures Act.

as suggested by the Sirois Report. This would require constitutional amendment. Tariff policy, however, is an exclusive Dominion prerogative, and all foreign trade, both import and export, will remain subject to federal control. Foreign exchange control likewise comes under existing Dominion jurisdiction.[11]

It is when we come to consider the internal economic controls and new plans for social security that the Dominion authority begins to become doubtful, if it does not vanish altogether. The Fathers of Confederation gave the national parliament a general control over trade and commerce, not restricted, as in the United States constitution, to trade and commerce with foreign nations and among the various states. Yet these restrictions have been read into the B.N.A. Act by the courts. The power to regulate trade within a province now belongs to the field of property and civil rights, and even the power to regulate interprovincial trade is of vague extent and hedged about with uncertainties which make it difficult to apply. Any general regulation of trade and commerce throughout the Dominion, on which might be rested a power to fix prices, as under the ill-fated Board of Commerce Act of 1919, or to control marketing, as under the abortive Marketing Act of 1935, seems to have vanished. Price regulation is in large part provincial. Wage control, outside of Dominion undertakings, is clearly a provincial matter in peacetime; the present legal requirement on employers to pay a war bonus related to the cost-of-living index will disappear at

[11]The War Conservation Exchange Act of 1940, designed to conserve foreign exchange, exists for the duration of the war only but would seem to be well within Dominion powers at any time.

the end of the war regardless of what the price level does. Canadian workers will soon learn that the government policy of granting a cost-of-living bonus, instead of a rise in basic rates as in England or the United States, has greatly weakened their bargaining position, since removing the bonus will not technically be a lowering of wages. We have frozen our former social stratifications. So, too, production control appears to be a provincial matter, if the Turner Valley experience[12] is any guide.

The Dominion might, however, declare certain "works" to be for the general advantage of Canada, and so secure control; this power has already been employed with regard to such things as provincial railways, grain elevators, the Beauharnois power development, and seems capable of much greater extension. Rent controls and control of instalment buying, on the other hand, seem outside the federal field in peacetime. Control of investment can be secured in part through the Dominion banking legislation, but the investments made by insurance companies, provincial corporations, and provincial governments escape direct federal regulation. The need to control inflation in Canada will outlast the War Measures Act; it will require many types of regulation, some of which, it can safely be assumed, will be found within the provincial field after the war.

It is always possible that a new attitude might appear in the Courts which would overcome some of our

[12]Control of natural gas production was considered to be within provincial powers as part of provincial control over natural resources. See *Spooner Oils Limited v. Turner Valley Gas Conservation Board*, 1933 Supreme Court Reports, 629.

constitutional difficulties. The almost revolutionary changes wrought in American constitutional law by the recent centralizing trend in the United States Supreme Court are well known. Old judgments have been overturned and restrictions on the federal power imposed during the heyday of *laissez-faire* have been removed.[13] By the simple process of barring from inter-state commerce the produce of factories employing child labour or indulging in other undesirable practices, a very considerable degree of federal control has been secured over economic and social matters otherwise reserved to the states. This method has not been attemped in Canada, save in so far as the barring of the mails to certain classes of material, and of the use of the railways for dangerous goods, may be considered as examples which might be extended. Nor have Canadian courts shown any sign of a desire to enlighten the old constitutional law with a new and more contemporary approach. Indeed, the Privy Council in its judgments on Mr. Bennett's "New Deal" legislation refused to follow even the mild liberal lead it had previously given in the Persons, the Radio, and the Aeronautics Cases. The United States has saved itself much of the slow and difficult process of constitutional amendment by a clear recognition on the part of the courts that a constitution is primarily intended, not to rivet on posterity the narrow concepts of an earlier age, but to provide a living tree capable of growth and adaptation to new national needs. Canada has not yet found such assistance from her judiciary, hampered as it is by the

[13]See, e.g., Arthur W. Macmahon: "Taking Stock of Federalism in the United States" (in *Problems of Modern Government*, ed. by R. MacGregor Dawson, pp. 46-73).

dead weight of the overlying Privy Council decisions of the past. One of the first steps toward post-war reconstruction might well be the enactment of the bill prohibiting appeals to the Privy Council.

Whatever may be the opinion as to government regulation of economic matters in the post-war world, there will be general agreement that our future society will need a well developed and co-ordinated system of social security. All democratic states recognize this obligation towards their citizens, and it appears in Article V of the Atlantic Charter to which all the United Nations have subscribed. Three important documents have recently been published which amplify this idea: the Beveridge proposals in England, the Marsh report for Canada, and the National Resources Planning Board's scheme for the United States. It can be taken as established, however, that no well-rounded system of social security can be provided in Canada under the pre-war constitution. Dr. Marsh's suggestions, if fully carried out, would involve considerable changes. Certainly his plan for contributory old age pensions cannot become really effective without amendment of the B.N.A. Act. Mr. Bennett's contributory Unemployment Insurance Act was held invalid in 1937. The legal capacity to legislate for social services lies principally with the provinces under the legislative head of "Property and Civil Rights", and provinces differ too much in income and in outlook to be able to give any lasting security or any sufficiency of coverage. The findings of the Sirois Commission make this quite clear. Its recommendations, involving a sharing of responsibility as between federal and provincial governments, and a revision of the whole policy of subsidies to provinces so as to make possible the maintenance of a national minimum standard of services throughout Canada, provide one possible and reasonable solution of the difficulty. There is no need to discuss these recommendations here in detail, save to stress the fact that they leave a wide field still open for provincial welfare activities. It is to be hoped, however, that Canadians will look upon this part of the Sirois Report not as suggestions rendered obsolete by the war, but rather as valuable contributions to the plans for post-war reconstruction. Unless some constitutional solution of the problem of the social services is found, one of the Four Freedoms, the Freedom from Want, is in danger of being lost on the home front.

Amending the Constitution

Changing the constitution is part of winning the war. This conclusion is forced upon us if we examine the existing law, assuming that we wish to secure post-war Canada from her pre-war ills. The question then arises, how should we amend the constitution? Shall we, by a bold and imaginative stroke, repeal the entire B.N.A. Act and frame a new constitution embodying the best ideas for the future? Or shall we merely make those few alterations which will be necessary to repair the damage caused by the courts and to enlarge the federal powers in keeping with the magnitude of the economic problems that must be solved?

There is much to be said for a general rewriting of the constitution. In the first place, the B.N.A. Act is not a Canadian constitution, but a British statute for Canada. It is written in English only, and not in the two official languages. Its name does not even include the name of our country. It is cluttered up with lengthy clauses, many of them obsolete. There is not one B.N.A. Act but nine Acts; there are eight others besides the original Act of 1867, each of which adds some new law that could well be part of a single document. A number of sections and one whole Act have been repealed or amended by later Imperial statutes. In addition, the Orders-in-Council admitting certain provinces contain further legal provisions, and there are an indefinite number of Imperial statutes which form a peripheral source of constitutional law. Nowhere is there a federal state with so inaccessible and so complicated a collection of legal documents passing under the name of a constitution. It is small wonder that the ordinary citizen of Canada is almost as ignorant of his constitution as he is of the differential calculus. "Preposterous as it may seem, no one knows where the constitution begins or ends."[14]

This condition of affairs can never be remedied until the whole basic law is contained within one great charter, adopted by representatives of all sections of the Canadian people assembled in constituent convention. Then the anomalies, antiquities, and absurdities could be cleared away and the clean metal of the national law made visible. The process of revising the constitution would itself be a creative act which, if successful, would immensely strengthen national unity and consciousness. If failure resulted, the worst that could happen would be a continuation of the former law. Out of the effort would come a clearer perception by Canadians of the nature of their society, of the princi-

[14]See H. McD. Clokie, "Some Basic Problems of the Canadian Constitution" (*Canadian Bar Review*, May, 1942, p. 395).

ples on which it must operate, and of the ends which it is supposed to serve. Such a proposal may seem visionary at this time, when internal class and racial frictions are only too evident. Nevertheless, it needs to be done, and could be done if enough people would make this effort on behalf of their country. In the common task we might find greater unity than we have ever known.

If a new constitution were contemplated, there would have to be acceptance of the present fundamental principles of the law which make of Canada a democratic federal state, possessing dual cultures and recognizing certain guaranteed minority rights. Any suggestion that the B.N.A. Act be revised, immediately awakens a fear in Quebec that minority rights may be threatened. English-speaking Canadians are often impatient with this attitude, since it implies that they are waiting for the opportunity to launch a major attack upon the French language, the separate schools system and other minority privileges. Both the fear and the impatience have perhaps some justification; the one is based on long historical memory, the other on an honest belief that constitutional revision is necessary simply for good government under present conditions and is not in any way an underhand attempt at racial domination. To resolve this opposition and to calm minority fears, there is a growing body of opinion that would favour the incorporation of a Bill of Rights into the fundamental law of the Canadian constitution. Not only could minority rights be thus defined and placed beyond power of change without minority consent, but other basic civil rights, such as freedom of worship, of speech, of association, and of the press, could also be protected. At present these latter rights are too easily set aside by provincial legislation. If the Bill of Rights were specially entrenched in the law, other parts of the constitution could be left more flexible. On this basis the structure could be re-designed so as to make it more simple, more just, and more efficient, and at the same time more secure against arbitrary action by legislative majorities.

Should a thorough revision of the B.N.A. Act be considered impractical, then the only other course is to seek specific amendments to achieve particular reforms, leaving the other parts of the constitution unchanged. This is a relatively simple process, apart from the political problem. New heads of legislative power must be added to those already existing in the constitution. One can suggest the general nature of these amendments. Among exclusive federal powers in Section 91 might be included (a) contributory social insurance, (b) the marketing of natural products entering into inter-provincial or international trade, and (c) a general power to regulate trade and commerce in all matters of common concern to the provinces. The first of these extends the Dominion's present partial control over old age pensions to include all contributory schemes of insurance. The second gives a legal basis to marketing schemes that have already been attempted by Ottawa with provincial approval but destroyed by the courts.[15] The last, the general power to regulate trade and commerce, is implicit in the original consti-

[15]*Attorney General for British Columbia v. Attorney General for Canada*, 1937 Appeal Cases, 377, set aside the Natural Products Marketing Act though supplementary legislation had been passed in every province.

tution and at one time was admitted by the courts but has since disappeared. The first of these suggestions is the only one that departs from our traditions of government in Canada, and if a general Dominion power over contributory social insurance is thought to be too wide, specific powers over, for example, contributory old age pensions and health insurance, could be named, though some argument has been made in favour of a concurrent power over health insurance. But, as Miss Whitton shows,[16] there is a strong case for giving all contributory insurance schemes to the federal government, leaving social assistance to the provinces. A federal power over industrial disputes seems also to be required in these days of nation-wide trade-union organization and industrial development; if this were granted it would restore the principle of the original Lemieux Act of 1907 which was accepted throughout Canada without complaint until set aside by the Privy Council in 1925.[17]

Then it might be agreed that three new subjects should be added to Section 95 which deals with the concurrent powers over Immigration and Agriculture. These subjects would be minimum wages, maximum hours, and the minimum age of employment, with health insurance as a possible fourth addition. This change would restore the right of Canada to enforce the I.L.O. conventions on these matters, and is in line with recommendations of the Sirois Report. By utilizing the idea of concurrent powers, provinces would still be free, as they are now with regard to immigration and

[16]Below pp. 109-14.

[17]*Toronto Electric Commissioners v. Snider*, 1925 Appeal Cases, 396.

agriculture, to make their own laws on these subjects as long as they do not conflict with any federal law. For example, they could improve on the federal minimum standards but could not lower them.

These suggested changes would go a long way towards providing a proper basis for post-war reconstruction. They can scarcely be called radical since most of them have already been the subject of Dominion legislation. More difficulty, perhaps, would be found in settling the vexed question of control over public finance and taxation. The vast increase in national income arising out of the full employment of our resources has greatly reduced the burden of provincial and municipal debt, and under these conditions the pressure for change is not so urgent as formerly. Nevertheless, the former system of financial relations between the federal and provincial governments could surely be improved. At present all income and corporation taxes are imposed and collected by the Dominion exclusively, and provincial portions are paid out to the various provincial governments. The Sirois Report suggested that this should be made a permanent arrangement, and in addition proposed a Federal Loan Council to control future borrowing by provinces. Australian experience suggests that a Loan Council would be useful, and there is much to be said for its adoption as a means of avoiding the reckless financing of the pre-war years. At the same time there is a legitimate field for provincial initiative in economic development on a regional basis, and a complete centralization of financial control at Ottawa seems undesirable. Between the chaotic conditions of the past and extreme centralization a new balance must be found.

Thus it appears reasonable to suggest that the constitutional changes necessary to post-war reconstruction need not be of startling magnitude. Those suggested above leave the provinces with a wide field of exclusive powers, since all other matters provided in the B.N.A. Act remain untouched. In particular, such forms of social assistance as workmen's compensation, youth programmes, relief for unemployables, health clinics and hospitals, and the control of education, would be provincial responsibilities. The co-operative movement in all its phases and the whole municipal field and town planning await development on provincial initiative, as well as agricultural betterment, soil surveys, rural electrification, road-building, forest conservation, and regional economic planning. Any provincial government that wants to take part in post-war reconstruction will find a wide field for action even if the suggested changes in the B.N.A. Act were made. No complete "centralization" is or should be contemplated. It must be reiterated that a proper distribution of legislative power in terms of present need would *not* lead to total centralization. Though our new means of communication have made a legislative union in Canada physically possible, our regional and racial differences will still exist after the war, and there is no solid argument and very little public opinion willing to support such a drastic change as this kind of union would involve. Only a revolutionary crisis could bring it about, and the best means of avoiding such a crisis is precisely by improving our legislative and administrative machinery so that we can master our national problems and make possible a rich and satisfying life for all Canadians. We can save our federalism only by making it workable.

It should also be pointed out that a grant of federal jurisdiction does not prevent a certain degree of decentralization in administration. A national minimum wage does not need to be exactly uniform in all sections of the country. There must be local officers carrying out the national law, and it is most desirable that they should be drawn from the region in which they will have to operate. Racial groups have a legitimate claim to fair representation on all administrative boards; Quebec's complaint that the war controls have been staffed with insufficient care for this principle can scarcely be refuted. Not only racial groups, but class and consumer groups also have a right to representation. Farm organizations, trade unions, and co-operatives should be drawn upon, as well as business. The principle of equality of representation has long been accepted in regard to the legislative branch of government; it must be applied also in the administrative work which is of supreme importance in the modern state.

Finally, consideration must be given to the method by which the desired amendments should be brought about. At present the standard practice is for the Canadian parliament to adopt an address requesting the British parliament to make the specified changes. Such a request is granted as a matter of course, since it would be contrary to established constitutional convention for London to oppose or alter the Canadian decision. In law no assent of provinces is required, nor is it likely that any objections they might make would prevail over the voice of parliament. Nevertheless, there is every reason for full consultation and discussion with provincial and other leaders before taking action. Plans for post-war reconstruction are not likely to succeed unless they command a wide assent among all sections of the Canadian people. They will obviously command more of this assent if they seek ends which appeal to common interests and common needs in all parts of Canada.

National unity can ultimately come only through agreement on great national objectives. We should concentrate on formulating these objectives in concrete terms. Since the Canadian parliament is primarily responsible, it is the duty of national political parties who compete for the control of that parliament to give the leadership to public opinion. The Four Freedoms are a mere guide; specific schemes must be put forward offering advantages for the great masses of the people, opportunity of useful employment for all, and freedom to minorities to make their own cultural contribution to our common nationhood. Even the Beveridge and similar plans, as Sir William himself made very clear, are not enough: "Income security, which is all that can be given by social insurance, is so inadequate a provision for human happiness that to put it forward by itself as a sole or principal measure of reconstruction hardly seems worth doing. It should be accompanied by an announced determination to use the powers of the state to whatever extent may prove necessary to ensure for all, not indeed absolute continuity of work, but a reasonable chance of productive employment."[18] What we face is not so much a constitutional problem as a challenge to our courage and our faith; if we can see post-war reconstruction in terms of a national revival, we shall quickly surmount the legal obstacles in our determination to build a juster social order.

[18]*Beveridge Report*, Macmillan edition, p. 163.

Chapter IV

THE RECONSTRUCTION OF THE SOCIAL SERVICES

Charlotte Whitton

"Social security" has become the slogan of the so-called people's war, and governments, in the Allied and Axis nations alike, hold it before their peoples as their guerdon when fighting shall be done. Little consideration seems to be given the fundamental question as to whether all risk can be eliminated from such a fluid and dynamic thing as human life and whether, were this possible, life, lacking the stimulus and strength of reasonable challenge and responsibility, would move on in enriching growth. Nor is this social security always explicitly defined, either by those who seek or those who promise it. In its narrower sense the term is being used to designate what might be called humane treatment of end-results in social break-down; in its broadest application, it is used to cover basic recasting of the whole social economy. Were the average citizen to put his social objectives in a few sentences, he would probably say that he asks of the state the assurance of such conditions (of production, distribution, and marketing) as will afford him the opportunity from his own labour to support himself and his dependants at a reasonably decent level of material well-being; and he seeks, further, the erection of reinforcing social defences which will allow no life within that state to drop below minimum levels of decency and survival, should the state or the worker prove incapable of assuring the first objective.

Obviously, with the states of the world so unequally endowed in natural resources and at such divergent levels in actual and anticipated standards of living, post-war policy can follow one of two lines. The first of these would simply assume the resumption, or even the heightening, of their standards of living by a few great powers, leaving the peoples of "less advanced" civilizations to hope for a "comfortable" but much lower standard. The second, on which much hope of abiding peace must be predicated, contemplates a radical change in attitude to a world planning in the use and development of economic power and resources, with the practical objective of reasonably comparable social security for the peoples of all states.

Few states are more directly challenged to alter their outlook than the United States of America and the Dominion of Canada; in fact, it is doubtful whether Canada can otherwise plan any comprehensive security programme. Her great natural resources give her a potential productive power which only an enormously increased consumer demand can sustain, and this will have to be developed within, as well as beyond, her own boundaries. Therefore, a more energetic and forward-looking policy in immigration and reciprocal trade than has characterized her thinking in the pre-war years or in these days of battle is essential. An expansionist programme in population, production, and marketing will involve, almost inevitably and at least in the transition period, the projection into the future of some of our restrictive controls over natural resources, manpower, and the spread in price between consumer and producer.

The Gainfully Occupied Population

It is assumed then that, as a post-war objective, gainful occupation for all of working age and, in its failure or impairment, reinforcing social defences are to be sought for all the Canadian people. A natural approach to the problem is, first, an over-all view of the normal distribution of gainfully occupied persons in Canada, and, against that, a study of some of the exigencies, general and specific, which thwart their ability to maintain themselves and their dependants by their own labour.[1] Two out of three Canadians will be found in the "working-age" levels, that is, between 15 years—the average age of compulsory school attendance—and 70 years—the age of eligibility, for public aid allowances to the aged. In this 7½ to 8 millions, about 2½ millions are homemakers, managing their own households and not included in the "gainfully occupied". Also excluded are children at home unless the major part of their time is given in actual assistance to their parents in the production of goods. Therefore the volume of the gainfully occupied is from 3½ to 4 millions, varying as to whether the measurement is of those in gainful occupation or in full-time gainful occupation. By the spring of 1943, war had added over 600,000 workers to those in recorded em-

[1]No census analysis, later than 1931, is available. The sampling reports of the 1941 census reflect war's shattering impacts on the general occupational structure. Possibly, therefore, the computations in the section on the Gainfully Occupied in the National Income of Canada 1919-38: Dominion Bureau of Statistics, showing fluctuations, by decades, between the two wars, is the most valid for general indications.

ployment, while 600,000 to 650,000 were in the armed services.[2] These totals involved a heavy shift from unemployed, own-workers, small employers, agricultural workers, homemakers, idle women, and adolescents in training. The corrected employment curve has tended to slow down in 1942, suggesting, with many other indices, that the Dominion is approaching her peak mobilization of civilian power at some point between forty and forty-five per cent. of the entire population, and between fifty-five and sixty per cent. of those in the gainful occupation age group.[3]

It might then be taken as a safe premise that, could the Canadian economy be normally geared to maximum working power, this would be the ratio of the gainfully occupied in the population. This would mean that the distribution of proceeds from gainful occupation would have to contemplate the maintenance by every two gainfully occupied persons in Canada, of about three others not so engaged. The latter would be those aged over seventy years, homemakers in the home, children under fifteen, and the ineffectives of all ages whom any army, civilian or active, must contemplate as falling out of its marching ranks.

It is also necessary to see clearly at what the "gainfully occupied" people of Canada work, if the state is to plan to keep them profitably active. Normally, about one in three of all Canadians, gainfully occupied, are found in the primary activities of agriculture,

[2]*The Employment Situation, Monthly Reports, Dominion Bureau of Statistics, October, 1942*, issued December 18, 1942, Dominion Bureau of Statistics.

[3]Progressive decline in production for civilian demand and release of man and woman power engaged therein will probably be offset by use of the latter in increasing transfer of other men and women to the armed forces.

forestry, fishing, trapping and mining, with 80 to 85 per cent. of all of these in agriculture. In ordinary times never less than one in four—often as high as one in three—of all gainfully occupied Canadians will be found in some type of farming.

The seven basic secondary industrial groupings listed below cover practically all the remaining two out of three gainfully occupied Canadians in other than these primary pursuits, "odd-jobs" workers ordinarily representing less than five per cent. of our gainfully working people—about 150,000 individuals.

Service normally absorbs about twenty per cent. of the gainfully occupied population, distributed nearly eight per cent. in personal service, six per cent. in the professions, three per cent. in public administration, two per cent. in custom and repair, and fractional percentages in business and in recreational services. However, the expansion of governmental activities has carried the number of state employees up very sharply since the war.

Manufacturing takes up, usually, fifteen to seventeen per cent. of the gainfully occupied, but between September 1, 1939, and December 1, 1942,[4] this index had risen ninety-two point three per cent. leaving all other industrial activities reflecting only a twelve to twelve and a half per cent. rise, and thus evidently itself absorbing personnel heavily from the unemployed and ordinarily non-working elements in the population as well as drawing heavily on workers in primary activities, especially agriculture. This abnormal bloating of the proportion of the population (over thirty-five

[4] *Annual Review of Employment and Payrolls, 1942,* **Dominion Bureau of Statistics.**

per cent. now) dependent on manufacturing—and so heavily on war manufacturing—is one of the factors that will loom large in the period of post-war adjustment.

Trade normally engages between nine and ten per cent. of the gainfully occupied, transportation and communication about eight per cent., construction six and a half to seven per cent., finance and insurance two to three per cent., electric light and power less than one per cent., and the "unspecified pursuits" of the odd-job worker a similarly small portion of the whole.

The gainfully occupied comprise four categories of workers: the employers, employees or wage-workers on wages, salaries, or fixed fees, own or own-account workers, that is persons in primary or secondary production or services who are their own "bosses" or work on their own resources, and the unpaid family worker. Over the twenty years between the two wars, 30 per cent. of working Canadians were working proprietors or own-workers; 60 per cent. wage-workers; 10 per cent. workers, unpaid, "for a living".

The status of the worker is significantly related to his ability to govern his own economic and social stability. The wage-earner is helpless in affecting or controlling his own retention in gainful occupation in any contraction of demand, while the own-workers, though masters of individual adjustments in business and living budgets, are equally helpless before the impacts of either economic or natural phenomena. Prior to the war, the proportion of own-workers gainfully occupied in the Canadian population was comparatively high, practically two out of five gainfully occupied, working either as employers, workers on their own, or for "no pay" or "just for a living". Own-workers predominate in agriculture in which no less than seventy-five per cent. of those engaged are so classified, while two out of three of all own-workers in Canada are found in this activity. Eighty-five per cent. of unpaid workers —that is working just for a living—are in agriculture.

In this last generation the shift in status of the Canadian worker from the comparative self-reliance of the own-worker to the dependence of the wage-worker has proceeded out of all due proportion to population increase.[5] From the beginning of 1929 to the autumn of 1933, the number of persons seeking work on an employee basis in Canada increased by 662,000, while the number placed in this status as workers numbered only 240,000—a growth of would-be wage-workers at three times the country's capacity to absorb them as such. War production, while, of course, affording temporary absorption of the wage-worker, increases the trend to this status as away from that of small employer or own-worker. In Canada there were over three and a quarter million non-agricultural wage-workers in the summer of 1942, as against two million and a quarter in August, 1939.[6]

Another factor of peculiar force in the development of dependency in Canada is the broken routine of much gainful occupation, rendered casual by climatic conditions. Agriculture, lumbering, mining, fishing, of the primary industries, are so affected and, in secondary pursuits, construction is particularly liable to heavy

[5]Valuable statistics, initiated by the late M. C. MacLean, Dominion Bureau of Statistics, and unfortunately abandoned with his death.

[6]Margaret Mackintosh, B.A., "War Labour Policies in Canada" (in *Annals of the American Academy of Political and Social Science*, November, 1942).

seasonal contractions. It is of the cruel essence of the situation that many of the activities in these seasonal undertakings call for but semi-skilled or even unskilled and low-paid labour, not easily trained or adapted to more skilled pursuits. Among these workers, idleness and resultant dependency are not problems of personal or emergency occurrence; they present a difficult, persistent aspect of gainful occupation in a country with Canada's physical features.

Major Causes of Need

These are some of the factors of significance in planning the gainful occupation of the Canadian income-earner if he is to be enabled to sustain the normal functioning of home and community life. The forces which may destroy his security may be economic or social in cause. The former may be widespread and general in occurrence, such as general economic depression, or emerge over a broad area and be extraneous in nature, such as drought, famine, flood, epidemic, devastating fire, and similar contingencies. Social need may arise from causes essentially individual in nature—bereavement, physical or mental handicap, or social disability or inefficiency—though some of these unpropitious visitings may occur over such large groups with such common manifestations as to be capable of generic classification, e.g., premature widowing, breakdown, ageing, mental disease, character instability, and the like. Social need, obviously, impairs the individual's capacity for self-support, quite apart from economic or other fortuitous circumstance.

It is implicit in both the criminal and civil codes of most western states that the family is regarded as the essential unit in an economically and socially stable state, and as a corollary, that the individual's responsibility for maintaining himself and those dependent upon him is primary to the community's responsibility.

But the *quid pro quo* of such a pact is the state's primary obligation so to order its economy that the competent and conscientious citizen may be self-supporting and that the actual background of his daily life accords with at least minimum conditions of health and decency. Settlement or continued residence in poor, unproductive, isolated, or "worked-out" lands, inhospitable and incapable of sustaining life for a group, within an area reasonably adaptable to community growth, means progressive dependency and deterioration for population so located. Poor housing, rural or urban, is similarly contributory to degradation and dependency with all their sequels—physical, moral, and social. Consequently, land settlement and resettlement, community rehabilitation or transfer, slum clearance and the control of over-crowding in urban and of under-settlement in rural or frontier districts, are vitally related to any broad plans for the prevention and the alleviation of related dependency.

Accepting these axioms of state and citizen relationship and responsibility, the next step in planning social security is to segregate those forms of need and resultant dependency that are reasonably predictable and therefore measurable. Cyclical economical fluctuations can now be anticipated, to some measure controlled, and their impact upon the national economy proportionately alleviated. The development of the science of statistics makes it increasingly possible for a state to predict with reasonable accuracy the probable occurrence of inability of the wage-worker or own-worker to market his labour, his skills, his service, or his goods, profitably or at all, the suitable retirement ages for varying occupations, the incidence of disease, or ill health, the actual death-rate among the major groups of all workers, and, in each case, to gauge the relative dependency, arising with these respective exigencies over respective groups. Consequently, reasonably reliable actuarial assessment can be made, within any state, of the likely occurrence of dependency and the cost of alleviating it, when arising from (1) loss or impairment of gainful occupation (a much broader and more complicated category than unemployment), (2) retirement, (3) death, (4) sickness, disease, ill health, or incapacitation. In other words, social insurance against need arising from any or all of these exigencies becomes as practical a possibility as it has long been a necessity in the life of the modern industrial state: its application to an economy like Canada's, however, calls for probable radial modification in the standard plans, predicated on predominantly wage-working populations.

Social insurance is exactly what the term implies. It is predicated upon the partnership of state and worker in the creation of protective reserves against exigencies likely to arise in the life of either or of both, and the fulfilment of the terms of a mutual contract, should the eventualities, stipulated therein, materialize. Obviously, the broader the coverage of social insurance, the greater its stabilizing power in the state; and the more effective its preventive features are, the greater will be its stability.

Upon unemployment insurance only has Canada as

yet embarked—first enacted by the Bennett Employment and Social Insurance Act, 1935, which provided also for exploration of health insurance. This statute being declared *ultra vires*, the British North America Act was amended to add "unemployment insurance" to the schedule of Dominion powers, and the Unemployment Insurance Act was passed in 1940, coming into effect in 1941. The Employment Services Co-ordination Act of 1919 was merged in the new statute and the Dominion-provincial system of employment offices operating thereunder was absorbed and widely extended under the employment services division of the insurance machinery, with these services later even more widely projected under selective service plans of 1942. Youth and emergency training provisions, being developed in 1937 and 1938, have also been broadened in scope and application in the war-training programmes, integrated between the employment service and the training facilities of the Dominion Department of Labour on the one hand, and between both and the provincial authorities in labour and education on the other. Consequently, Canada is attempting, under war's almost intolerable pressures, at one and the same time, to bring to maturity the guidance, training, and placement characteristics of a sound employment and insurance plan, and to evolve and operate its new tripartite state-employer-employee insurance scheme. Between two and two and a half million workers and over 150,000 registered employers are already contributing approximately one and a half million dollars weekly to the Fund. Employment is at an all-time peak and the accumulation of reserves proceeds under especially favourable circumstances. But the Canadian system is entirely industrial, and even within its industrial application, limited to reasonably stable occupations. The coverage includes all employees, that is, persons working on a wage basis, in receipt of less than $2,000 per annum.[7] Excluded are workers in agriculture, forestry, fishing, lumbering, logging, workers in air or water transportation, in stevedoring, in hospitals, charitable and benevolent institutions, and in private domestic service. The calculation, preliminary to the preparation of the legislation in 1935 and 1940, estimated that approximately one in three Canadian wage-workers would not be covered and, of course, none of that one-third of our gainfully occupied population "on their own" would be included, no matter what their income level or continuity of annual activity.

Consequently, without benefit of insurance in case of dependency, there remain somewhere under two million working Canadians, outside the scope of present legislation: (1) all own-workers in any occupation, (2) all wage-workers earning more than $2,000 per annum, (3) all wage-workers in the excepted pursuits, (4) all dependants of insurable workers, to whose maintenance benefits do not extend and, in addition, (5) those insured whose benefits expire in any case of idleness, following on short employment, or in any case of greatly protracted individual or general unemployment. All these groups, with the lapsing of Dominion unemployment and assistance measures, in 1941, remain the liability, when in need, of provincial and municipal authorities. They are in exactly the same statutory

[7]Regulations provided at the time of writing for the inclusion of all those up to this basic wage, disregarding variations occasioned by war cost-of-living bonuses.

position, in respect to Dominion, provincial, and municipal liability, as prevailed from 1915 to 1920, in which latter year the Dominion first made any grant to unemployment aid. It would appear that more adequate rounding out of provisions for the alleviation or relief of distress in this first area of need arising primarily from economic cause calls for immediate consideration and the examination of some system of *occupational income insurance* for the own-worker of low income, parallel to *unemployment benefit* for the wage-worker, and a complementary scheme of assistance at need for the non-insured or for expired insurees under either plan. Crop insurance, acreage subsidy, and prairie reclamation measures indicate some approach to such provisions for the agricultural own-worker.

Provision for Retired or Aged Persons in Need

In the second area, herein described as that of need due to social cause, neither Canada nor any of the provinces has yet evolved any contributory provisions.[8] The largest single group among these needy are the aged for whom provision now runs along three lines.

First there is the Dominion-provincial scheme of direct assistance on a non-contributory basis, shared seventy-five and twenty-five per cent. respectively. Under this, in the fiscal year, 1942-3, about forty million dollars will be distributed to just under 200,000 beneficiaries over seventy years of age, on the approximate means test of supplementation of existing income

[8]The Dominion Government annuities scheme does provide for a solely individual saving against dependency in old age, but it can hardly be described as social insurance since it is purely voluntary and the state's participation is limited to administration costs.

by a maximum of $20 per month to a total of $365 per annum.[9]

Non-eligible aged may receive assistance, on a straight basis of actual need, either in their own homes as "outdoor relief" or in the form of custodial care in institutions as "indoor relief" varying with the provisions or lack of them in the different provinces. In all the provinces the resources of voluntary services, especially of religious bodies, provide a good measure of the more humane and imaginative care of our aged.

Assistance to the necessitous blind, amounting to about a million and a half dollars annually, is an adaptation of the system of allowances to the needy aged, with payments possible at the age of forty, instead of seventy years. Non-eligible blind are also similarly the responsibility of provincial or municipal authorities, with a large measure of actual supervision and provision extended through the Canadian National Institute for the Blind, a voluntary service, receiving also substantial public grants.

Survivors and Dependants of Deceased or Incapacitated Workers

The needs of survivors or dependants of deceased or seriously incapacitated workers are met through three major provisions, all provincial or municipal, one contributory, two non-contributory.

In all the provinces except Prince Edward Island workmen's compensation legislation applies over a broad range of occupations, in which specified accident or disease, or both, render the workmen's compensa-

[9]Cost-of-living bonus adjustments have been provided on a war basis in some of the provinces.

tion fund, assessed upon industry, liable to payments to the worker or his survivor in accordance with a schedule pro-rated to his ordinary earnings. Gross claims, adjusted in a year, in the Dominion, now (1942) exceed 200,000, with compensation and payment of medical aid aggregating twenty-one to twenty-two million dollars.

In the same eight provinces, systems of mothers' allowances prevail, payable, in all but Alberta, from provincial funds alone. Within varying categories and differing qualifying terms, in all the provinces but New Brunswick and Prince Edward Island, widowed mothers, or mothers under varying social or physical handicaps, or with incapacitated husbands, are eligible in behalf of children, under stipulated ages, for monthly allowances for themselves and such dependants. Payments of this nature, forming really a specialized form of assistance or relief from provincial funds, now run about twelve million dollars per annum, in respect to 83,000 mothers and minor children.

All other categories of dependency, arising from loss or impairment of the income earner through death, accident, illness, or handicap, rest back upon provincial or municipal or voluntary funds, or upon various combinations thereof, varying with the different provinces, and municipal practice within each.

Cost of Illness and Health Care

It is, however, in the area of the provision of health care and costs that protection against dependency varies most widely, and is, on the whole, either inadequately extended or seriously lacking in integration.

The British Poor Law Commission, 1909, attributed

about thirty per cent. of the dependency then prevailing to ill health, the costs of sickness, and the loss of earning power of the worker occasioned thereby. There are few Canadian statistics, but the 1931 census indicated that one in every twenty-three workers in Canada (that is, more than four per cent.) lost, on the average, over twelve weeks in the year because of illness, or an average loss of ten full days per annum over the whole working population. Any major treatment or prolonged illness is apt to mean for the average worker the loss of his savings or a mortgage on his home. Almost a fifth of our annual hospitalization is extended to indigent patients, indicating somewhat the relevancy of the cost of sickness and dependency in the Dominion.

Social protection against the impact of ill health, accident, and disease presents more intricate problems than does the extension of material aid. It calls for dual provisions: first (as in occupational, retirement, and survivors' insurance) compensating benefit for the loss of earning capacity and benefit in lieu of income; and second, the purchase, not merely of material needs or custodial care, but also of professional skills. These are presently largely the prerogative of private professional enterprise, though the hospitals and clinics wherein these skills are practised and the training for proficiency in them is made possible, are provided, almost entirely, by state and community enterprise and public funds and voluntary donations.

To provide compensation for the loss of earning power due to ill health and, at the same time, to meet the costs of health care, state health insurance has emerged in social insurance, and, like unemployment insurance, retirement insurance, survivors' insurance, it provides certain benefits, if certain conditions arise, on the possibility of which certain payments have been made by the mutually contracting parties—generally the state, the employer, and the wage-worker—again with the own-worker, so important in the Canadian economy, omitted! These benefits are usually of two kinds: out-of-work benefit, and provision of medical, hospital, nursing, optical, dental, etc., costs varying with the extent of coverage, and generally provided from a panel of practitioners, and with stipulated hospital accommodation at an agreed cost schedule.

Of such pure state health insurance[10] there has so far been no development in Canada, though various publicly approved but privately incorporated ventures have been developing with considerable success in various parts of the Dominion, notably the Associated Medical Services, Inc., in Ontario, and various group hospitalization projects in Winnipeg, in Kingston and other Ontario centres, in Montreal, etc.

Many as are the difficulties that present themselves, the mutually responsible state health insurance scheme is comparatively simple in that it provides co-operatively contributed funds and stipulated benefits, to be

[10]The first draft bill, submitted in the British Columbia plan of 1934, offered true insurance as to eighty per cent. of those covered, combining straight state medicine principles for the indigent. Cash benefits were also on the insurance principle. But this was greatly modified in 1936 amendments and the scheme, then offered, provided for a system of state supervised rather than direct state health insurance. Even this modified plan was later abandoned in the face of strong opposition by the medical profession. The so-called Health Insurance Act, passed in Alberta in 1935 and also left in abeyance in face of similar opposition, really provided not insurance but an inclusive state health service, covering every legal resident in the province through a tax on all income-earners and funds from general revenue.

purchased for each contributing member on a basis of joint responsibility within a fund's actuarial capacity. It is, however, when aid against dependency and health care have to be extended, not as of right under contributory benefit, but at need as a straight public grant (as in unemployment aid, aid to aged, and aid to survivors and to the necessitous, not insurable and distinct from claim and benefit) that real problems emerge. State aid to the idle, the aged, the survivor, the needy, is not contractual benefit, to which the needy citizen is entitled under stipulated contract of social insurance, but it is direct aid from state funds, subject to public prescription and control upon ascertaining of need and the means required to meet it. Identical in principle, nature, and source (that is, solely from public funds) is any system which provides health care and grants of material aid to the sick on a non-contributory "insurance" basis, since the care or relief extended is really a specialized form of social assistance, *not* sick benefit paid from jointly contributed insurance funds. Any system or services under which such wholly state-provided care or assistance or both are extended cannot therefore be described as health insurance but properly only as state medicine and sickness assistance. A citizen cannot, with logic or sound economy, ask for public provision of health care in need, and insist upon retention of the right of exercising his own private enterprise as to where and how he shall satisfy those needs in terms of his personal preference or prejudice. To cite a parallel situation, the entire system of public education would break down were the individual citizen free to live in one area and place his child in any existing school in any existing school district at the public cost, without payment of special fee to indulge his preference.

In the United Kingdom, with the most successful system of health insurance and public services as yet in operation, the lines of different services are clear-cut. The citizen, paying his own costs, is free to go to any practitioner whom he chooses and to the "voluntary hospital"; the insured person has free choice of any practitioner, willing to stand on the medical panel (in respect to which the latter is limited to 1,000 patients per year), and the local medical services to the insured are supervised by a local board, with the majority of its members lay persons. The non-insured, in need of medical or health care, come under the service of full-time district medical officers, retained and supervised by the public assistance authorities who also provide hospitalization in their own hospitals or their wards in other hospitals, the "council hospitals". Consequently in the United Kingdom today private practice, health insurance, and state medicine operate side by side in an integrated system.

In the public extension of care on a non-contributory basis and in the protection of the public health (both, in principle, of the nature of state medicine), there has been considerable development in every province in Canada in the provision of hospitals, mental hospitals, and tuberculosis sanatoria, wherein care is given at varying standards of private, semi-private, public-pay, and public provision. Clinical provisions have extended remarkably on similar bases; but most significant has been the development, in western Canada, of the municipal hospital and, more recently, the municipal doctor plan. Under the latter scheme, on the basis of income or land tax, as the case may be, community provision of professional care is assured to all residents, with special provisions for special consultants at special schedules, and also for service to indigents.

The next step in progress to health protection in Canada would appear to rest upon the clear establishment of these distinctions between:

(1) State health insurance, on a contributory basis, with benefit and individual choice of health facilities, hospital and professional personnel, within the terms and schedules of the insurance contract; and

(2) State medicine with public provision of care at public cost for the non-insurable, non-contributory public in need, on conditions and under controls as to hospitals, professional staff, etc., prescribed by the public authority, with whom the responsibility of payment for these provisions rests.

While maternity benefits are usually contemplated as part of any comprehensive health insurance benefits, the inclusion of family allowances would appear to introduce a purely gratuitous compassionate grant into what should be actuarially and economically sound work and insurance plans, based on the relative cost of a unit of work in the production of goods. A different principle is at once raised if a man's or woman's remuneration is to be based on the power of reproduction instead of production! Nor would such a basis be practicable or socially just in Canada as a levy on the income of the whole country for redistribution with diverse racial strains, revealing extreme variations in the birth-rate and with different population elements holding diametrically opposed views on such matters as family limitation and sterilization of the feeble-minded.

It is submitted that, for economic stability and equity, insurance and social assistance and any system of subsidy to the birth-rate should be kept distinct in social planning and statutory and fiscal provision. A sound, healthy, intelligent, reasonably secure population is sought. It is doubtful whether this objective would be attained by a principle of state grants in ratio to the number of offspring in a family; rather is it more likely to be reached by insistence upon the organization of production on a basis, recognizing a decent return for labour as a prime item in costs; by the provisions of social insurance with benefit proportionate to earned income; and by the extension of social assistance, honestly as such, on the basis of individual need and individual merit in all circumstances where supplementary help can be shown to be required. Encouragement of the birth-rate among the healthy, sturdy, and self-supporting could likely be most directly assured not by direct subsidy but preferential rebate in tax deductions, proportionate to rate assessed.

Thus there is visualized, as a sequence in greater social security for the Canadian people: greater stability in gainful occupation, assurance of reasonably sustaining returns therefrom, and social insurance and social assistance, available in any break-through in these first lines of defence.

All this means recognition of equal pay for equal work, with remuneration of human labour at rates of minimum decency as a primary charge upon production.

One Inclusive Insurance Scheme for Predictable Need

Through each of the major categories of economic or social break-down, the fear of which haunts the average citizen through all his years of discretion, a reasonably clear distinction can be drawn between those which are predictable and reasonably assessable, and those which arise with peculiar personal characteristics or emergency. Those which can be anticipated and assessed can be submitted to actuarial control and insurance contract. There would, therefore, appear to be solid argument for immediate examination of the present unemployment insurance provisions of the Dominion from the point of view of gradual inclusion, within one generalized insurance system, and by the payment of one premium, of provisions covering (1) retirement insurance at an earlier age than old age non-contributory allowances can or should provide,[11] (2) survivors' and dependants' allowances, integrated with the present system of workmen's compensation, and (3) health insurance,[12] that is, in cash benefits for sickness.

At the same time, the basis of social insurance should be modified to include provision for the own-worker, especially the agriculturist, on the basis either of service or land income tax, as the individual contribution, and the state's *pro rata* of the premium. This would be justified in the greater hardship of ordinary living con-

[11]This could be simply done by an adaptation in the present Dominion annuities scheme providing for compulsory contributory provisions within the same limits as the unemployment insurance scheme now covers.

[12]This naturally assumes concurrent action to amend the British North America Act, extending Dominion jurisdiction to all forms of cash insurance.

ditions for the average primary producer, among whom so many of our own-workers are found, and also, in the desirability of maintaining our present, or, if possible, an enlarged population on the land and in forest conservation and development.

Such a development in insurance would eventually lift from the provinces and municipalities over a period of fifty years—a spell in the life of nations—by far the major portion of their present costs of care of aged, of survivors and dependants of the occupationally maimed or handicapped, and the sickness costs of all insured. In the transition period, actuarially calculated grants, in decreasing amount, could be extended to each province, as each category gradually shifted from the non-contributory to a contributory basis.

Provision could also be made for the establishment of certain "norms" in employment and gainful occupation, and, when an agreed deviation therefrom developed, the Dominion could proportionately subsidize the respective provinces to permit, within their constitutional integrity, the continued functioning of their services for assistance at need to the non-insured employee or own-worker. Or alternatively the Dominion, under these circumstances, could assume obligation for direct payment of actual costs of such assistance, provided on the same basis and through the same machinery as local assistance and relief, for categories, prescribed and individually certified as to status by local employment services, but as to need by the local assistance authorities. The procedure has worked with approval in assistance to dependants of aliens during the present war.

Relative Financial and Administrative Responsibilities

Social Insurance

This development would thus assign the responsibility and administration of all social insurance, on a contributory basis, to the Dominion authority under one comprehensive plan national in scope, cost, and administration. This would include insurance against dependency arising from unemployment, impairment of gainful occupation, sickness, premature ageing, death or incapacitation of the income-earner, and retirement insurance at stipulated age. Need, predictable and assessable and covered by insurance, is relieved, when it arises, within the framework of the pre-determined contract and the rights thereby established. Such provisions are therefore generally applicable and susceptible to competent handling through one general policy and service, and under common schedules of benefit, determined by relation to income and premium paid. There is therefore no scale of aid to be established, no ascertaining of individual circumstances, and no adjustment varying with home conditions, community, and province.

Social Assistance

Quite different, however, are the requirements and process of the relief of distress, on the basis, not of right and contract, but of need and public assistance. Immemorially and not erroneously, the ascertaining of the need and the provision of treatment and care for the sick, the needy, the young, the aged, and the handicapped, have rested, in western practice, where the problem arose—within the milieu of the individual's background and relationships, against knowledge of which his re-establishment or adjustment should begin. Here, circumstances require careful inquiry as to the causes leading to the need, general or individual, their treatment and removal, and, if at all possible, the re-establishment of the individual concerned. Processes, principles, and procedures are quite different, and must be much more humanized and localized than in the automatic issuance of contractual benefit within fixed schedules. In very recent years in Canada, a tendency has arisen to disregard these fundamental administrative requisites in the treatment of need and to approach the problem, not from the basis of humane procedures so much as from that of retention of major taxing powers and revenue in one unit of government, and adjustment of all other things thereto, as though these divisions of revenue rights were immutable and not susceptible to transfer or subsidy as human needs might require.

All these services for help at need have developed in Canada within her provinces and municipalities. Her hospitals and clinics, her charitable institutions, her provisions for outdoor aid are, on the whole, fairly well developed on a municipal or provincial basis, albeit with some distance still to travel in municipal-provincial integration. Under such direct administration from coast to coast, there now exist, in close to three-quarters of our 4,200 municipalities, provisions for the alleviation of various forms of distress, while in all the unorganized territory of the provinces from Ontario west, the province itself assumes such liabilities directly. In Nova Scotia the vote for the unsettled and transient poor provides a practically equivalent recourse. Upon these services now depends all assistance, except that available under unemployment insurance and administration of the old age allowances to which the Dominion contributes. If these provincial and municipal resources are not adequate to continue effective operation of all these services, do disruption or centralization offer the only alternatives? Is the way of sounder progress not to seek an integration and a strengthening, continuing (especially in a country of such diverse provincial backgrounds) the development to maturing of these experienced services, and seeking such financial and administrative adaptations as to encourage and assure such a consummation? Should not the administration of all assistance at need, on a non-contributory basis, therefore, rest with the provinces and municipalities where natural requirements, broad experience, and widely developed facilities presently exist? Should all such non-contributory provisions not be classified in this one major category of social assistance with all measures for the alleviation of distress at need, either "outdoor" or "indoor", centralized as to legislation, planning, and supervision within provincial authority, and so including:

(1) assistance to all non-insured in need because of loss or impairment of gainful occupation;

(2) assistance to all non-insured aged, infirm, etc.;

(3) assistance to necessitous mothers, and child dependants not covered within survivors' benefits or workmen's compensation;

(4) generalized assistance or relief to persons in need for various unclassified causes, not covered by insurance benefit, particularly to non-insured sick, and their dependants?

Social Utilities

But back of the defences of *social insurance* and back of the provision of *social assistance* there must run also the third line of defence of the well-ordered community life, through what might well be described as the *social utilities*, extending specialized care that can only be practically given, on a corporate basis, as in education, by the resources of the whole community, no matter what the private means may be of those who utilize it, on the basis of relative charge, varying with capacity to pay or private preference. Such are the hospitals, various charitable and benevolent institutions, child care and protection, family welfare, and similar social agencies. Such are our clinics, our visiting nurse services; such should be, as they develop, the medical and nursing and other professional panels, and the hospitalization services developed for the actual treatment and care of the non-contributory patient benefiting by the social assistance provisions under state medicine.

Here, again, actual working services and personnel are already widely developed under provincial-municipal provisions. Over 900 hospitals—607 public, 292 private—with 56,000 beds annually shelter some 900,000 patients cared for by personnel exceeding 40,000.[13] Sixty tuberculosis sanatoria or special hospi-

[13]Dominion Bureau of Statistics' *Annual Hospital Report, 1940*. Dominion hospitals include nine veterans' hospitals, eight marine, nine in Indian affairs, and seventy-seven operated by the army or the R.C.A.F.

tal units, with 10,000 beds, serve thousands of "in" and clinical patients annually, their cost exceeding eight million dollars; fifty-nine institutions for mental care accommodate 57,000 patients, on annual aggregate budgets of sixteen to seventeen million dollars. Provincial and municipal services, caring for the public health, expend over eighteen million dollars annually. More than 450 charitable and benevolent services, under provincial supervision, care for our children, our aged, our infirm, at annual costs of over nine millions, while schools for our deaf, blind, and handicapped children also operate under provincial authority. All these social utilities require closer integration within their respective provinces, and, therein, as between the province and the municipal authority on the one hand, and between both and voluntary charitable or philanthropic enterprise. But, here, within province and municipality they exist and operate, available, as any utility, for purchase by the private citizen, by the beneficiary of social insurance, by the public authority for those dependent on social assistance. Surely the way of progress is to strengthen, not to absorb or duplicate them.

Rather would it seem practicable for the insurance or assistance authority to purchase, from the well-administered social utility, the specialized service which it might desire for itself or on behalf of contributor or client. It would appear to be so unjustifiable as to be inconceivable for a Dominion health insurance fund to duplicate diagnostic, clinical, or hospital facilities where these could be purchased by its beneficiaries, or for their use, from existing services. Insured and homeless aged could be housed at fair payment in good existing facilities; children, eligible for survivors' benefits entrusted, with payment of costs, to children's aid societies with proven experience in guardianship, etc.

Larger Units of Local Governments

The exact demarcation in cost and administration, as between the provincial and municipal authority, would vary with the differing conditions in each province, but it is a *sine qua non* that any such re-alignment of services would involve a strengthening of local government, a *desideratum* requisite for better handling not only of public welfare, but of all the business of local administration. This development might well be explored and encouraged along the lines of larger co-operative units. For the urban area, there is a promise of strength in the metropolitan area or borough of the larger cities and suburban municipalities (as in the county boroughs of the United Kingdom and the interesting developments of Greater Vancouver and Greater Winnipeg). In the rural area there is the proven success of the county unit in the older provinces (characterized in the remarkable county health units of Quebec, and the successful county children's aid societies of Nova Scotia and Ontario) and the regional unit on the basis of the judicial district or its own area, now operating, with remarkable promise, in Manitoba and British Columbia, and in the broader hospital and school districts of the three prairie provinces.

A Dominion Social Insurance Fund and Board

Such an expansion and re-alignment of the major social services of the state contemplates Dominion leadership, but in conference and planning with the provinces, and is predicated upon elimination of the expediency and log-rolling which have been tragically characteristic of too much of the spasmodic Dominion-provincial and provincial-municipal extension of such services in the past. Nothing less than the entire security of the people of this land would be tied up in the comprehensive general insurance provisions suggested. Consequently, the Dominion and all the provinces and the major elements in the life of the state should be directly and continuously associated therein, with every possible safeguard erected against Dominion domination whether political or bureaucratic.

This could probably be best assured by avoiding the creation of any Dominion ministry in this field with its natural culmination in ministerial ambitions and the danger of development of vested departmental interests. Since constant integration of Dominion and provincial activities would be required, it is suggested that, on an analogy with the Bank of Canada, a National Insurance Fund should be created, under its own board of governors, but that the latter board be constituted from the nominees of the nine provinces, with a lesser number of co-opted members, elected for a term of years by the representatives of the various occupational categories who are covered in the Fund. The Board—it is suggested—should report to parliament, through its chairman, who should be a Minister without portfolio, free to give his undivided attention to general policy but without administrative responsibility for the Fund, which would rest with a comptroller, like the auditor-general of Canada, removable only by a vote of parliament and for cause.

Voluntary Welfare Service

Such a broad concept seems to indicate the recession of the voluntary welfare services: it does, not by their contraction but by comparison with the expansion of public responsibility for the welfare of the people. The voluntary services would continue in a relatively smaller but vitally important category, comprising—(perhaps under some such designation as the social facilities or just this simple category of the voluntary services)—all these services and activities which any group within the state may want to, rather than are forced to, undertake for themselves or for others or for both themselves and others. Pre-eminently do experiment, demonstration, and research in social principles and practice belong to voluntary initiative and direction; only those policies and procedures, found feasible upon trial, being justifiable for the broader and permanent structure of statutory provision from general taxation. The same considerations suggest that this category would also include all those undertakings in which the need of absolute freedom and discretion argues against restraint within the statutory and audit requirements of public finances.

As the more complete organization of assured gainful occupation for all the working population and the reinforcing social insurances would bring greater stability into individual life, a large number of those enjoying the resources of the social facilities or of the voluntary services would be doing so as participants and beneficiaries rather than clients. Case work and counselling agencies of a purely voluntary nature would probably be increasingly consulted by persons in receipt of a self-sufficient income or of untrammelled contractual benefit under social insurance.

Voluntary citizen effort will probably find a satisfactory outlet for its activities through membership on advisory and administrative boards rather than through the financing of welfare projects, for conferences and effective planning on a wide and continuous scale will be required. In the care of the very young and the very old, the infirm and the mentally afflicted who together constitute a group unimportant in electoral power and inarticulate as to their special needs, humane interest should dictate exactly such efforts particularly by women citizens in advisory capacity and administrative supervision of many public projects.

Nor will the support of the social utilities by public funds necessarily mean in all provinces or groups that such operations should cease to utilize private personnel, especially such organized entities as religious orders. Indeed, it may be considered practical to grant subsidies to approved, licensed and regularly supervised agencies under private management but public incorporation.

Voluntary citizen effort can therefore be visualized as having something of the function of the snow-plough—breaking new highways, opening those in which drifts may threaten to settle from public indifference or neglect, and continuously travelling accepted routes, keeping them free and clear for the human traffic that may need special encouragement and direction thereon.

Summary

In such projected developments in the Canadian social services, *social insurance* would be basically national, provided under Dominion statute and supervision but with provincial participation; *social assistance* and all the *social utilities* (in which state medicine would be included) would rest within provincial direction and control with municipal partnership strongly developed in planning and administration. While the *voluntary services* would occupy a smaller arc in an enlarged circle of provision, it would be one of vital supplementary and discretionary responsibility, and lay citizen participation would be anticipated in administrative and advisory machinery, at all levels of government. Moreover, the deputizing to voluntary services of specific responsibilities in management and of certain types of agencies and care under public supervision, would not necessarily be precluded on any level of government.

This discussion of more adequate welfare provisions for the Canadian people is based on a fundamental assumption, that it is the purpose and function of government to *assure* conditions whereby the citizen may attain full gainful occupation, and, in partnership with the state, participate in measures designed to reinforce his own efforts to achieve and maintain social stability for himself and his dependants. In other words, the evolution here visualized contemplates the free play of the individual in a democratic society, limited, as is all true freedom, by its adjustment to the equal freedoms of one's fellow-men. It rejects even a benevolent autocracy. In the organization of the state's life for the well-being of the subject, can any other concept assure individual security and justice with freedom, for such an approach accepts the eternal diversity of every human being, where the state as the inclusive directing, dictating authority denies it! Government can and government should provide, through legislation and supplementary provisions, the general framework under which ordinary life may be, presumably, happily lived, but the attainment of individual well-being and happiness will forever be conditioned by the human being himself.

CHAPTER V

CANADA AND THE WORLD

F. H. SOWARD

MILITARY critics often complain that it is the besetting sin of generals to fight a new war with the weapons of the last one. Unless the opponent has committed the same error such a time-lag in their thinking proves fatal. The strategy of the French High Command in 1939-40 bears unwilling witness that this charge is justifiable. In the political sphere such a tendency is less prevalent, possibly because the contemporary politician has been obliged by sheer pressure of events to become more receptive to ideas if he is to survive. As a consequence Allied political leaders in this war have shown themselves aware of the limitations of the promises and policies of their predecessors in the First World War. Even a cursory examination of the Atlantic Charter and the Fourteen Points will show in the former a more complete recognition of the urgency of economic and social problems. The "Four Freedoms" of President Roosevelt and the "Free World" concepts of Vice-President Wallace have been ridiculed as starry-eyed idealism by the cynic. But they are a conscious effort to express the spirit of a people's war, such as this has become, for which there is no consistent parallel in the speeches of Clemenceau, Wilson, and Lloyd George.

What is true in the wider sphere of Allied statesmanship is also applicable to Canada. Our entry into the Second World War was prefaced by a separate declaration of war based upon the approval of the Canadian parliament—a deliberate reminder that the Canada of 1939 had advanced a long way in status from the Canada of 1914, which was committed automatically by the action of the British cabinet. After Pearl Harbor, possibly more by accident than design, Canada's declaration of war upon Japan actually preceded that of Britain or the United States. The significance of this policy has been noted by specialists in Canadian constitutional history[1] and stressed by the Prime Minister. Speaking in New York in June, 1941 to the Associated Canadian Organizations of New York City and over a national radio network, Mr. King told his audience:

"The Canadian people entered this war of their own free will. As one people we made the momentous decision by the free vote of a free parliament .... We in Canada were as free to make war or to abstain from making war as the people of the United States are free to make war or abstain from making war."[2]

Two months later the Prime Minister addressed a luncheon in the London Guildhall which was also attended by Mr. Churchill. To the distinguished audience he again stressed the fact that "ours was not an automatic response to some mechanical organization. Canada's entry into the war was the deliberate decision of free people, by their own representatives in a free

[1]See F. R. Scott, *Canada and Hemisphere Solidarity* (Chicago, 1941), p. 141 and Chester Martin, ed., *Canada in Peace and War* (Toronto, 1942), pp. 3, 4.

[2]W. L. Mackenzie King, *Canada's Contribution to Freedom* (Ottawa, 1941), p. 4.

parliament."[3] These statements, and the trend of Canadian policy to date indicated in such matters as the control of Canadian troops, the "Canadianizing" of the Royal Canadian Air Force, and the deliberate abstention from membership in an Imperial War Cabinet, make it safe to assume that the next peace conference or whatever replaces it should not like its predecessor become an arena where Canada will feel it necessary to lead the Dominions in securing international recognition of their changed status.[4]

While Canada should have no major difficulties about status, and her stature, both military and economic, has grown since 1939, the question of the type of Canadian representation at the next peace conference deserves careful consideration. At the last one Canada secured a double representation, as one of the Allied and Associated Powers and as a member of the British Empire with its panel delegation. As a small power Canada had little influence on the deliberations, since the great powers, speaking through Clemenceau, voiced their determination to make the peace and invited the small ones only to attend plenary sessions, of which there were six, or meetings when their interests were especially affected. Membership in the British panel proved to be less important than was expected because in practice only two delegates from the United Kingdom attended meetings of the great powers. On the other

[3]"*The Lord Mayor's Luncheon in Honour of the Prime Minister of Canada. Addresses by Right Hon. Sir George Henry Wilkinson, Right Hon. W. L. Mackenzie King, Right Hon. Winston S. Churchill*" (Ottawa, 1941), p. 7.

[4]F. H. Soward, "Sir Robert Borden and Canada's External Policy 1911-1920", *Canadian Historical Association, Annual Report 1941*, pp. 75-81. The experiment at Quebec of having a joint meeting of the British and Canadian War Cabinets was an interesting innovation.

hand, Canada benefited from the numerous informal conversations with British and American delegates and access to British records.[5]

It should be remembered the British Empire peace delegation grew out of the Imperial War Cabinet as it operated between 1917 and 1919. No such institution has been evolved in this war for all of the Commonwealth. In the near future the Canadian Government should decide whether it wants to endorse the panel system in a British Empire delegation again as a convenient device for group consultation within the Commonwealth, reconstituted in some way to avoid the apparent subordination to the United Kingdom that was reflected in the method of signature employed at the Paris Peace Conference. But whether the panel system be ruled out or not, it is time that the value of the concept of the United Nations should be examined by Canadians. To date, the nearest approach to a meeting of the United Nations have been the conference held at St. James' Palace, London, in September 1941 to discuss the Atlantic Charter about which, incidentally, the Dominions enjoyed no prior consultation, and the Food Conference at Hot Springs. This war is run by the firm of Roosevelt and Churchill, advised by the Combined Chiefs of Staff in Washington, and operating in conjunction with the British ally and the lend-lease partner of the United States, the U.S.S.R., through the contacts afforded by visits of leaders or their intimates like Churchill, Molotoff, Beaverbrook, Harriman, and Hopkins. It is true that a Pacific War Council also exists in Washington, but

[5]See G. P. de T. Glazebrook, *Canada at the Paris Peace Conference* (Toronto, 1942), pp. 53-6.

apparently for purposes of information rather than for consultation. The arguments that have been raised in certain quarters, that it is time to give reality to the concept of the United Nations by convening its members in wartime and allowing them a chance to develop machinery for peace and rehabilitation that will be ready and waiting for the difficult days to come, deserves careful consideration by both parliament and cabinet.

Again, Canada should consider, from the standpoint of domestic politics, the membership of her peace delegation. Should it be based upon the one-party organization of the existing government or should it represent all the principal parties in parliament, as will the British delegation and those of many of the governments-in-exile? Last time the government represented a coalition and also took the trouble to send to Europe the secretary of the Canadian Trades and Labour Congress, who played some part in the discussions which preceded the formation of the International Labour Organization. Since then we have grown accustomed to both employer and labour representation in the Canadian delegations to the conferences of the I.L.O. Surely that device might also be used for the peace in view of the numerous social and economic problems which this war has created.[6]

In retrospect we realize that the struggle for status in 1918-19 was largely the task of a handful in high political circles and was not forced upon them by an

[6]G. P. de T. Glazebrook, *Canada at the Paris Peace Conference.* Professor Glazebrook points out (p. 28) that there is no record of any Canadian government committee examining plans for the peace conference and that parliament in the same period was "singularly silent".

aroused public opinion.[7] The very fact that Canadians only slowly realized what had then been accomplished in Paris made them more inclined to look upon the League of Nations as the latch-key for a young country which had come of age and not as a weapon by which peace might be preserved. For them, as a distinguished French student of Anglo-Saxon ways once wryly observed, collective security was "only a conviction *de luxe*."[8] The few in Canada who tried to combat this characteristic North American attitude towards the League fought a losing battle for two decades. For them it is sorry consolation today to find that many of their former opponents now frankly admit that Canada often played the part of a Caspar Milquetoast in Geneva when the clouds darkened over the international horizon. Commenting on the Hon. J. T. Thorson's remark in the House of Commons in June, 1942, that most Canadians were isolationists before 1939, a Western liberal newspaper observed that "our foreign policy from the time Mr. King took office was a policy of hiding under the bed", and admitted that "with one or two exceptions in the press of Canada, to which this newspaper cannot claim to have belonged, Canada played the ostrich." It also added, perhaps optimistically: "The simple fact is that we were wrong, nearly all of us, before the war, but we have learned our lesson."[9] In an address to the annual meeting of the Council of the League of Nations Society, Mr. J. W.

[7]See Gwendolen Carter, *Consider the Record: Canada and the League of Nations* (Toronto, 1942), pp. 4-5.

R. A. Mackay, "Canada and the Balance of World Power" (*The Canadian Journal of Economics and Political Science*, May, 1941, pp. 741-2).

[8]André Siegfried, *Canada* (London and Toronto, 1937), p. 304.

[9]*Vancouver Sun*, edit., June 10, 1942.

Dafoe, the Canadian Cassandra of collective security, was less exuberant in his comments on the change in Canadian opinion but did feel that "we are on firmer ground, that we have a clearer idea of the road before us and a stronger will to travel that road."[10]

It is not surprising that the Prime Minister has been less explicit in his statements. Yet in his more recent public addresses there are warnings that Canada cannot in future escape the perils of the wider world. After his visit to England Mr. King said to the Canadian Club of Ottawa in September, 1941: "If there is one thing that the last two years have made plain, it is surely that as a means of escape from the encircling danger which threatens the entire world, no nation which wishes to see freedom survive can now look to anything so old-fashioned as its own sovereign rights or as restricted as its own unaided strength."[11] Five months later in inaugurating the Second Victory Loan, the Prime Minister told the Canadian people that "The fortunes of battle since the outbreak of war; the fate of nations that lie today prostrate beneath the heel of the aggressor; the terrific tasks which face the nations still battling their freedom—all these go to show that neutrality has become a snare and isolation an illusion."[12] Parallel statements could be quoted from Mr. King's address of August 19, 1942, on "Manpower and a Total War Effort", of September 1, 1942, on "Three Years of War", and of December 2, 1942, to the Pilgrims of the United States.

[10]*Report of the Annual Meeting of the National Council of the League of Nations Society in Canada* (mimeo., Ottawa, 1942), p. 8.

[11]*Servitude or Freedom* (Ottawa, 1941), p. 8.

[12]*The Inauguration of the Second Victory Loan* (Ottawa, 1942), p. 3.

Although we may agree that arguments over status and delusions about our security in a "fire-proof house far from inflammable material" should not preoccupy our statesmen when peace comes, it remains true that our leaders have, like Mr. Churchill, been wary of drafting too precise blueprints of the shape of things to come. The Hon. T. A. Crerar, the first Canadian cabinet minister to visit Britain after war began, did express Canadian willingness to accept a limitation of national sovereignty in the interest of peace. His colleague, the Minister of Agriculture, the Hon. James Gardiner, has envisaged the need after the war for an international police force. But their leader has been more circumspect. He has spoken of the unshakable purpose of the British and American people to establish "a freedom, wider and more deeply founded than ever before in human history."[13] He has expressed the belief that the alliance of the United Nations will become the foundation upon which " . . . nations may hope to build an enduring order of peace and good will."[14] He has argued that "if that new order is not already on its way before the war is over, we may look for it in vain."[15] But this realistic comment was followed by warnings against putting too much stress on paper plans since a new world order is "not a matter of parchments and seal."[16] Then came vague references to the new relationship of men and nations beginning its slow but sure evolution which, said the Prime Minister, "is based not on fear, on greed, on hate,

[13]Speech of June 17, 1941.

[14]Speech of February 15, 1942.

[15]Speech of March 24, 1941, *A New World Order*, p. 8.

[16]This simile was used again in his Guildhall Speech of September, 1941.

but on mutual trust and the noblest qualities of the human heart and mind. It seeks neither to divide nor to destroy. Its aim is brotherhood, its method co-operation."[17] On still another occasion Mr. King interpreted the supreme lesson of the war to be that nations must be made to serve and save humanity. He foresaw a new order in which "the rights of man will be determined not by privilege derived from inheritance, position, or possessions, but increasingly by men's own contributions, through their own lives to the common need and the common good."[18] These are fine sentiments but they serve as sign-posts rather than road-maps towards the world of tomorrow.

To date the Prime Minister has permitted himself only one specific comment on post-war organization. No Canadian will be surprised to know that it deals with Canadian-American and Anglo-American relations—the time-honoured objects of our affections. After the Ogdensburg Agreement of September 1940, which created the Permanent Joint Board on Defence between the United States and Canada for the defence of "the northern half of the western hemisphere,"[19] the House of Commons was informed that it constituted "a part of the enduring foundation of a new world order based on friendship and good will," and that in further-

[17]Speech of March 24, 1941.

[18]Speech of September 17, 1941. In December, 1942, the Prime Minister told the Pilgrims of the United States that "in the new order economic freedom will be as important as political freedom."

[19]Professor John P. Humphreys of McGill University has advanced the interesting speculation that this vague phrase commits Canada to a "certain responsibility" for the defence of Latin America. See his article, "The Twenty-Second Chair—Is It for Canada?" (*The Inter-American Quarterly*, October 1941, p. 9), and his book *The Inter-American System, A Canadian View* (Toronto, 1942), pp. 17-19.

ing this order "Canada, in liaison between the British Commonwealth is fulfilling a manifest destiny."[20] Subsequently the conclusion in April, 1941, of the Hyde Park Declaration was interpreted as the economic corollary of Ogdensburg—"nothing less than a common plan of the economic defence of the western hemisphere."[21] These arrangements, and the Anglo-American success in reaching agreements over the exchange of destroyers and naval bases and the Lend-Lease Bill, encouraged Mr. King to tell both British and Canadian audiences that "nothing had been more significant in recent months than the deepening interdependence of the British Commonwealth and the United States."[22] The attack upon Pearl Harbor which forced the United States into war necessarily brought the British and American peoples into even closer union. On that union, Mr. King is convinced, will be based the foundations of the new world order whose principles are expressed in the Atlantic Charter.[23] That remains to date almost his sole formula for the future.[24] Like the Duke of Wellington the Prime Minister has his lines of Torres Vedras and from them he will not easily be lured![25]

[20]*Canada, House of Commons Debates*, November 12, 1940.

[21]The Hyde Park Declaration, House of Commons, April 28, 1941. See J. S. B. Pemberton, ed., *Ogdensburg, Hyde Park and After* (Toronto, 1941).

[22]Speeches, September, 1941.

[23]Speech of February 15, 1942.

[24]However, in December, 1942, Mr. King did tell the Pilgrims of the United States that the peoples of the British Commonwealth and the United States would be "part of a larger company" and that "in that company, all the nations now united in the defence of freedom will remain united in the service of mankind."

[25]Professor F. R. Scott would add that Canadians who are "almost as silent about world affairs and Allied policy as if they were already occupied by an enemy" have themselves to blame. See his article "Canadian Nationalism and the War" (*Canadian Forum*, March, 1942, p. 367).

But war has ever been the great accelerator of political maturity and Canada is being forced to enter upon new experiences. War exigencies have sent Canadians literally to the four corners of the globe. The value of Greenland as a Nazi observation post impelled us in 1940 to send a consul there in common with the United States. The location of Iceland forced us, after the occupation of Denmark, to co-operate with Britain in extending that remote island Allied protection which it reluctantly accepted. Our first professor of naval history has recently described how Newfoundland ". . . for so many years the isolated ship has become a fortress, the north-eastern bastion of the other great geographical unit of North America."[26] There we have spent tens of millions on fortifications and established a garrison and air base. There, too, has a High Commissioner taken up residence to promote friendly relations between two peoples who have recognized that they were neighbours but little else. Similarly the menace of Japan has led us to grant the United States ready permission to build a highway through our territory to reach its colony of Alaska, and has in turn compelled the United States to utilize our airmen, gunners, and sailors in defending that vital area.[27] Possessing for the first time a navy capable of performing important functions we have wisely cut our

[26]Gerald P. Graham, "Britain's Defence of Newfoundland" (*Canadian Historical Review*, September, 1942, p. 278). More graphically the *Round Table* described Newfoundland lying across the St. Lawrence "like an orange in the mouth of a sucking-pig" (March, 1941, p. 356).

[27]On October 10, 1942, the Canadian Minister in Washington told an American audience: "The Canadians in the Aleutians are in fact the first foreigners since Lafayette to join Americans in defending American soil against an invader."

coat to our cloth and developed a force of destroyers and corvettes that has done admirable patrol and convoy duty, assuming with Great Britain charge of the convoy tasks in the North Atlantic. In the Prime Minister's anniversary address on three years of war he reminded us with legitimate pride that "for a full year from June, 1940, until June, 1941, Canada next to Britain was the strongest power actually at war with Nazi Germany."[28] The Mediterranean area has never loomed as large in our consciousness, as it must for three other Dominions, but Canadian ships operated there, Canadian engineers helped to strengthen the defences of Gibraltar, Canadian airmen played a prominent part in the "Battle of the Desert", and Canadian munitions and motored vehicles were being utilized in North Africa in large quantities. So, too, has Canada furnished sorely needed supplies for Soviet Russia.[29] Out of the enforced partnership of the two countries in stopping Hitler has come a deep-seated Canadian respect for the heroism and endurance of the Russians which made the nation welcome the exchange of ministers with the U.S.S.R. in 1942 and draw a hasty veil over the days when we firmly declined to "shake hands with Bolshevism".[30] Not only is Ottawa the centre of the British Commonwealth Air Training Scheme and the meeting-place of a United Nations Air Training Conference. It is the refuge of the heiress to

[28]*Three Years of War* (Ottawa, 1942), p. 6.

[29]The Minister of Munitions, Mr. C. D. Howe, told a Toronto audience in December, 1942, that the Soviet Government had praised the tanks made in Canada as the best they had received to date.

[30]The list of patrons for the Aid to Russia fund opened at the close of 1942 and the generous response of Canadians to the appeal are symptomatic of public opinion.

the Dutch throne. It arranges for the despatch of cargoes of flour and wheat to the famished Greeks. It expands its diplomatic list to include ministers from victims of oppression like Yugo-Slavia and Poland, from neutrals like Sweden, or from leading Latin American states such as Argentina and Brazil. It welcomes High Commissioners from every Dominion. It has arranged for the housing of the International Labour Organization at McGill University. In Washington, Canada has representation on the Pacific Council, the Combined Production and Resources Board (the embryonic economic general staff of the United Nations), and on six Canadian-American joint committees that co-ordinate the defence and economic policies of the two countries.[31] In London, as Mr. Churchill has indicated, Canadian membership in the Imperial War Cabinet may be had for the asking. Viewing these appointments, an envious Chinese, if such there be, might well remark with a remembrance of his own country's experience that seldom have so few gained so much with so little sacrifice. He might fail to be much impressed by the announcement of Canada's willingness to surrender extra-territorial rights in his country—since the announcement came only after previous declarations had been made in the names of Great Britain and the United States.

The economic forces at work in Canada since the outbreak of war are already making themselves felt in the political sphere of Canadian-American relations. Even

[31]Canadian external policy, 1939-41, may be traced in R. MacG. Dawson, ed., *Canada in World Affairs: The First Two Years of War* (Toronto, 1943); see page 243 where Professor R. A. Mackay has suggested that a joint commission between Canada and the U.S. on war aims is perhaps as urgent a requirement as the Joint Board on Defence.

before 1939 careful observers like H. A. Innis pointed to the increasing importance of the pulp and paper, newsprint, and gold-mining industries, all dependent upon the American market, as a significant trend with political overtones.[32] The protectionist mood of the early nineteen-thirties, partly a reaction from the Smoot-Hawley tariff, had aided the Conservative Party, the historic protagonist of high tariffs, and influenced the Ottawa Agreements of 1932. But by 1938 the enthusiasm for those agreements, except in British Columbia, had visibly waned and the Conservative Party in opposition could find little to criticize in the two Canadian-American trade agreements negotiated with Mr. Hull. The war has inter-meshed even more closely Canadian and American economies, has abolished tariffs on munitions, raw materials, and some food-stuffs, while at the same time reducing the amount of Canadian indebtedness to Britain and expanding Canadian industries.[33] Thus, no criticism has appeared to date of the exchange of notes between Canada and the United States on November 30, 1942, by which the two governments recorded their agreement on the broad principles of post-war international economic policies. Such an agreement rules out, for the near future at least, a return to the Ottawa Conference policies and makes the slogan of thirty years ago—"No Truck nor Trade with the Yankees"—sound quite silly. The Port Hope Conference of the young Conservatives in August, 1942, marked, in the opinion of the *Round*

[32]H. A. Innis, "Economic Trends", in *Canada in Peace and War*, ed., Chester Martin (Toronto, 1941).

[33]See F. R. Scott, *Canada and Hemisphere Solidarity*, pp. 149-55.

A. N. Reid, "Canada and the War", *Canada and the United Nations* (Toronto, 1942), pp. 33-40.

Table Canadian correspondents, "a fundamental change on the Tariff question."[34] It paved the way for the national party conference in Winnipeg, which chose the former Progressive Prime Minister of Manitoba as its leader, adopted the name of Progressive Conservative, and likewise repudiated high tariffs. This shift of policy on the part of the party of Macdonald, Borden, and Bennett will simplify political negotiations in future with the United States. On the American side of the line economic factors have also helped. Canadian wartime economic policies have been studied with respect and more than once have been paid the compliment of imitation. This in turn has increased Canadian self-confidence and furthered maturity. Canadian credit was never higher in New York, as the speedy flotation in January, 1943, of a $90,000,000 loan demonstrated. Canadian problems of pioneer construction in the far north are much more of a reality to the American engineers who laboured to construct the Alaska Highway. Likewise the significance of Canada in world aviation as lying across the Great Circle routes has come to be amply realized by American commercial aviation companies.[35] In that field of enterprise there may be some dangers of dispute but, in general, economics have eased rather than bedevilled the prospects for harmonious post-war political co-operation between the two countries.

With deeds rather than words expanding Canadian prestige and power in wartime, it remains to be seen

[34] *The Round Table*, December, 1942, p. 82.

[35] A Canadian Press despatch of January 25, 1942, describes the preparatory studies of the Canadian-American Joint Economic Committees on the possibilities of collaboration in the peacetime development of northern British Columbia, the Yukon, and Alaska.

what Canada will do when peace "breaks out". The Canadian Minister to Washington has combined our traditional attitude towards world affairs with our new-found appreciation of global war by dwelling on peaceful relations between Canada and the United States as an example of international amity and then expressing the hope that "surely in the future . . . we will have enough sense to realize that for Pan America, as for Europe and Africa and Asia, peace can only be preserved by an acceptance of the fact that it is indivisible."[36] The great Canadian speech on the undefended North American frontier has lost its savour for most, and has so little to do with the case for the rest of the world that it is time it was decently forgotten. But the reminder that peace is indivisible, a concept which the Soviet diplomats first popularized, or global, as Mr. Willkie emphasizes, needs constant repetition everywhere in North America if provincial continentalism is to be held in check. It is as true of Canada as of the United States that, in the words of Mr. Cordell Hull: "After the last war, too many nations, including our own, tolerated, or participated in, attempts to advance their own interests at the expense of any system of collective security and of opportunity to all."[37] But the United States has begun to admit its error. Mr. Hull told his countrymen bluntly: "It is plain that some international agency must be created which can by force if necessary keep the peace among the nations in future." His chief assistant, Mr. Sumner Welles, came out in favour of the United Nations undertaking " . . . the maintenance of an international po-

[36]*Canadian Press* despatch, October 10, 1942.

[37]Speech of July 23, 1942.

lice power in the years after the war to insure freedom from fear to peace-loving peoples until there is established a permanent system of general security promised by the Atlantic Charter."[38] While advocating this police power the then Under-Secretary of State strongly favoured the retention of the present inter-American system which, with some exaggeration, he described as "the only example in the world today of a regional federation of free and independent peoples . . . a cornerstone in the world structure of the future."

Should the United States support these policies, and to date no American political leader of any consequence has opposed them, Canada's position in the post-war world will be simpler than it was after the last world war. Then the absence of the United States from the League became an example and a warning to many that gave strength in Canada to the steady pull of continental isolationism. "Close your eyes and you might almost think that the voice of America was speaking," was the comment of a discerning Frenchman upon Canadian oratory in Geneva.[39] But with the United States co-operating in police power, general association of United Nations, or whatever circumlocution may be substituted for the Wilsonian phrase "League of Nations", Canada will certainly find her position easier as "the linch-pin of the English-speaking world".[40] To have been the permanent partner of an isolationist United States in a defence agreement for the northern half of the western hemisphere only, as Ogdensburg

[38]Speech of May 30, 1942.

[39]André Siegfried, *Canada*, p. 290.

[40]Mr. Churchill's phrase in an address at the Lord Mayor's luncheon in honour of the Canadian Prime Minister, September 4, 1941.

makes possible, and at the same time to have remained a member of a British Commonwealth pledged to further world order, and, in the case of Great Britain, at the very least compelled to do so if Europe is not to relive the experiences of 1919-39, would have created a dichotomy which even the dexterity of Mr. King could not long have made endurable. But a United States and British Commonwealth marching together to further an indivisible peace—the glowing spectacle which Mr. Churchill held out before the American congress in December 1941—would free Canada from the dilemma which a Canadian correspondent of the *Round Table* envisaged shortly after Ogdensburg. He argued that "being the tail of one kite (i.e., Britain) is bad enough but to be the tail of two at the same time will be tragic, and what is perhaps worse, ridiculous .... In other words, if Canada can develop no positive policy of its own it will be the sport of the policies of the two larger powers, and seeing that these cannot be expected to keep in exact unison indefinitely, it will come to grief."[41] The only hope of escape the writer saw was "such a condition of harmony between Great Britain and the United States, such a thorough 'mixing-up', that whatever the political form, the great wound of 1776 will heal." That consummation, devoutly to be wished for, seemed remote in the spring of 1941. Since Pearl Harbor there are more solid grounds for its existence.

If, then, we assume that the British Commonwealth and the United States, together with the U.S.S.R., China, and the lesser United Nations, will form a

[41]Anon, "The Canadian-American Defence Agreement and its Significance" (*Round Table*, March, 1941, pp. 356-57).

continuing quasi-federal international organization to police Europe and Asia while a peace settlement is slowly and painfully worked out,[42] the Canadian task begins to take shape. In this immediate transition period when Europe and part of Asia will be enfeebled and desperate, Canada has it within her power to make two positive contributions. The easiest, from the standpoint of sacrifice, will be the economic one. A Canada that has helped to feed Britain, Greece, and Soviet Russia in wartime, without worrying over considerations of cost, can well afford to aid in restoring life and vitality to oppressed peoples deliberately starved, as Marshal Goering frankly admits, by their masters. Without the assurance of rapid and ample food supplies tired peoples may be lured into desperate paths by the type of national gangster that the last post-war period produced. In enemy countries as well, the distribution of food supplies by the United Nations may help the decent elements to take heart for the stupendous task of rebuilding the political and economic structures which Naziism and Fascism had razed to the ground.[43] On the problem of grain reserves conversations have already taken place and plans been formulated between Argentina, the United States, Canada, and Great Britain. With proper planning the prediction of the American Secretary of Agriculture that food will win the peace may be justified.

The United Nations must exercise a police function in distracted Europe and Asia. To that international

[42]More than one statesman has agreed with Mr. Harold Nicolson that the rapid establishment of a peace settlement would be an error.

[43]See Gilbert Jackson, *If Thine Enemy Hunger* (Toronto, 1941).

force Canada could also make a positive contribution, and for such a purpose the Royal Canadian Air Force seems an admirable instrument. Tempered in combat over a longer period than any other arm of our fighting services, it is manned by a personnel more adventurous and less "set" in civilian life than its opposite numbers in the army and navy. The nature of its duties and its weapons has made the R.C.A.F. the most flexible and mobile striking force that Canada has ever created. Among a body of men who already exceed two hundred thousand in number, by the close of the war it should not be difficult to secure a Canadian quota for the international air force for police duty in Europe and Asia. With the enemy deprived of its air force, a compact efficient air arm, in which Canadians would rank in quality with the fliers of any United Nation, would play a vital rôle. Such policies as outlined above are a long way from our timidities and uncertainties of the past two decades but as a Canadian historian pointed out: "One thing is certain: that if through the fatigue of war the body militant of the United Nations rejects its larger purpose and dissolves into its futile sovereignties, its impossible neutralities, its destructive autarkies, the last condition will be worse than the first and the crisis of the twentieth century will be indefinitely perpetuated."[44] A President of the American Historical Association, Professor Arthur M. Schlesinger, reached the same conclusion. In an analysis of American foreign policy published in the *New Republic* he argued that ". . . no lesson of history stands out more

[44]W. E. C. Harrison, "The United Nations in War, Victory, and Peace", *Canada and the United Nations* (Toronto, 1942), p. 19.

boldly than that collective security is the best safeguard of American security."[45]

Although enlightened self-interest may lead the United States to stay in a world peace organization after the battle has ended, it is most unlikely that they will abandon, as superfluous, hemispheric associations such as the Pan American Union. In the speech of former Under-Secretary-of-State Sumner Welles in May, 1942, there was a reminder that future opportunities should not be gained at the expense of past advantages, with the pointed comment, "I cannot believe the peoples of the United States and the western hemisphere will ever relinquish the Inter-American system they have built up." For Mr. Welles, as for Professor P. E. Corbett, the hope of world order rests in a subordination of regional groupings to a universal authority.[46]

Before 1939 Canada was a member of a universal organization, the League of Nations, and of an imperial one, the British Commonwealth of Nations. Should Canada join a third grouping, the Pan American Union? Such a possibility was mildly canvassed in the thirties but attracted little general interest. Now that Canada is more closely linked with the United States than ever before in her history and has exchanged diplomatic representatives with three South American states, now that the western hemisphere has shown, despite the attitude of Argentina, the greatest solidarity against an aggressor in its history, the stock

[45]Arthur M. Schlesinger, "War and Peace in American History" (*New Republic*, September 21, 1942, p. 340). In 1938 Mr. Winston Churchill asked an incredulous House of Commons: "What is ridiculous about collective security?" and answered: "The only thing that is ridiculous about it is that we have not got it."

[46]P. E. Corbett, *Post-War Worlds* (New York, 1942), pp. 188-89.

of the Pan American Union in Canada has risen. So also has Canadian stock risen elsewhere in this hemisphere. The Minister of Trade and Commerce, the Hon. J. A. MacKinnon, found in every Latin American country he visited in 1941 a desire that Canada become the twenty-second member of the Union.[47] The argument that adherence to the Pan American Union during the war would be regarded elsewhere in the Commonwealth as a form of continental isolationism and a weakening of loyalties, which Professor R. G. Trotter has vigorously propounded, has some substance. In his view: "To join now would not be expressive of a wider internationalism on Canada's part . . . It would strengthen those who would minimize attitudes and practices of consultation and collaboration among the nations of the British Commonwealth."[48] Another more dubious argument for non-membership expounded by Mr. Trotter was the contention that until the United States exhibited a more continuously responsible attitude in world affairs, participation in the Pan American Union might deepen in Canada the latent forces of isolation. With Latin American states like Mexico and Brazil playing an increasingly active part in the war, with several others discharging a real interest in the work of the I.L.O., with the United States having world co-operation thrust upon it by the experience of this war, it would seem that membership in the Pan American Union in the post-war era should not be much of a risk even for a people as cautious as

[47]*Canadian Press* cable, October 15, 1941.

[48]Reginald G. Trotter, "Canada and Pan Americanism" (*Queen's Quarterly,* Autumn, 1942, p. 257). See also his article, "More on Pan Americanism—A Reply to Professor Corbett" (*Inter-American Quarterly,* January, 1940, pp. 5-11).

ourselves. Our membership could strengthen the forces for world co-operation in the Americas at a time when faltering of will would be damaging. It might give Canadians a chance to demonstrate in the western hemisphere that small powers under the shadow of a big one may still exert considerable influence as Canada has done in the British Commonwealth. The implications of our being a North American state, just as Australia is a South Pacific state, is something which a considerable number of Canadians have been slow to grasp. Yet it is significant that Canadians from the three leading parties such as Senator Gouin, Mr. M. J. Coldwell, and Mr. Howard Green, have recently publicly favoured adherence to the Union.[49] They would accept Mr. Humphrey's contention that "Canada has a service to perform in this hemisphere. Together with other American nations she must work for the creation of an organized international American community based on the principle of justice and democracy. In so doing she will be serving her own best interest, the interests of the hemisphere, and ultimately the interests of the universal world community."[50]

In the future Canada may be expected to view the Far East with more interest and attention than in the past.[51] The loss of almost 2,000 troops at Hong Kong, the threats to the safety of the British Columbia coast since Pearl Harbor, and the amazed realization of how

[49]The most recent analysis of western hemisphere co-operation is to be found in John P. Humphrey, *The Inter-American System—A Canadian View* (Toronto, 1942).

[50]*Ibid.*, p. 291.

[51]Recent studies of Canadian policy in the Orient are C. J. Woodsworth, *Canada and the Orient* (Toronto, 1941), and A. R. M. Lower, *Canada and the Far East—1940* (New York, 1940).

formidable an enemy Japan is, have gone a considerable distance in counteracting the strong tendency in Canada to think of the world in terms of Europe and the western hemisphere. China has gained immensely in prestige with a better realization of the magnitude of her resistance to Japan since 1937. The announcement that Canada would follow the Anglo-American lead in renouncing extra-territorial rights in China was followed by the appointment of the first Canadian Minister to Chungking, Major-General V. W. Odlum of Vancouver. His fellow-citizens in British Columbia are becoming increasingly aware that the present Chinese Exclusion Act, which their insistence secured from the Canadian Government in 1923, offers a slight to a proud and self-respecting nation that it can scarcely be expected to accept indefinitely.[52] When it is recognized that China is not interested in large-scale emigration to British Columbia but in the disappearance of "an unequal treaty" and in some consideration for Chinese scholars and businessmen, it should not be impossible to negotiate a new reciprocal treaty which will be equally acceptable to both nations. In the peace terms Canada also should offer no objection to China's recovery of such territories as Formosa and Manchuria. She should look with sympathy and give practical assistance to the international schemes that must emerge for aiding China in the reconstruction of her shattered economy. Canadian businessmen have learned by now from our Trade Commissioners in the Far East that the much heralded vast Chinese market can only become a reality as Chinese living standards are raised and Chinese commodities find a market abroad.

[52]See *Vancouver Province*, ed., Jan. 18, 1943.

As far as Japan is concerned Canada shares the expressed resolve of the United Nations to render that nation incapable of becoming a threat to world peace for a long time to come. Such policies as the disarmament of Japan, the elimination of the militarist influences which have made a mockery of her parliamentary institutions, and the creation of a regional security system in the Pacific as a guarantee against aggression in future, should find general acceptance from a nation which the aeroplane and submarine have brought nearer the Orient. The most difficult domestic problem for Canada arising out of the war in the Pacific will be the resettling of the 22,000 Japanese evacuated from the British Columbia coast to the interior of the province or to other parts of the country. A British Columbia member of the federal cabinet, the Minister of Agriculture in the provincial government, the Mayor of Vancouver, and the Union of British Columbia municipalities and the B.C. Command of the Canadian Legion publicly urged the repatriation of all Japanese. Such a policy bears harshly upon those Japanese born in British Columbia (Niseis) and thoroughly Westernized.[53] Those Canadians who deprecate its harshness can only moderate British Columbia opinion by demonstrating a willingness to accept the Niseis elsewhere in Canada. A policy of dispersion would meet the fears on the Pacific coast of a solid block of Orientals difficult to assimilate. If Canadians are not prepared to consider dispersion, the extremists' demands in British Columbia will be difficult to evade.

A new problem is emerging in south-east Asia with

[53]See "Minorities of Oriental Race in Canada" (Canadian Paper No. 1, Eighth Conference, Institute of Pacific Relations, December, 1942).

which Canadians are little acquainted. That is the method of restoring colonial administration after the war in such areas as Burma, Malaya, Indo-China, and the Netherlands Indies. There the American demand for the end of imperialism, as voiced by Wendell Willkie, is being met by some colonial experts, such as Lord Hailey, with the suggestion that, in the Pacific, colonial administration should be restored to the former governments but should be subject to international supervision and "third party judgment". Such a scheme would also be dependent upon international guarantees for security, which lends further point to the suggestions that a regional Pacific Council be created. As one of the few Pacific powers without colonies or aspirations for them, Canada might well be called upon, in common with the United States, to aid in the international supervision to which reference has been made.[54]

Canadians, while sympathetic with Indian aspirations for self-government, have been generally content to leave the Indian problem to Britain.[55] The transmission by the Canadian Government to the British of certain suggestions for mediation in India, sponsored by the C.C.F. Party, was an innovation. But Canada could make at this time one gesture of sympathy with India which would be welcomed by both Britain and India. That is the enfranchisement of the thousand or more Sikhs in British Columbia who have, like other Orientals, been denied the vote. Such a policy is now

[54]For a liberal view of Canadian policies in the Pacific, see "A Canadian View of the Pacific", prepared by the Toronto branch of the C.I.I.A. (Canadian Paper No. 4, Eighth Conference of the I.P.R., 1942).

[55]The publication of *India To-day* by three Canadians, Messrs. Duffett, Hicks and Parkin (Toronto and New York, 1942), is a new sign of interest.

being advocated in some quarters in that province and might be tactfully aided by public opinion elsewhere. It would help to make India a little more convinced that membership in the British Commonwealth has reciprocal advantages.

In September, 1938 an unofficial conference in British Commonwealth affairs was held in Australia attended by delegates chosen from the Dominions and the United Kingdom to represent as many points of view as possible. Inevitably there were divergencies of opinion on the issues discussed but, in the opinion of the official Recorder of the conference proceedings, Mr. H. V. Hodson, a measure of agreement was reached on the rôle of the Commonwealth in world affairs. "In the march towards a world order," he wrote, "the British Commonwealth, if it survives, will certainly be in the van; for the discussions showed at least one thing plainly—that the Commonwealth cannot prolong its life as an end in itself but only as a means to still greater things."[56] More than four years have passed since those discussions, the capacity of the Commonwealth to survive has been put to its severest test. The strain of war superimposed upon unhappy relationships such as persisted between Britain and Ireland or Britain and India have created severe handicaps to the efficient prosecution of the war. On the other hand the contributions of other Dominions both in quality and quantity have equalled and at times surpassed their achievements in the last world war. We have demonstrated that a free association of nations when animated by a common purpose can function

[56]H. V. Hodson, ed., *The British Commonwealth and the Future* (London, 1939), p. 279.

effectively without a centralized control. There are some, including Lord Bennett, who feel that continued unity of purpose and action can only be maintained by the evolution of a common foreign policy for the Commonwealth. To them Lord Cranborne on behalf of the British Government said in reply, in the House of Lords on July 21, 1942: "I see no other way, apart from consultation, by which unanimity may be sought, and no other way, at any rate, which is consistent with the complete independence of opinion which exists in the British Empire." This reply, with which Mr. King would certainly be in full agreement, negates the prospect of any move under official British sponsorship for a federation of the empire, a "Union Now" within the Commonwealth. The Dominions will continue as in the past to co-operate in special arrangements for special needs; they will work with Britain in a common effort for world order but they will not subordinate Ottawa or Wellington to Whitehall.[57] Anomalous as it seems, it may be easier for each member of the Commonwealth to accept a diminution of sovereignty for an international order than for an imperial one. Such a policy entails a willingness to accept responsibility and an awareness of world problems which has not been conspicuous in the past in Canadian policy. Canadians have been too inclined to slip into the rôle of those who also serve by only standing and waiting—and usually

[57]"In the British Commonwealth the notion of federation is probably more remote than it was thirty years ago." Harold Butler, *The Lost Peace* (New York, 1942), p. 224.

An American expert describes the British Commonwealth in its present form as "one of the few successful experiments in world organization." R. L. Buell, *The United States in a New World. Relations with Britain* (*Fortune* Reprint, 1942, p. 9).

only waiting for something to turn up. They forget that a minor power need not necessarily be a silent or passive one, as New Zealand demonstrated within the Commonwealth, and that it was a small power such as Norway which produced a servant of the world like Nansen.

This war has also shown that only a few states are capable of enduring the sort of total war which mechanized weapons have brought to the battle-field. Only Germany, as at present constituted, the United States of America, the U.S.S.R., and the British Commonwealth have at their disposal the physical assets and economic organization essential for survival.[58] Three of these powers are compact continental states and two of them possess within their own boundaries most of the sinews of war. In contrast the British Commonwealth girdles the globe and suffers accordingly in a global war where the aeroplane menaces its ancient bastion, sea-power. The effects upon Commonwealth policies have already been striking. Britain has formed a twenty-year alliance with the U.S.S.R. for both war and peace, and has leased key naval and air bases to the United States in exchange for destroyers. It has lost its jealousy of American sea-power that strained Anglo-American relations in the days of the Coolidge Conference. Canada has formed a permanent alliance with the United States. Australia has preferred a Pacific Council in Washington to one in London for regional defence, and greeted with lusty cheers the arrival of an American general as commander-in-chief of all forces based on its shores. New Zealand has forgotten its prejudices against legations abroad and has sent one of its ablest cabinet ministers, Mr. Walter

[58]See Harold Butler, *The Lost Peace*, pp. 188-89.

Nash, to represent it in Washington. He has pleaded more than once for a World Reconstruction and Development Council "to ensure maximum production after the war of all commodities essential to human welfare and their distribution where needed."[59] In short, the realization has been borne upon us that the British Commonwealth cannot achieve security for its members by itself. It must, like some of the far-away countries of which it once knew nothing, combine with other groupings of states in an effort to guarantee peace for all. It must be in the van of the march towards world order as was suggested at the British Commonwealth Conference in Australia.

If Canada is to play a fitting part in the British Commonwealth, the Pan American Union, a Pacific Council, and whatever form of world organization the United Nations devise, her political leaders will have to display more faith in their countrymen's courage and common sense. Last September the British Foreign Secretary, Mr. Anthony Eden, told his constituents that "questions of foreign affairs are no longer matters that can be left to experts—the world has grown too small for that."[60] Before 1939 not the Canadian public, not members of parliament, and possibly not even all of the cabinet were encouraged to peer into the secret mysteries of foreign affairs.[61] In pre-war days M.P.s

[59]Walter Nash, "Steps to World Organisation" (*Pacific Affairs*, September, 1942), and "New Zealand Today" (*Manchester Guardian*, August 28, 1942).

[60]Speech of September 26, 1942.

[61]See W. E. C. Harrison's comment, in summarizing the proceedings of a 1942 Round Table Conference of the Canadian Institute of International Affairs: "There has been a strong ministerial tendency to bar debate on the floor of the House of Commons, and even to avoid continuous scrutiny in the cabinet", *Canada and the United Nations*, p. 23.

were repeatedly urged before periodic diplomatic crises not to utter comments which might imperil negotiations, or were told during a crisis that the time was too serious for uninformed speculation. Such cautionary advice has its occasional value but should not become habitual.

Similarly, cabinet ministers were only too ready in Geneva to suggest that the Canadian people, who had not been consulted, were opposed to full use of international machinery. Thus the Hon. C. H. Cahan told parliament in May, 1933, after his equivocal performance in the Manchurian crisis, that he had been asked in Geneva: "How many thousands of troops would Canada . . . put into the Far East as part of a joint international force?" and had answered: "I did not believe that under the then existing conditions the parliament of Canada would appropriate a single dollar for maintaining a single company of troops in the Far East for that purpose."[62] Mr. Cahan may well have been right in refusing support of an international police force, but it would be hard to find where and when a parliamentary debate gave him the information on which he based his judgment. Canadians are cautious, almost colourless, in their public appearances in the international arena but they are not cowardly. Give them a courageous lead, with adequate explanation of the reasons for it, and they will play their part in world affairs as willingly as the men called upon to bomb Berlin or to test the Nazi fortifications at Dieppe.

This lack of confidence in public opinion is sometimes paralleled by an apparent lack of confidence in the wisdom of expressing the policy of the statesman him-

[62] *Canada, House of Commons Debates*, May 16, 1933, p. 5066.

self, even on a question about which Canada could justifiably hold definite views. When on January 28, 1942, the Prime Minister was asked a question in the House about the future of the islands of St. Pierre and Miquelon in the Gulf of St. Lawrence, recently seized from Vichy France by the forces of General de Gaulle, his answer was: "I shall be pleased to give the House a statement in the matter as soon as I am advised by the governments of Great Britain and the United States that so far as they are concerned, it will be quite satisfactory that a statement on which they are agreed can be made in the Canadian House of Commons."[63] A parallel case of valorous discretion seems indicated in the Duff Commission's report on the Hong-Kong expedition. If the Department of External Affairs was consulted on the diplomatic aspects of the decision to send troops by the Department of National Defence, it does not appear in the record. If in turn it consulted with American experts in the Department of State or on the Permanent Joint Board on Defence where questions of strategy in the Pacific are presumably legitimate topics of discussion, there is also no record. Such methods of negativism and of evasion are neither effective nor creditable. No reasonable man expects a Canadian Government to talk and act like a great power, but its policies can be more effectively coordinated. Surely by now we have learned that the mere avoidance of initiative presents no solution to a problem and that the absence of long-range commitments may create only too often short-term calamities.

Like any other power great or small, Canada must learn to act courageously and live dangerously in

[63]*Canada, House of Commons Debates*, Jan. 28, 1942.

peace as well as in war. But a courageous policy abroad implies a degree of unity and agreement at home which depends upon the balance of social and domestic forces. A survey of pre-war public opinion[64] revealed in all parties a desire to maintain Canadian unity by evading contentious issues in foreign affairs. As Mr. King remarked in May, 1936: "I believe that Canada's first duty to the League and the British Empire with respect to all the great issues that come up is, if possible, to keep the country united."

Only a crystal-gazer or astrologer would offer positive predictions about our political behaviour in the post-war world but the historian may venture to comment on the implications of certain contemporary trends. Economically, as we have seen, Canada has developed a much more mature economy. The increase in the size and extent of her industries and the much greater industrial efficiency of her workers makes her less dependent on other countries for certain finished goods than in the past. Britain's need of Canadian products of all sorts has wiped out almost completely Canadian indebtedness and necessitated the gift of a billion dollars of supplies in 1942, a gift which was exhausted three months ahead of the expiration of the government's fiscal year. The war has also increased our need for markets abroad, with the result that the Canadian manufacturer is going to share to a far greater extent the interest of the farmer and lumberman in foreign trade. It has likewise produced a state of full employment which has given the Canadian people a sense of their capacities and a desire not to return to the miser-

[64]See F. H. Soward, J. F. Parkinson, N. A. M. MacKenzie, and T. W. L. MacDermot, *Canada in World Affairs: the Pre-War Years* (Toronto, 1941).

able economic muddle of the thirties. Though few Canadians, as a Gallup poll revealed in January, 1943, know the precise terms of the Atlantic Charter or the Four Freedoms, they are desirous of furthering security economically and socially at home and will demand that the state use its powers for that purpose. That fact is well illustrated in the welcome given to the Marsh Report, a counterpart of the Beveridge Report. Is it too much to assume that under future Canadian legislation, a guarantee of security under the social services of a character similar to that envisaged in the Beveridge Report will be attempted? Such policies must lead to a greater appreciation of the work of the International Labour Organization and the value of implementing its recommendations than has been shown in the past by the Dominion and provincial governments.

Before this war has ended perhaps 500,000 Canadians, men and women, will have seen overseas service and will have had forcibly brought home to them the effect of foreign affairs upon their lives.[65] Unlike their predecessors in the first Canadian corps they cannot anticipate a return to "normalcy" and will accept less passively the task of finding employment as civilians. That the government is well aware of this circumstance is indicated by the fact that the schemes for post-war rehabilitation are much more generous now than in 1918. Once again let it be remembered that all schemes of rehabilitation and reconstruction must be predicated upon co-operation and security in the international arena.

[65]Radio, motion-pictures, etc., have helped to make the significance of foreign affairs more real to their friends at home.

In the present political parties there has been a shift, through death and retirement of the older leaders whose ideas were formed in the last two decades of the nineteenth century when expansion and progress were axiomatic. More and more the leadership of the parties will be shared by men who served in the last war or this one, who are accustomed to uncertainty and taught by bitter experience to battle with insecurity. Both the Progressive Conservative and C.C.F. Parties already reflect these tendencies, the one choosing a new leader of unusual background and adopting more progressive policies, the other shedding gradually the isolationist and pacifist tendencies which handicapped its effective criticism of pre-war political policies. Like the British Labour Party the C.C.F. is also keenly aware of the challenge of Communism, and the immense influence which the heroism, endurance, and efficiency of the people of Soviet Russia have exercised upon popular opinion. The Liberal Party still struggles with the problem of retaining the allegiance of isolationist Quebec. This struggle leads to such formulas as "Conscription (for overseas) if necessary, but not necessarily conscription", or the two titles for the Prime Minister's latest volume of speeches: *Canada at Britain's Side* and *Canada et la guerre.* All parties need Quebec's support but none has profited by its bloc vote so much as the Liberals since 1917. If the solid front be broken by the switch of urbanized French-Canadians to a party offering more progressive social and economic policies or if schisms among the French-Canadians weaken their political power the tendency to hold back from international collaboration, when it involves positive action, may be appreciably reduced. The argument that isolation is a North American way of life can also be more readily challenged if the United States remains a willing and eager partner in international collaboration. We may not be able to produce Dantons as audacious leaders but, as a country with a strong Puritanical strain, we might take to heart the advice of Oliver Cromwell, the greatest Puritan of them all: "God has not brought us hither where we are but to consider the work we may do in the world as well as at home."

SECTION II

ECONOMIC POLICIES

Chapter VI

THE PROJECT OF FULL EMPLOYMENT AND ITS IMPLICATIONS

D. C. MacGregor

I

Some of the answers to the question: "How can full and effective employment for labour and capital be secured?" have been known to economists for a long time. Since the end of the eighteenth century one of the main conclusions of economic argument has been that in the absence of restrictions upon commodity prices, wages, and interest rates, upon production, trade, and the movement of labour and capital, the community's and indeed the world's resources would in the long run be employed fully and to the best advantage. The argument related to the very long run, reflecting the outlook of men of affairs schooled in astronomy and mathematics and in the long views of the classical scholar, the historian, and the philosopher. Although usually known as classical economics it may also be described as the long-term principles (or "theory") of full and efficient employment. (The meaning of the term "full employment" is discussed below, pages 172-8.) It was a simplified treatment, the underlying reasoning usually omitting the effect of wars, manipulation of the currency, and other disturbing influences. These omissions were intentional and probably reflect the desire of early economists to see beneath disturbances from war finance and beyond the decaying regimentation of their own times.

In marked contrast with the older long-term principles are the short-term principles advocated by writers of recent years. To them, changes in the community's outlay for durable goods are a major cause of fluctuations in employment and prosperity.

At present the short-term proposals which attract the widest public interest are those made by Professor (now Lord) Keynes in 1936 and a popular restatement for American readers by Professor Alvin Hansen in 1941. Lord Keynes' views are expressed mainly in his volume *The General Theory of Employment, Interest and Money*, hereafter referred to as his *General Theory*; Professor Hansen's in his *Fiscal Policy and Business Cycles*, hereafter referred to as his *Fiscal Policy*. The essence of their views is that a strong tendency to recurring depressions is inherent in a system of private enterprise which is rapidly increasing its capital equipment and paying for it out of money savings; as antidotes they have recommended properly timed and directed public expenditures and low interest rates. Both have written mainly with the depressions of the interwar period in mind. Their volumes were not intended as prescriptions for post-war reconstruction. In this paper it is assumed that the reader is familiar with the basic economic ideas.[1] The argument is long and intricate and cannot be presented here, but the rough summary presented in the following section may prove useful.

[1]Keynes' main principles are summarized in Hansen's *Fiscal Policy*, Chapters 11 and 12, and his earlier proposals for dealing with unemployment appear in *The Means to Prosperity* (Macmillan, 1933).

II *Basic Ideas*

Both Keynes and Hansen have been classified by one writer as belonging to the "under-consumption" or to the "psychological" schools of business cycle theorists.[2] They hold that while most persons and enterprises able to do so make a fairly constant effort to save a part of their incomes, periodic breakdowns of confidence lead to incomplete utilization of the savings thus set aside. *When money which is saved is not spent directly by its owner, nor indirectly as the outcome of a transaction between lender and borrower, that money is for the time being rendered as useless to the rest of the economic system as if it had been hoarded by a peasant and buried in the ground.*[3] As a result, the goods which would otherwise have been bought lie unsold upon merchants' shelves; the houses or factories or roads which might have been contracted for are not built; and men who would have worked to replace the merchants' stocks or to carry out the building contracts are idle. Owing to the ensuing spread of unemployment and the decline of corporate earning power, the ability of individuals and corporations to save is checked, and as the amount which they manage to save declines, the contractive power of unused savings is correspondingly reduced until the eco-

[2]G. Van Haberler, *Prosperity and Depression* (League of Nations, 1941 edition), Chapter 8.

[3]The reader may wonder why the countries in which hoarding of money is most common, such as India or France, have not experienced deeper or more frequent depressions. The answer appears to be that since the hoards are numerous and small, and set aside mainly against death and marriage rather than for speculation, they are in the aggregate dis-hoarded as fast as they are hoarded, the gold which one peasant buries being offset by the gold which another digs up. In India the continuous importation of specie (until recently) also served to offset hoarding.

nomic system finally levels off into the trough of a depression.

If the saving effort of individuals and corporations were flexible and controlled by infinite wisdom and foresight, if in the aggregate they tried to save only an amount equal to that being currently borrowed and spent for new capital outlays, then acute depressions of the type encountered in the 1930's would not occur. In the world as it is, however, saving habits are fairly constant and must remain so, partly because of the human tendency to make financial outlay a routine affair for the sake of simplicity, and more especially because of prearranged or contractual savings such as insurance and annuity premiums and payments of principal on mortgages, serial bonds, and sinking funds.

Now if on the one hand the saving habits of the community are fairly constant while on the other hand business sentiment and investment outlays are changeable[4] and beyond the control of individual business concerns acting independently, it follows that the much-to-be-desired equality between the saving which is attempted and the current investment outlays of business enterprise will occur only occasionally and fortuitously. Since this equality is necessary for busi-

[4]Both writers also mention long-term contraction in investment. Keynes thinks this is not far off and Hansen, in an effort to explain the failure of deficit spending in the United States, argues that that country has reached "economic maturity" and will not require appreciable amounts of new privately financed capital equipment in future. (Hansen's view has been effectively disposed of by J. W. Angell in his *Investment and Business Cycles*, Chapter 13.) Both writers appear to ignore the obvious lack of capital equipment over probably 90% of the settled area of the world, the reality of obsolescence, and the possibility that improved fiscal and international banking arrangements and a lower burden from existing debts may enable enormous purchases of capital goods in the future.

ness stability, and since neither savers nor enterprises can be held individually responsible for maintaining it, the situation calls for the attention of a powerful outside agency. There is only one such agency, the state.

The character of the state's action remains to be determined. Keynes envisions public investment timed to make good the periodic lapses in private investment, together with a policy of low interest rates, favouring at the same time a minimum of intervention in private enterprise with a view to maintaining business confidence. Hansen, in addition to emphasizing the need for public spending as an offset to depressions, stresses the importance of using all the fiscal powers of the government; in particular he favours the use of income and social security taxes as a means of controlling the ability of individuals and corporations to save, and certain tax reductions as an inducement to invest. He does not emphasize the importance of low interest rates, at any rate for the United States, and in this he differs markedly from Keynes and other British writers.

On the post-war problem at large Lord Keynes has not yet published his views, and it might be a mistake to assume that he considers the indications of his *General Theory* (which did not emphasize international problems) closely relevant.[5] Professor Hansen, on the other hand, has published a number of popular articles in which he applies the principles of his *Fiscal Policy* to a reconstruction period.[6]

Parenthetically, it may be remarked that important

[5]A recent British proposal for post-war stabilization of exchange rates is widely attributed to Lord Keynes.

[6]See for example *Harper's Magazine*, April, 1942; *Atlantic Monthly*, October, 1942; *Fortune*, November, 1942; *Survey Graphic*, May, 1943.

changes in the attitude towards interest rates have occurred in recent years. It used to be held that if, at the current rate of interest,[7] the flow of saving tended to exceed the amount demanded by borrowers, the rate was too high, and if saving fell short of the amount demanded the rate was too low. From this it followed that if interest rates moved up and down more freely in response to conditions in the capital market they would thereby maintain a continuous flow of transactions, preventing a glut of investment funds at one time and a shortage at another. (As some rates such as those on mortgages had hitherto responded extremely slowly to alternating periods of dearth and plethora in the capital markets, and as others were influenced more by transactions in outstanding securities than by the market in new contracts, e.g., the return on speculative bonds and common stocks, the need for more flexibility in some rates and less in others became evident.) Recent experience and research[8] have shown that a rapid fall in the more flexible rates is not able to induce much more borrowing (unless the rate becomes negative, which is equivalent to a subsidy) when other conditions are unfavourable. From the lending or supply side, it appears that a decline to very low levels of say under two per cent. may lead to an almost complete drying up of the willingness to lend except in the case of

[7]For simplicity, it is customary to write as though there were a single rate of interest. Actually there is a complex structure of rates, comprising pure interest plus compensation for the money costs and the inconveniences of lending, and for risk.

[8]See J. E. Meade and P. W. S. Andrews, "Oxford Economic Papers", *Summary of Replies to Questions on Effects of Interest Rates;* also two papers in the February, 1940, number of the same publication, by P. W. S. Andrews and R. S. Sayers.

enormous amounts loaned for short periods on prime security,[9] while a marked rise from very low rates would create a serious decline in prices of all long-term bonds. In short, the rate of interest is no longer regarded by itself as a major instrument of control.

Two new principles which now command almost universal agreement among trained economists are of basic importance to both writers. The first is that *general* efforts at retrenchment and a *general* scramble for liquidity by dumping inventories and securities in a time of depression defeat their own end by further depressing prices. The second new principle is that government outlay to offset a depression may afford more support to the economic system than the immediate employment provided, owing to the multiplicative character or "leverage" of spending. In a construction undertaking, for example, there is first what is known as "on-site" employment, such as bricklaying, carpentry, and plumbing. Second, there is the "off-site" employment required for making the mason's bricks and so on. "On-site" and "off-site" together comprise *primary* or direct employment. Secondary employment is that arising from the disbursement of wages earned in direct employment and comprises the provision of the workers' clothing, food, fuel, transport and amusement, as well as government services, and upkeep of existing capital. Third, there is a type of ensuing employment for which no satisfactory word exists, namely, that arising from additions to existing capital equipment which are undertaken to serve the expanding purchasing power arising from "on-

[9]This refers to treasury bills and commercial paper, large dealings in which are confined to financial centres.

site", "off-site", and secondary employment. These by no means exhaust the repercussions of expenditure, especially in Canada where they are complicated by the unusual significance of exports and imports, and the important influence of large outstanding debts.

In common with most economic reasoning, the Keynesian theory of employment starts with a hypothetical economic system isolated from all other countries and technically described as a "closed economy". Although thinking in these terms, Keynes obviously had his eye on the United States and Russia, both of which bear a marked resemblance to the closed economy. His principles were not designed for Canada or Australia or Newfoundland or Jamaica or Trinidad or any other area which depends heavily upon foreign customers, and they are far from appropriate even for Great Britain, unless they are applied to other countries at the same time. No doubt full employment schemes, American model, are more relevant to Canada than to Newfoundland, but at the same time it should be remembered that Canada's economic structure is probably closer to Newfoundland's than to that of the United States.

III *Policy for the United States*

Turning from the underlying theory to its expression in practical policy, our inquiry now proceeds by two stages. First we examine counter-depression or full employment schemes as they are likely to be applied in the United States. Second we discuss, in section V, the feasibility of applying similar policies to Canada. As a preface to the Canadian discussion the meaning of the term "full employment" will be examined in detail in section IV.

Let us suppose that a depression has begun in the United States. This will probably be marked by the usual declines in the demands for and the prices of common stocks and commodities, by a moderate curtailment of merchants' orders for finished goods and of manufacturers' orders for materials, by a sharp reduction in the amount of building contracts awarded, by a reduction of employment and of wage payments, and by a falling off in retail sales especially of automobiles and household furnishings. In an effort to offset the contraction, the authorities at Washington with more or less co-operation from state governments and municipalities decide to enlarge the amount of public investment mainly through larger outlays for the upkeep and extension of public works.

Will these emergency outlays of governments be large enough to offset the decline in private investment? The answer is not reassuring. The various governments can secure the required sum of money but are not likely to spend it quickly enough because their activities are not sufficiently wide to permit investment on a sufficient scale. The simple truth is that private activities cover a much broader field than those of government (except when a country is at war) and that private spending is correspondingly larger. The predominance of private investment in the United States[10] is shown by a simple comparison: private investment in durable

[10]Comprehensive figures are not accessible to the writer but partial comparisons relating to new "plant" but excluding "equipment" will be found in a paper by George Terborgh in *Federal Reserve Bulletin*, September, 1939 (Washington D.C.), p. 731.

goods in 1929 was from three to five times greater than the highest level of the government's anti-depression expenditures in later years.[11] Similar evidence is available for Canada.

There is a further reason for doubting the adequacy of compensatory spending upon public works. The reduction of private spending is by no means confined to the field of fixed capital. Lower purchases of raw materials and reduced pay rolls for working them up into finished goods for consumers may be an even more depressing influence,[12] especially in the early stages of a slump. It follows that measures to maintain the flow of business spending in this field may also be necessary, such as special reductions in carrying charges, extra provision for losses on inventory and lower taxation of ensuing inventory profits, government purchase of a variety of basic commodities, and so on. Hitherto government efforts in this field have always come too late and been too small to be of much use. In future, we may find it advisable to experiment with a general subsidy on production as an alternative to cutting wages.

But simple arithmetical comparisons of public and private spending are only the beginning of our inquiry. If government outlay breeds loss of confidence among

[11]The same relation may be shown by comparing the federal deficit with the decline in private investment: the largest federal deficit in the thirties was not much more than a third of the deficiency in the new investments of private enterprise, and this largest deficit occurred not in 1932 or 1933 when it was most needed, but in 1936. (See Hansen, *Fiscal Policy*, pp. 87-8.)

[12]The importance of a reduced investment in inventory is hard to estimate or portray in figures. Published accounting records do not give a clear picture. The swiftness with which the decline in spending occurs, the tendency for it to be spread over many industries (both evidenced in the general decline of commodity prices early in a slump) are the basis of this view.

private enterprises, the compensatory influence of spending may be offset and perhaps more than offset by a further reduction of private disbursements. Loss of confidence among private enterprises may develop in several ways: it may arise directly from government outlays, if in order to spend enough the government invades industries formerly reserved for private enterprise; or it may arise from the associated increases of taxation or public debt, and more especially from uncertainty as to how the resulting tax burden is to be distributed in the future; or it may arise from a disturbance of foreign exchange rates effected by government intervention.

Again, loss of confidence may arise from such measures as tariff warfare or self-destroying price maintenance schemes. Even proposals which are desirable from a long-run standpoint, such as fiscal reforms or laws for social security or the control of business, may be harmful to confidence if introduced at a time when business men are still rubbing their eyes after a collapse of all their plans. In the early days of the Roosevelt regime it was argued that for political reasons reforms can be brought about only at times when the need is greatest, that is to say, in periods of economic distress. If this argument be accepted, we face the dilemma that reform can be achieved only at the expense of further dislocations of the economic system whose defects the reformers seek to remedy.

To stress the need for business confidence may seem platitudinous, but it cannot be too strongly emphasized; recent developments in the study of depressions and their antidotes concentrate above all on the importance of the anticipated net return from new investments

(Keynes' "marginal efficiency of capital"), on the state of confidence or "expectation", and on the changing desire to hold bank deposits rather than bonds or stocks ("liquidity preference"). At the same time is it too much to hope that men of affairs may in future be more tough-minded as to the forces which keep our economic system running? In the 1930's businessmen took fright at minor squeaks and rattles and overlooked or even accentuated the real sources of trouble in the machine.

IV *Policy for Canada*

Before appraising British and American full employment proposals as a guide for Canadian policy we must first examine the meaning of the term *full employment* as it is likely to be used in Canada after the war.

1. It should be made clear at the outset that the term does not imply a precise number of persons which can be neatly counted or estimated to within a fraction of one per cent. of accuracy. Full employment is, statistically speaking, a zone rather than a point, an amount which is anywhere within perhaps eight or ten per cent. above or below some agreed upon figure.

2. The term full employment does not imply that everyone is at work all the time. Experience in many countries has shown that an appreciable fraction of employable persons will not be at work on any given day even at the peak of prosperity. Some are absent owing to sickness or to bereavement or because they are moving to a new residence or making other domestic arrangements; some are taking a holiday which if it does not come at a conventional time is often called absenteeism; some are looking about for, or

are on their way to, a new job. Several (but not all) of these forms of absence from work contribute to the substantial percentage of unemployment shown in statistics even in good years. As an indication of the minimum level, unemployment among members of Canadian trade unions fell to a low point of 4.9 per cent. in 1923, and 4.4 per cent. in 1928. In Great Britain, where the information covers a much wider field and extends over more than half a century, the lowest proportions of unemployed were 2 per cent. in 1899 and 2.1 in 1913. It is important to remember that an economic system in which all the labour, all the machines, all the houses, shops, locomotives, and power plants were fully occupied (i.e., in which there were no reserves) would be almost completely rigid. If, for example, there were no vacant housing in a town, and a number of people needed to move, their chances of securing appropriate accommodation would be very small and they would probably give up the attempt.

3. Full employment before and after the war is bound to be less than the highest level of employment attained during the war. At present (August, 1943) there are probably hundreds of thousands of persons in gainful occupations[13] who would not ordinarily be so employed. Such persons include (a) young people of both sexes who would otherwise be at school or college, (b) unmarried young women who would otherwise be living with their parents and assisting in purely household duties pending marriage, (c) young women already married who would otherwise be keeping house and rearing children, (d) older able-bodied women, single

[13]The term is here used as in the Census and does not include homemakers.

and widowed, who ordinarily depend on their relatives or live partly on their own means, (e) young war widows most of whom will marry again and become home-makers, (f) married women who are going out to work for patriotic reasons or to maintain their standard of living in the face of higher taxes and living costs, and (g) persons of advanced age who would ordinarily have retired or been laid off. When the war is over the majority of these persons will (we hope) return to their former peacetime situations and cease to be among the gainfully occupied. Their return will be hastened if the economic transition from war to peace is swift and orderly, if young men are able to bear the costs of marriage, if men already married are able to support their wives in the home and send their children to school and college, and if young men and women demobilized from the forces are able to continue their education. We thus reach the important paradox that, if employment conditions are good and wages and farm incomes are high after the war, the number of people seeking work for wages will be considerably reduced.

4. In Canada, seasonal influences are an important factor in defining full employment. Monthly statistics show that the highest level of employment is usually reached late in August or September, when the number of employees is from ten to twenty per cent. above that in January. It follows that something approaching full employment on a peacetime basis will be attained, if at all, during the summer months. This paper is not concerned with the special problems of seasonal unemployment.[14] That is a separate topic on which

[14]See another treatment of these issues in Chapter IV.

Canada, one of the world's principal victims, will have to design her own policy.

5. The terms *unemployment* and *full employment* are usually applied only to wage-earners, that is, to those working for a wage, salary, or commission. There is a tendency to think of wage-earners as the whole of the labour force—as a fixed number of persons whose occupational status does not change. In the British Isles no great error arises from this view but the situation is far different in Canada. Consider the following table which shows that for every ten wage-earners there are five other gainfully occupied persons.

STATUS	Census of June 1931[15] MALE	FEMALE	TOTAL (in thousands)	Census of June 1941[16] MALE	FEMALE	TOTAL (in thousands)
1. Wage-earners and salaried workers.....	2022	548	2570 (65.4%)	2088	720	2808 (66.9%)
2. Own-account workers.....	550	55	605	733	61	794
3. Employers...	388	19	407	237	9	246[17]
4. Unpaid workers.....	301	44	345	272	75	347
5. Total gainfully occupied....	3261	666	3927	3330	865	4195

[15] *Canada Year Book*, 1937 (Ottawa), p. 144.

[16] *Census Bulletin: Occupations and Earnings, No. 2* (Dominion Bureau of Statistics, Ottawa, 1942). A study based on a ten per cent. sample.

[17] The decline in the number of employers owing to a reduction in hired labour on farms is more than counterbalanced by the increase of own-account workers.

During the war a great many persons who would ordinarily work on their own account or as employers have become wage-earners, transferring from groups 2 and 3 to group 1. In addition a large number of unpaid workers comprising mainly farmers' sons (who would ordinarily have moved into group 2 as they became older, through becoming farm operators on their own account) have likewise moved into group 1 and become wage-earners. If these additions to the wage force do not return after the war to their former pursuits as own-account workers, employers, and unpaid workers, the number of persons seeking employment for wages will be considerably greater than in 1939, especially after demobilization has been completed.

A similar movement into the wage-earning group occurred in the three or four years ending in 1929. In that period the number of wage-workers grew more rapidly than the whole working force. To some extent this growth reflected the absorption of unemployed and persons from the fringes of the occupied population, but a considerable shift from own-account to wage work also seems to have occurred. To a large degree this shift is the same as the movement from rural (mainly agricultural) to urban occupations, and it would not be far from the truth to say that, after the unemployed, the rural population is, from the standpoint of employers in the towns and cities, the second line of the country's labour reserve.[18] As a labour reserve the rural population differs from the unemployed in that it is a less permanent part of the

[18]This has an important bearing on the size of the labour reserve required for a smoothly functioning system.

industrial working force, at any rate until it has become well established in wage work. In times of urban unemployment its members exercise the alternative of remaining on farms and in other rural situations; in times of high employment they move into the cities, unless farming is very prosperous,[19] and in a succeeding wave of unemployment only a fraction of the newcomers return to their former pursuits in the country. All this is the natural way for urbanization to proceed (in the absence of overseas immigration flowing directly into towns and cities). It reinforces the statement already made that if farm incomes are high the number of people leaving the farms will be reduced with the result that fewer people will seek work for wages in the towns.

6. It is an open question whether *structural unemployment* should be allowed for in reckoning the level of full employment. Structural unemployment arises from the long-term decline of an industry, or from an unusual competitive situation which may not, however, last indefinitely. Since 1920 this type of unemployment has been a conspicuous feature of the British coal and cotton textile industries, of the New England cotton textile industry, of most North American steam and electric railways, and of sawmilling in eastern Canada. It may arise from a change in technique or loss of a foreign market, from exhaustion of resources, or from an improved competitive position of a substitute. It is a condition which exists in a few industries even at the top of a boom.

[19]Even prosperity for the farmers will not stem the movement to the towns if mechanization of agriculture is meanwhile reducing the need for farm labour.

Subject to these qualifications, the term "full employment" will be used in this paper for want of a better.

V *Applicability of Hansen Proposals*

We now return to the question: "Is a project for maintaining full employment, of the type sponsored for the United States by Professor Hansen, applicable to Canada?" The answer is a qualified "no" with a reminder that the Hansen project may not succeed in the United States either, though its chances of success there are far greater than in Canada.

To be successful, a Canadian anti-depression programme must take place under the following conditions. First, and above all, the governments of other countries, especially our principal customers, Great Britain and the United States, must pursue spending policies similar to our own. Moreover, they must do so at the same time or a little earlier and on an equivalent scale and with proportionally good results. Second, the impact of each country's internally induced revival must be allowed to spread to other countries by means of international trade. To this end, restrictions in the form of tariffs, quotas, arbitrary valuations, clearing agreements, and such, must be greatly reduced. Third, enterprises and consumers, borrowers and lenders, must be given whatever assurances are necessary to justify them in making long-term commitments. For instance, satisfactory spreads between selling prices and costs (especially for new investments) must come into being; there must, moreover, be reasonable hope that profitable conditions will continue over an average of a good many years, and that occasional strokes of good luck may be enjoyed. In order to keep down costs, the cost-raising activities[20] of tariff monopolies, labour monopolies, patent monopolies, and monopolies arising from large-scale production, must be brought under control, while at the same time the action of buyers' monopolies must be restrained, especially in a "buyers' market". Furthermore, borrowers and lenders must have confidence that the value of money will not change violently and that contracts will be enforced in an orderly and reasonable fashion. Finally, the taxation of private enterprises and individuals must be established on a basis which reconciles the often conflicting claims of equity and aspirations for reform on the one hand with economic necessity, security, and convenience on the other. In the last year we have heard a great deal about the need of social security for the individual and almost nothing about the need of business security for enterprise. Measures to promote business security are not a good vote-catching device for governments which hope to stay in power after the war, but they lie at the heart of a successful reconstruction policy.

Unless the foregoing conditions are met, public spending for investment will, as Dr. Coats has recently said, "lack staying power".[21] The writer sees little hope of satisfying so many conditions by ordinary parliamen-

[20]The extraordinary situation which has grown up in the running trades of the steam railways, one of the oldest fields of labour union activity in North America, is described in the *Reader's Digest* for March 1943 under the title " 'Featherbedding' Hampers the War Effort". On patents see a recent article from the *Economist* of January 16 and 23, 1943. On monopolies, see L. G. Reynolds, *The Control of Competition in Canada* (Cambridge, Mass., 1940).

[21]See R. H. Coats, "The General Economic Setting" (Chapter 1 in *Reconstruction in Canada*, ed., C. A. Ashley, Toronto, 1943).

tary methods in less than a generation, especially in view of the well-known sources of revenue of the older political parties, and the equally compromised position of new parties which rely upon generous promises rather than upon campaign funds. No doubt governments will go through the motions in order to secure public approval but this gives little assurance that each separate part of the task will be completed, and none whatever that an integrated policy will be carried out under parliamentary leadership. (The outlook was summed up recently in a discussion group when someone asked: "Can any federal party appeal to the electorate in the future without promising full employment?" In reply another member asked: "Has any federal party *ever* appealed to the electorate without promising full employment?") In view of the slow and ineffectual operation of parliament in matters touching economic policy, the post-war period will almost certainly require an extension of emergency powers granted to the cabinet. This need not mean the disappearance of democratic government—it may, on the contrary, be one of the conditions of its survival.

It may be argued that if many countries were to adopt spending programmes and if other external and internal conditions were met, Canada might reap the benefits without incurring any of the costs, enjoying what has been described by Mr. R. B. Bryce, as a "free ride on the recovery of others".[22] This is a point of view which should appeal especially to the more radical and calculating isolationists, who have adopted a similar attitude towards the extent of this country's war effort.

[22]R. B. Bryce, "Basic Issues in Postwar International Economic Relations" (*American Economic Review*, Supplement, March, 1942, p. 169).

But in the peace as in war, the welchers and the counters of narrow gains will earn a bad name and all that follows upon it. Those who imagine that Canada can reap all the benefits of American or British recovery measures without incurring any of the costs should remember that tariff reprisals can follow in a matter of months from Washington and London.

We may next inquire what would happen in the absence of the first two conditions of a successful anti-depression scheme. Under these circumstances other countries would buy fewer Canadian products, export prices would fall, and our export trades would be depressed at least as badly as they were after 1929. It would soon be found that expenditures for construction work and other investment outlays, even at a rate of many hundreds of millions per annum, gave little or no help to the depressed export trades. What advantage, for example, would be enjoyed by wheat farms, copper mines, salmon canneries, or paper mills, if the Dominion government confined itself to letting building contracts for the purchase of steel rods, cement, and construction labour? Of course such contracts would indirectly increase the purchase of Canadian-made clothing, food, and housing (and also increase the purchases of goods made in other countries) but only a negligible benefit would be conferred upon predominantly export industries.[23] At best, farm hands and miners and loggers would have an opportunity to become road-builders and construction workers. At worst, the export industries would gain nothing but the prospect of higher

[23]Except in cases where the exportable surplus has been very small (e.g., butter) larger internal demand may then create a shortage and bring an appreciable rise of price.

taxes to cover interest payments on the enlarged public debt.

It is evident, then, that if Canada is obliged to pursue a full employment policy without co-operation from abroad, aid to exporters must be combined with aid to domestic investment and should probably be given priority. Aid to exporters may be given in three ways: by subsidies and valorization schemes, by depreciation of the Canadian dollar abroad, and by a lowering of production costs.

(a) The most obvious way to support export industry over short periods is for the government to subsidize export products by purchasing them at higher than world prices and selling them for what they will bring in world markets, absorbing the loss out of taxing and borrowing. This would be most agreeable to exporters, and there is much to be said for the policy if other exporting countries do not object (as Canada does) to competition from subsidized exports, and if buying countries do not dislike (as Canada does) bargaining with the resulting government monopolies. This country has already cushioned collapses in wheat quotations by small subsidies. The total amount of expenditure required to sustain exporters might equal or exceed that needed for aiding internal investment.

(b) Depreciation of the Canadian currency on the foreign exchanges may benefit exporters by bringing them higher prices in Canadian dollars (provided that prices in United States funds or pounds sterling remain unchanged). For example, it can easily be seen from a study of wheat prices in the thirties that, when the Canadian dollar fell in London, wheat prices rose in Winnipeg, and that, when the Canadian dollar rose in

London, wheat prices fell in Winnipeg, other changes having been allowed for.

Against the benefits enjoyed by exporters must be set the losses of importers who in buying cotton, wool, oil, coal, rubber, and other imported products must pay a premium on the required foreign currency. During a depression, however, the buyers of these imported materials usually reap a more or less fortuitous advantage from lower world prices so that the higher costs arising from a premium on foreign currency are offset by the unusual cheapness of imports. The main disadvantages of depreciation fall rather upon debtors who must make fixed payments of interest and principal in the more costly foreign currency, and upon those who must buy foreign goods whose prices do not fall appreciably in a depression.

In short, a depreciation of the Canadian dollar, in so far as it tends to raise export prices, is a method of helping export industries with a minimum outlay by the federal government. The costs are borne by the groups who lose from depreciation. The gains and losses raise complex problems; sometimes depreciation leads to lower commodity prices in London or New York so that the last state may well be no better than the first; in others, it leads the buying countries to impose more obstacles to importation so that the last state is quite definitely worse.[24] In view of the importance of this problem, the information at present available is scanty with respect to particular commodities such as lumber, newsprint, aluminium, and asbestos. The one product

[24]The principal survey for Canada is a study prepared for the Royal Commission on Dominion Provincial Relations by Professor F. A. Knox entitled *Dominion Monetary Policy* (Ottawa, mimeo., 1939).

which has hitherto enjoyed the full benefit of depreciation has been gold.

(c) Lower production costs for materials, labour, and capital equipment, and for taxes, freight, and miscellaneous items, have long been one of the main needs of export industries, particularly agriculture. The lengthy and on the whole abortive attempts to secure substantially lower costs by tariff reduction indicate that as a means of combating sudden dislocations little is to be expected from this method. Nevertheless, a satisfactory relation between domestic costs and export prices is probably the most important long-term condition of a high standard of living in an exporting country. Short-term monetary stimulants are in themselves mere palliatives and if used continually may leave a hangover that does not wear off.

The foreign exchange rate is also of importance in imposing limits on government spending. If outlay for government works has the desired effect of adding to the public's total disbursements, part of the additional purchases will be directed to foreign goods; this will in turn lower the value of our dollar abroad in the absence of sufficiently powerful offsetting forces. As the exchange rate falls it approaches a level where the disadvantages of depreciation more than cancel out the advantages already noted. At this level we reach the limits of government assistance both to export and to investment goods industries. No comparable limits exist for the spending policy of the United States, owing to the smaller importance of foreign trade in that country.

Fortunately the fall of the Canadian dollar abroad may be controlled to a degree by restrictions on imports, capital movements, and travel abroad, as well as by gold movements and, under favourable conditions, by raising foreign loans. (If the internal schemes of the big countries fail, these countries can at least assist revival by giving the small countries a chance to maximize their own measures.) With drastic controls, perhaps requiring the rationing of imported goods to Canadian consumers, the limits to government spending could be stretched perhaps hundreds of millions per annum before the exchange rate became unwisely low. Such an operation calls for some of the paraphernalia of a war economy including a foreign exchange control board, perhaps a prices and rationing board, appropriate inter-departmental arrangements, and the delegation of certain parliamentary powers.

Persons who have no direct experience with foreign trade often suppose that depreciation of the Canadian dollar is an unmitigated evil. They argue that depreciation casts doubts upon the country's ability to pay its debts abroad or that depreciation threatens the internal value of the currency or the soundness of the banking system. Enough has now been said to show that there are definite advantages in depreciation for certain purposes and within certain limits and that most fears on the subject are groundless.[25]

VI *Sources of Funds*

To return to the general subject of compensatory spending: the reader may well have thought: "Com-

[25]Uncontrollable depreciation on the foreign exchanges may arise from efforts to maintain payments on a large foreign debt when commodity trade is insufficient, or from excessive issues of currency for internal purposes.

pensatory spending is a nice idea but where are the enormous sums of money to come from and how much can be secured?" The answer is somewhat reassuring but not simple.

First, suppose that the government raises an additional million dollars in taxes or loans from persons and corporations who would otherwise have spent all of this money themselves, or have loaned it to others to spend.[26] When the government disburses this million dollars, the combined outlay of the public and the government is no greater than before. All that has taken place is that the government spends more and the citizens less as a result of which the government's reputation as a good uncle is increased and the output of post-offices, roads, and so forth has risen at the expense of the tax-payers' purchases of houses, furniture, automobiles, and industrial equipment. There are more of some jobs and fewer of others, and while this may benefit those who have suffered most from lack of work, the total number of jobs is probably unchanged.

Second, suppose that the government levies taxes or borrows from those who would not otherwise have spent or loaned their money. The disbursement of the proceeds will then create a net addition to the total spending of the nation and employment will be increased. So far so good, but it is not easy to segregate the non-spenders and the non-lenders from the rest of the community for purposes of taxing and borrowing. One method of segregation is to tax large incomes (which are one of the principal sources of savings) more heavily

[26]Putting money into a savings account instead of spending it is not likely to result in a loan to someone else by the bank.

by personal and corporate income taxes, at periods when little investment is taking place. The defect of this method is that such taxes are likely to be perpetuated into a period when the would-be hoarders might have become investors; the levies then become a drain on the funds available to private enterprise and check the desired revival.

Third, funds may be secured by borrowing from the banking system. Provided this type of borrowing does not lead to any contraction of bank credit available to business, the funds so borrowed are a net addition to spending power and constitute an increase in the supply of money.[27]

In view of the foregoing, we are obliged to regard bank credit as the principal source of government receipts for combating a contraction of employment. The limits to the amount of bank credit which may be safely granted to a government depend greatly on the circumstances. As a rule, the total amount of bank credit (roughly equal to loans plus investments) can be extended safely up to about ten times the cash reserves of the banking system. The limits to cash reserves depend partly on the internal policy of the Bank of Canada but ultimately on Canada's foreign exchange position. Under the gold standard (now understood as a system permitting free settlement of international balances by shipments of monetary gold between countries) the basic reserves of the Canadian banking and currency system are highly sensitive to changes in

[27]The supply of money in use in Canada for the purposes of this discussion, is the sum of (1) coin and notes in circulation and (2) all deposits in the chartered banks.

the international balance of payments.[28] No great extension of bank credit above the usual amount is feasible under the gold standard, therefore, unless other countries are likewise extending credit and thereby increasing their purchases of Canadian products to the same extent as we increase our purchases of their products.[29] If the gold standard is not in force, an increase of Canadian bank reserves and bank credit and employment will be followed by heavier imports and a tendency of the Canadian dollar to depreciate, if other countries are not extending credit and increasing their imports at the same rate. As the dollar depreciates, it eventually reaches a point already referred to in this discussion, where the disadvantages of depreciation, to purchasers of foreign funds, cancel out the benefits to exporters. As hitherto argued, arrival at this point may be delayed by the use of controls, provided always that these mechanisms are acceptable to the countries which buy our exports.

Since the funds for compensatory spending are to be secured mainly by borrowing, it remains to inquire into the burden of the increased public debt. Whenever controversy arises over public debt, two bodies of opinion at once appear, the optimists and the pessimists. The optimists hold that the payment of interest on internal debt is no more than a transfer of funds from one pocket to another. Such a transfer of funds imposes no significant burden, they argue, since the cost

[28]A description of the items entering into Canada's balance of international payments, and their amounts, will be found in any recent volume of the *Canada Year Book*.

[29]Recent proposals for a world clearing-house for international transactions would permit somewhat greater latitude in the movements of balances of payments.

of collecting the taxes and paying the interest charges is not usually more than two or three per cent. of the sums handled. Nor is repayment of the principal of the debt regarded as a problem; refunding is considered satisfactory and it is argued with much truth that a general repayment of public debt would prove embarrassing to the larger holders. In short, the optimists regard the debt-service as little more than a self-cancelling system of book entries, without economic or political significance.

The pessimists are divided into at least two schools. There are the "individual analogy pessimists", some of whom, reasoning from private experience, conclude that a state which never pays off its debts must sooner or later declare itself insolvent; others, looking at a war debt and finding no tangible offsetting assets in the government's hands, conclude that the state is already bankrupt. Both these views arise from a mistaken analogy between the individual and the state and they are on the same level with the argument that because the individual must die the state must die.

A more sophisticated school of pessimists begins by agreeing that the internal debt service is merely a transfer of funds from one pocket to another pocket. Then he asks "Whose pocket? Does the state take money from Peter's left pocket and put it back into his right, or does it rob Peter to pay Paul?" If, in the first place, the money is merely taken from Peter's left pocket to his right, that may not seem serious to those who think merely of offsetting entries, but how does it seem to Peter? Peter made a loan to the government and now he finds himself obliged to pay it back to himself. The interest on his capital is employed in revolving around the seat of his pants and it dawns upon him that we have a capital levy in fact if not in name.

If instead the state taxes Peter to pay Paul, almost anything may happen as a result of the debt-service. If the Peters are rich and the Pauls poor, debt-service has a levelling effect and reduces personal saving. If the Peters are old and the Pauls young, it redistributes income in favour of the young. If the Peters live in one part of the country which we shall call A and the Pauls live in another part called B, then A will lose and B will gain. If the Peters are free spenders and the Pauls are thrifty then saving may be increased and *vice versa.* All this is on the assumption that taxes are assessed on personal incomes. If, instead, taxes are assessed on particular commodities or on buildings, the output of the taxed articles will almost certainly be hampered by taxation and the total loss to the country may be much greater.

In short, the two-way process of taxing and of paying interest charges may be far from neutral in its effects. To secure neutrality of effects from debt would require a delicate adjustment of the whole fiscal system to this one end, at a time when the system is called upon to serve many other purposes. Moreover, as men naturally seek to lighten their burdens at the expense of others, political disturbances will undoubtedly bring about a rolling of the tax burden now here and now there. Each change will alter somewhat the effects of the debt-service.

It should be noted that even the most optimistic views on debt relate only to internally held national obligations. The debts of provinces and municipalities, even though held in Canada, may create serious problems as Canadian experience has demonstrated all too clearly.

VII *Some New Fallacies*

In the last year the problems dealt with in this paper have been widely discussed in conferences, radio forums, and the press. In the course of these discussions a new crop of mistaken economic notions has sprung up. From these I have culled three which deserve attention: the assumption that what we can do in war (i.e., in creating and maintaining a boom) we can do in peace, the declarations of businessmen that they have an obligation to provide employment, and the belief that social security schemes offer a solution of post-war problems.

What we do in war is dominated by the demands of a single great buyer, the national government, which purchases enormous amounts of war goods. To our own government's spending is added the wartime buying of other countries and other governments, some of whom have not in time of peace bought much from Canada and may even have raised heavy duties against our products. This growth of government spending is made possible by heavier borrowing, undertaken in the belief that bad as a swollen national debt may be, a national defeat is worse. Greater spending is also made possible by much heavier taxes, especially on persons with small incomes, by more or less inflationary bank loans not only to governments but to the buyers of bonds, and by the extension of international credits through lend-lease and other emergency arrangements. For the most part these are money-raising devices which few people would wish to see employed continuously on anything like the present scale, since it appears that unlimited expansion of currency and one-sided debts and one-sided gifts would soon create a situation abhorrent alike to the principles of any known financial and legal system and to human nature in a free community. Some readers will feel that this statement indicates a stodgy and reactionary point of view, and to them I reply that any other conclusion appears to be the product either of wishful thinking, or of an attitude which would forbid human beings from asking or even expecting the state to honour its contracts, and which would compel them to make unlimited "gifts" to other persons and even to other countries, against their will.

To fill the urgent demand for war goods in the shortest possible time, and regardless of the cost in dollars, the capital equipment of industry must be extended more swiftly than during an ordinary boom. Plans and specifications must be prepared, mines must be enlarged, pipelines and power plants built, and new factories and machines set up. All this creates a most abnormal demand for labour especially in certain branches of construction work and the metal trades, a demand so intense that it might not be equalled once during twenty years of peace.

In addition to being large and urgent, the government's demands are (within limits) certain. Purchases are usually made by letting contracts to the producers, with the result that the goods are sold before they are produced, in marked contrast with peacetime conditions when the bulk of consumer goods and raw materials are made in advance of sale, that is, on a speculative basis. In wartime, in other words, the government (i.e., the community) bears not only the current cost but also the risk of carrying inventory. In many cases too it bears the risk of capital investment in equipment made specially for war purposes. To do the same in peace would involve the tax-paying public in most of the losses incurred by businessmen.

Wartime demand also differs from normal demand in that it is comparatively free from seasonal fluctuation. This makes it possible to utilize industrial equipment and labour more fully throughout the year, and is a most desirable change which it should be possible to perpetuate. In this connection it would be of great interest to know how far the elimination of seasonal demand has increased the annual output per worker in Canadian automobile assembling plants, which formerly operated for only about five months in a year.

Returning to the international aspects of demand, it is evident that warfare obliges all the combatants to increase their purchases simultaneously, thereby enormously augmenting the expansive effect of both government and private spending. If someone were to discover how to keep the economic policies of all the nations in step after the war, now to quicken and then to slacken the industrial tempo, one of the world's hardest politico-economic problems would be solved.

All in all, then, the war economy differs so much from that of peace that an effort to perpetuate its merits after the close of hostilities will be exceedingly difficult. The confident statements of publicists that "it must be done" are about as convincing as the promise of the alderman that after his election no cats will yowl and no dogs bark.

Another popular notion concerns the obligations of

private enterprise. Businessmen have begun to talk about the "obligation to provide employment", as if an individual firm or group of firms could fix the scale of output and employment without regard to the state of the market. It need hardly be said that no enterprise, either public or private, could shoulder such an obligation unless its support were guaranteed from the public purse. An enterprise which seriously tried to live up to such an undertaking without regard to the condition of its market and without government aid would soon have neither a dollar in its till nor a postage stamp in the drawer. It is true that private business has many obligations, as defined by the particular contracts into which it has entered and by the laws and customs under which it operates, and there is no doubt that the community would benefit by a more scrupulous fulfilment of these obligations, but it is hard to see what can be gained by adding to these already numerous responsibilities a new and fantastically burdensome one which the realities of business itself would be the first to prove impracticable in the event of a depression.

Finally, misunderstanding may arise from several elaborate post-war schemes which have recently appeared, such as the "Beveridge Report" in Great Britain, the report of the National Resources Planning Board in the United States, and the "Marsh Plan" in Canada. There seems to be a general belief that these schemes offer a solution of the main post-war problems. The British and Canadian proposals relate almost solely to the extension of social insurance and welfare devices, suggesting the payment of additional benefits and the inclusion of new risks not hitherto covered. They are of great long-term significance in that they recognize the importance of the family and the dangers inherent in the fall of the birth-rate, but it should be clearly understood that they have not been devised for the stabilization of employment.[30] Instead they assume quite explicitly that the basic problems of employment discussed in this paper have been solved, that a bigger and better pie has somehow been brought down from the sky, and that all that remains is to divide it among the national family in a way more agreeable to the majority of voters. This "assumes away" the most difficult part of the whole problem, namely how to maintain the employment and output and money income of the various nations at a high and stable level.[31] The American plan frankly recognizes the problem and makes proposals for maintaining output and employment but can hardly be said to contribute to the subject.

* * * * *

In carrying out a programme of public spending (on the assumption that the long preparatory work has been completed) a variety of important decisions must be made. Some of these must be reached by the Cabinet alone, others by deputy ministers and subordinate administrators, while still others should be in the hands of experts in economics and finance, to be put

[30]It is true that the payment of unemployment insurance and other benefits is itself an anti-depression measure in that it assures a minimum of income and hence of buying power in a period of unemployment, but the power of these payments in sustaining employment is necessarily limited and they may even have a depressing effect if the schemes are supported from ill-devised levies.

[31]A good British summary of the underlying problems usually neglected by advocates of social security measures will be found in a recent statement entitled *The Problem of Unemployment*, published by Lever Brothers and Unilever Limited in Great Britain, and by Lever Brothers in Canada.

into effect as soon as the Cabinet's approval is secured.

Consider for a moment the problems upon which a verdict must be given:

(a) When is compensatory government spending to begin? This is primarily a matter for economists specializing in the current movements of the business cycle and international trade, but if the technical question of when to commence spending in order to sustain employment conflicts with the political question of spending to sustain the government's position at the next election, there is not much doubt as to the outcome. Those who consider this observation cynical should compare the employment index for highway construction in Ontario with the dates of provincial elections in that province.

(b) How much money should be spent per month, and when should the amount be increased or reduced? This is mainly a technical question for economists, but it will soon dissolve in the administrative question of how much *can* be spent in view of the existing outlets for expenditure, and the extent to which plans and legal arrangements and agreements with other governments et cetera have been made.

(c) How should spending be directed in order to create the maximum amount of employment? This too is mainly a technical question, which experts are not fully prepared to answer, but their decision should be closer to the mark than anyone else's. It can readily be seen that allocation of expenditure between regions, industries and even between towns, and as between direct outlays, subsidies, guarantees, and tax remissions, raises political as well as technical problems.

One of the largest and most controversial problems is the division of public assistance between the public and the private sectors of the economy. Should government spending be designed to widen the field of publicly controlled output or to narrow it, or to leave the present division as between public and private output unchanged?

(d) When should public spending be tapered off, and when should the federal government begin to budget for an over-all surplus? The answer to this question is ideally a technical one but it rests upon so many judgments which cannot be precise that the politician will probably take advantage of these uncertainties to warp the verdict in his own favour.

(e) How far should a Canadian full employment programme be carried, in the event that schemes in other countries are not started soon enough, or for some other reason fail to stimulate Canadian exports? As already argued, the answer rests mainly upon the level to which the Canadian dollar can wisely be allowed to depreciate in New York. Here as elsewhere technical and political considerations are so intermingled that only a statesman with exceptional breadth of view, courage and integrity can be relied upon to give full heed to the public interest.

In short, the success of even the best devised measures to sustain employment (and in our present state of knowledge the best is far from good) may be threatened by a conflict between technical and political considerations, and by a generally stormy political atmosphere. The natural tendency of mankind in earlier post-war periods has been described as follows by one of the greatest students of the relation between war and politics:

"Nor is it enough for the security [of men] that they be governed and directed by one judgment for a limited time, as in one battle or one warre. For, though they obtain a victory by their unanimous endeavour against a forraign enemy; yet afterwards, when either they have no common enemy, or he that by one part is held for an enemy, is by another part held for a friend, they must needs by the difference of their interests dissolve and fall again into a warre amongst themselves."[33]

[33]Hobbes, *Leviathan*, Pt. II, Ch. XVII.

Chapter VII

PROBLEMS OF INTERNATIONAL ECONOMIC RECONSTRUCTION

J. F. Parkinson

Reconstruction in Canada can hardly be planned *in vacuo*. The ultimate success of any programme of economic reconstruction will depend, above all else, upon the kind of world economy in which the country must operate after the war. That is, Canadian "prosperity" will be determined, in large measure, by the extent to which Canadian exports are given access to world markets, and by the volume and strength of world demand for exports generally. If world trade can be raised to a level much higher than has been achieved in the past, there is some prospect of Canada being able to maintain employment for a substantial portion of the vast number of people now engaged in the production of export commodities, including in this term many war materials. In the future, as in the past, such determining factors as geography, climate, and population, together with a recognition of the advantages to be obtained from international exchange, will set the limits within which domestic economic policy must operate if it is desired to maximize economic welfare.

The existence of these limiting factors can hardly be ignored. Canada is lacking in many of the raw materials essential for an industrial civilization. Moreover, the domestic market is too small to produce all manufactured articles as cheaply as some other countries, even if she possessed all the necessary raw materials. On the other hand, Canada does possess certain abundant resources that the rest of the world can acquire advantageously from her. And the same condition holds true also for many manufactured goods, so long as manufacturing industries can enjoy the economies of large-scale production. These, then, are the circumstances dictating that Canadian economic welfare is served best when international exchange is widely practised.

If anything, the war itself has strengthened the case for economic internationalism, so far as Canada is concerned. The urgency of the needs of the United Nations has given rise to a vast expansion of production in most of the traditional staples of the Canadian economy—foodstuffs, forest products, and metals. Some diminution of production in these areas may be inevitable. However, the smaller the decline in production from the high levels of wartime the more easily the economy will be able to cope with the inevitable dislocations induced by the shrinking of the "munitions" industries. On this last point, however, the war effort has also demonstrated the ability of Canadian industry to produce cheaply manufactured goods of the most complicated types where the circumstances are favourable. A significant feature of Canada's experience with the production of war materials is that it has been confined to a fairly limited range of products and—for that reason, and because of the heavy requirements among the United Nations—conducted on a large scale. In these circumstances, Canadian-produced war supplies have been made available in such quantities and at such low prices as were thought feasible only in a much larger and more industrially developed country. If Canadian products have easy access to the markets of the world after the war there is no reason to believe that our exports would be confined mainly to raw materials, foodstuffs, and semi-manufactures. On the contrary, it is almost certain that highly fabricated goods would constitute a much bigger proportion of the total than in the past.

The Trend to Economic Nationalism

As is well known, the events of the decade 1929-39 posed a serious problem for those countries whose economies were based upon the expectation of an expanding world economy. This period witnessed a serious disintegration of the world economic order. The breakdown of this system was characterized by the growth of an exaggerated protectionism, a shift towards bi-lateral trade arrangements, and the bi-lateral balancing of the international accounts, including the strengthening of imperial preferences. It was marked by the abandonment of the gold standard—the technique and the symbol of world economic unity—the instability of the foreign exchanges everywhere, and the virtual cessation of international investment and migration.

The explanations of the drift towards economic nationalism vary in their emphasis and obviously there were many contributing factors. There was the loss of economic resilience, as emphasized by the growth of monopoly or imperfect competition; the removal of the stimulus to production caused by an expanding population; the disappearance of geographical frontiers; the mis-use of political nationalism. All these and some other ingredients went into the making of economic nationalism and imperialism. But a prominent place must be given to the increasing incidence of mass unemployment; few would deny the importance of this factor in promoting the drift towards economic nationalism in the thirties. But the world depression of the thirties in turn had its roots in the economic developments of the last war. The middle twenties saw a confused attempt—riddled as it was with inconsistencies—to revive the world economy, but this effort broke down with the onset of the world economic depression. Thereafter, the disintegration of the system was rapid, and, in that part of Europe dominated by Germany, it was wellnigh complete. Any consideration of the future of world economic relations must reckon with the fact that similar pressures towards economic nationalism will recur, and will endanger the prospects for reconstruction unless they are handled differently.

The failure of all efforts to find a solution to the world economic collapse should be a warning to the "dependent" economies of the bleak future that must face many countries unless the problem is tackled in the spirit of international collaboration.

While the framework of the world economic order was seriously cracked by the events of the depression decade, the exigencies of war have led to a further disturbance of the structure in a way that promises to aggravate the earlier trend towards economic isolationism. For example, the needs of war have altered or restricted the flow of goods and services between the United Nations, not to speak of the disappearance of all trade with enemy countries. Within the United Nations, a substantial proportion of the wartime trade is composed of strictly war materials and munitions. The present level of production and exchange of these materials can hardly be expected to continue when the war is over. But there will be, as there should be, desperate efforts to turn such production to civilian uses, and to find external as well as internal outlets for the new products.

Practically the entire continent of Europe has been affected by the economic domination of Germany, and the various national economies have been twisted to fit the requirements of the "New Economic Order". From producing consumer goods for domestic use, or for export, they have had to shift to the production of foods, raw materials, and war materials for Germany. In agriculture, the production of grains has been increased at the expense of livestock and other protective foods, a development which, if it is not reversed, bodes ill for the future of the grain-growing countries overseas. By the end of the war, if not already, an economic unity of sorts will have been imposed upon Europe. This is the kind of economic omelette that will not be unscrambled very easily.

Elsewhere in the world the same forces that operated in the last war to destroy the bases of an international economy have been at work again, this time with probably greater effectiveness. The blockade and counter-blockade, the shortages of shipping, the difficulty of obtaining supplies from such universal providers as the United Kingdom and the United States, have all combined to encourage a greater degree of economic self-reliance everywhere. The industrialization of the less mature countries has, consequently, been speeded up. The results of these developments can be seen most clearly in South America, in Australasia, and, not least of all, in Canada.

It is also clear that in the United States, the United Kingdom, Canada, and to a lesser degree elsewhere, there is an impressive development of new industries to manufacture substitutes for products formerly obtained abroad, of which synthetic rubber is the most striking example. The chemistry of the First World War was based upon coal; the chemistry of this war is utilizing petroleum to a much greater degree. Many of these wartime techniques will survive the war. The outcome of this is not easy to determine but it seems likely that the increasing use of oil for the production of rubber or for plastics (for example) will disturb the balance of world economic resources; it will certainly disrupt established systems of international commodity exchange.

The Position of the United Kingdom

The difficulties to be faced in re-creating a world economy can be brought to a sharp focus if we examine, for a moment, the probable position of the United Kingdom after the war. The pivotal rôle performed by the United Kingdom in creating and maintaining a unified world economy during the last century or more is a familiar theme with the economic historians, and there is no need here to do more than emphasize the fact that the size of the consuming market, combined with a free trade policy, made the United Kingdom the most important and most dependable outlet for the raw materials and manufactured products of the world.

Britain was able to pay for its heavy import surplus by the sale of manufactured goods, and with certain earnings derived from banking commissions, shipping services, and the like, and with the earnings from foreign investments. At the same time the international financial operations conducted in the city of London were usually so contrived as to preserve some kind of international economic equilibrium, and to lend continuous support to the forces making for world economic unity.

It is now clear that, whether we consider Britain's ability to satisfy her own essential import requirements, or her ability to contribute to the smooth working of the international economy, her position—which had already been seriously jeopardized by the events of the thirties—has been made even more difficult by the war. The external requirements of the United Kingdom will be at least as urgent as ever; her external economic strength, on the other hand, will have been seriously weakened. Export markets for manufactured goods of the types that were familiar in the twenties will be reduced; the industrially immature countries are, of necessity, learning to produce for themselves, and will not easily return to the pre-war status. Britain's shipping earnings may be seriously curtailed because world shipping is being built and operated more and more in the United States. A substantial proportion of Britain's immense foreign investment has been sold off to acquire foreign exchange, and the real resources owned in the Far East have been made useless for some time to come as the result of Japanese conquests. At the same time, pre-war holdings of gold and foreign exchanges have already been spent.

This paper has emphasized the economic position of

the United Kingdom because of the sharp contrast which will exist between Britain's post-war political status and her probable economic situation, and because of the crucial importance of a prosperous United Kingdom to the operation of the international economy. But other industrial countries, such as Belgium, Holland, the Scandinavian group, and of course Germany itself, will find themselves in a similar dilemma. They are not as worried as we are on this continent about the possibility of mass unemployment; the opinion is held that the sheer task of physical reconstruction will look after that problem for quite a while. There is a problem, however, as to how they are to pay for the foodstuffs and raw materials needed for the restoration of standards of living and for the rebuilding of the physical plant and equipment. They are concerned, in other words, as to how they are to maintain a standard of living in the post-war world comparable to that which they have enjoyed in the past.

There have been suggestions that the most appropriate solution to this dilemma is for the United Kingdom to use what bargaining strength she still possesses to obtain trade concessions wherever possible, to offer entry to the British consuming markets to those countries whose need for markets may compel them to discriminate in favour of British manufactures, and to continue with government monoplies in the import trade so as to preserve the bargaining advantages of the mass buyer. In other words, the suggestion is that Britain might find it necessary to engage in the type of bi-lateral bargaining which reached technical perfection in pre-war Germany!

It should be said at the outset that such proposals have not received official approval; on the contrary they have been disavowed in those wartime agreements to which the United Kingdom is a party, including the Atlantic Charter. It is everywhere recognized that bilateral arrangements of the pre-war type would do violence to the principle of international specialization and to the rule of non-discrimination. Bi-lateralism lends itself to the exploitation of weaker countries by the metropolitan powers and, however well intentioned, is bound to provoke resentment and recrimination on the part of countries both inside and outside the circle. Moreover, if one of the principal economic powers should embark upon a development of this kind, the number of such separate economic empires could hardly fail to multiply, and, perforce, to give rise to political conflict between the groups. It might be added that for countries which have strong economic ties with two or more of the predominant powers likely to be found in opposite camps—and Canada is only one of many countries in this position—the job of choosing sides would be politically most unpleasant, while the outcome would probably be devoid of any economic compensations.

As has been mentioned already the actual declarations made by the United Nations all renounce the bilateral approach and the case for internationalism does not lack for support in the United Kingdom. There is no difficulty in showing that, taking the long view, the prosperity of the older industrial countries will be served best by the restoration of multi-lateral trade and the expansion of the world market. But we have no assurances that a solution to the problem which meets the requirements of the *short run* will be found. And it is that need which so frequently governs public policy.

Wartime Economic Collaboration and the Transition

So much then for the difficulties in the way of post-war international collaboration created by the war itself. The next question is: has the war contributed anything of positive assistance to the solution of the problem?

It may be argued that the wartime experience of the United Nations in joint economic planning will present them with a starting-point when the war comes to an end; that international economic affairs are becoming so "mixed up" that we shall not be able to disentangle them, even if we wish to; that measures which have proved mutually advantageous in war can be adapted to the conditions of peacetime trade.

This judgment, it is suggested, exaggerates the potentialities of wartime arrangements. For one thing, collaboration in wartime is made easier by the fact that the United Nations have a common objective, and recognize the need for common sacrifices. Economic arrangements are, therefore, made in an atmosphere of tension and urgency that is not likely to be reproduced in time of peace. Moreover, the practice of a greater degree of international specialization is easy when every country concerned is experiencing something comparable to an economic boom. It is possible to reach an agreement that country A shall make the Bren guns and country B the tanks, in strict conformity with the principle of comparative costs, when resources are fully employed, and there is too little rather than too much labour to go round. But in normal circumstances, full employment is rarely approached.

Further, it is a mistake to assume that the area of economic collaboration is, necessarily, very wide in time of war, since the possibilities are strictly limited by factors of military strategy, by the shortage of shipping, and by the over-riding consideration that economic plans were already too set in national moulds to permit of anything more than marginal adjustments during the war itself.

For the most part, the type of co-operation achieved in wartime is concerned with equalizing the burden of shortages common to the Allies, on which it is not so difficult to reach agreements. More important still, wartime arrangements are not hampered by any insistence that international aid must be based upon complete reciprocity. The inter-allied financial arrangements, thanks to Lend-Lease and other such measures, are gradually evolving a system of international pooling of exportable resources; the balance of payments problem has been virtually abolished for the duration. But it is Utopian to expect that this principle can be extended indefinitely when the crisis has passed.

Nevertheless, as a device appropriate for the transition period of reconstruction, the principle of pooling has much to commend it. Moreover, while some of the other machinery of wartime collaboration does not seem to be entirely appropriate to the more permanent circumstances of peace, it can play a very significant rôle in the emergency period of reconstruction, which may well last for some years after the war. This immediate post-war period will resemble wartime in many respects. Shortages of food and of many materials will continue to be acute. The need for food, clothing, and medical help, along with the equipment required for the elementary stages of physical reconstruction, will be urgent. The distribution of this type of assistance will call for allocation on the basis of need, a task for which the collaborative machinery of wartime is well suited. The United Nations may need to continue to control the use of shipping, food, and raw materials in collaboration with each other as they are doing today.

It should, therefore, be recognized that, for many countries, collaboration and pooling cannot be operated on a completely reciprocal basis for some time after the war. In all those regions which have become or will become battlegrounds, the destruction of cities, of productive equipment and agriculture, and the loss of external assets and external markets will make it impossible for them to reciprocate fully in external economic relations. Sheer self-interest—that is, an appreciation of what the alternative would involve—should dictate that the countries with potential surpluses in terms of the balance of payments should continue to put into the world pool of resources more than they need to take out. This means that the entire American continent, which is now and will be for many years the only major area able to export more than it needs by way of imports, should continue to participate in the exchange-pooling devices practised today. It may mean the continuance of many of the controls and much of the involuntary rationing which this involves. But it will enormously simplify the economic adjustments needed in the transition period, and, by the same token, will help to reduce the pressure in favour of isolationist solutions. Needless to say, the time to formulate this kind of arrangement has already arrived.

Pre-Requisites for International Collaboration

It will be assumed, therefore, that for several years at least after the war the principle laid down in the Atlantic Charter, namely, that nations should have reasonably easy access to the economic resources of the world, will be served by some sort of exchange-pooling after the manner worked out by the United Nations in wartime. But this can only be a temporary arrangement, appropriate to the emergency conditions of the immediate post-war period. In the long run, world economic relationships should and can provide for a reasonable degree of reciprocity. More important still, the essential task of the long run is to provide for an improvement in economic conditions over as wide an area as possible. This goal will not be achieved without the resumption of international specialization, international investment, perhaps international migration, and certainly not without international collaboration. By what methods shall the goal be pursued?

Before trying to answer this question, there are certain broad issues to be clarified. First and foremost, there is the question of the political settlement after the war. Obviously, economic collaboration can only be achieved if the world political environment is congenial; without national security there can be no real progress in the direction of international economic inter-dependence. This means that the peace settlement must provide guarantees against external aggression. Economic co-operation also involves the absence of those ideological conflicts (which need not mean uniform social and political objectives) which stood in the way of political and economic collaboration in the thirties. These matters are outside the scope of this paper, but everything suggested herein hangs on their solution.

However, assuming that political obstacles are overcome, there remains a further complication. It is almost certain that the nations of the post-war world will be affected by different degrees of national planning. In some, government controls will be confined to only small, but probably strategic, sectors of the economy; in others, the ramifications of control may reach down deeply into the economic structure. Whatever the scope of government controls, it is certain that external economic relations will be directly or indirectly affected thereby. Indeed, the evidence of the thirties suggests that control is likely to begin in this particularly strategic area. If this is so, the concrete procedures of post-war international policy will have to be viewed in appropriate terms. For example, while the objective of "freer trade" may be unchanged, international agreements to reduce tariffs would not be much of a contribution to this objective if tariffs have ceased to be the principal means by which imports are controlled. The task of promoting international trade will, therefore, require a much more complex brand of international machinery than was required in the nineteenth century.

By the same token the direction and promotion of economic relations between countries will have to take in many new spheres of activity. Such international agreements concerning economic matters as have been reached in the past have been mainly negative in character. There have been conventions not to raise tariffs, not to discriminate between countries in respect to import restrictions (the M.F.N. clause), not to depreciate exchange rates deliberately, and so forth. The assumption in these cases, like the assumptions behind the *laissez-faire* principle in the domestic sphere, was that automatic forces would provide for the expansion of trade so long as the practice of free competition, and no favours for anyone, was upheld. In the main, the contribution of the League of Nations to world economics was, through no fault of the League organization, directed to this kind of agreement. It represents, of course, an approach that is now recognized to be inadequate in the domestic sphere. Conscious direction of the economy is now recognized as a government responsibility. The same conclusion holds good for international economic relations.

Mass Unemployment an International Problem

Among the factors that led to the extension of economic nationalism before the war was the increasing incidence of mass unemployment. The attempts of the League (or of any individual country) to promote tariff reductions inevitably proved abortive in periods of substantial unemployment or depressed agriculture. When a country is faced with depression at home it can hardly refrain from increasing the tariff or manipulating the exchanges or from following any other tactic which promises to give at least temporary relief, notwithstanding the damage done thereby to foreign producers. Or again, plans for promoting employment at home may turn out to be of more benefit to the outside world than to the country concerned unless that country is protected from external depressive contagions. Hence the growth of tariffs and other impediments to cheap imports. In other words, the economic isolationism of the thirties was not the product of original sin on the part of governments, but was in no small part the outcome of attempts to grapple with domestic difficulties within the only sphere in which governments believed they could operate, that is, within the limits of national sovereignty.

International collaboration in the future must therefore primarily concern itself with the prevention of mass unemployment, partly because the other objectives of international statesmanship have small chance of success unless the world is free from economic depression, and also because for most countries domestic plans for economic recovery cannot succeed fully unless world recovery is proceeding simultaneously. The isolationist and imperialist approaches to the problem (and they will usually be found to be synonymous) only retard the prospects of permanent recovery by provoking retaliatory punitive measures from other quarters.

The first objective of world economic collaboration after the war, therefore, ought logically to be the achievement of as high a level of production—and hence of consumption—as is reasonably possible for every country prepared to co-operate to this end.

Fortunately, the importance of this economic strategy is now recognized by the present administration in Washington and by other governments. Thus, what few joint declarations of international policy have been made by the United Nations have emphasized their intention to collaborate in the prosecution of policies to combat unemployment and to raise standards of living generally. The numerous Lend-Lease agreements, for example, all contain a clause which provides that, when the time arrives for a final settlement, the terms shall include agreed action by both countries "directed towards the expansion of production, consumption, and exchange, by appropriate international and domestic measures".[1] If this means anything it should mean that the United Nations agree that they will each formulate policies and plans for the maintenance of the maximum possible levels of national income, and, where these plans are affected by or dependent upon the policies of other countries, that they will collaborate with such countries so as to bring their policies into harmony.

Now there is no evidence that the United Nations (or even, say, the United Kingdom and the United States) have considered in detail what concrete measures of a joint nature will be needed to promote the expansion of production. It may be inferred that the present administration in Washington has in mind certain fiscal and monetary policies of "full employment" now being expounded in the United States. Internationally, it may mean that the countries concerned should agree jointly on certain specific questions concerning the treatment of imports, the scope of international lending, and the levels of prices, interest rates, and exchange rates to be maintained. It should certainly involve a joint and synchronized control over the aberrations of the business cycle.

[1]While Canada has not been a party to Lend-Lease, an almost identical agreement was made in an exchange of notes between Canada and the United States in December, 1942.

It remains to be seen whether there is enough political and economic wisdom in the world to permit the principal nations to collaborate at this level. The complexities involved in social and economic planning in the domestic sphere alone are great enough; to extend the area affected to the international plane will increase the difficulties enormously. Nevertheless, the attempt must be made because there are no tolerable alternative solutions.

If, to begin with, the larger economic powers can seriously attempt to harmonize their fiscal and monetary policies, enlarge the mutual exchange of goods, and promote a revival of international lending, other countries would be able, without risk, to integrate themselves more closely with the world economy. Such a programme would ultimately involve a new code of international economic ethics. It might mean, for example, that a country which sought a "free ride" to prosperity on the back of its more venturesome neighbours would not be regarded as making its fair contribution to world economic improvement. It would mean the renunciation of those measures, which were almost standard practice in the last decade, whereby countries sought to achieve domestic advantages at the expense of their neighbours. It should mean that the kind of international behaviour which led to the breakdown of the World Economic Conference in 1933 would be repudiated. At that time, the British and American Governments were committed to economic measures which were mutually incompatible; in effect, their monetary and exchange rate policies were working at cross-purposes. In retrospect, this failure to co-operate can be seen as one of the most unfortunate episodes of the decade.

The first task, therefore, must be to enlarge the agenda of international economic statesmanship, and to give priority to the need for joint anti-depression policies. However, there would be little sense in trying to blueprint in detail the kind of joint action necessary. It may be that such domestic measures as are envisaged in the Beveridge Report might be paralleled by comparable social security plans in the United States, Canada, and elsewhere. A joint plan for the promotion of international capital development might well be regarded as an essential step towards maintaining employment in those countries that will end the war with surplus manufacturing resources. Whatever the concrete tasks, special international agencies will have to be set up for their planning and promotion.

International Investment

One such agency would be something in the nature of an international investment corporation to promote the lending of funds by the mature capital-surplus countries to the new and less developed countries of the world. For a century or more, one of the characteristic features of the world economy was the international movement of capital funds. Such investment originally was typically private or corporate; in a free trade and nominally *laissez-faire* atmosphere, government control or sponsorship of the flow of investment funds was only minimal. By and large, the system was beneficial to borrowing and lending countries alike, in that it accelerated the economic development of new regions and provided the old world with cheap food and raw materials, as well as outlets for an expanding level of exports. In time, a good deal of this foreign investment came to be part and parcel of a programme of economic imperialism ("dollar diplomacy") and came into conflict with the growing force of political nationalism in the debtor countries. International recriminations multiplied and foreign capital (and foreign capitalists) were, in many countries, regarded with suspicion. At the same time, the trend in the new countries was towards more governmental responsibility, if not ownership, of public utilities, or of enterprises concerned with the exploitation of natural resources. Private international capital investment was not usually appropriate to this situation. In the twenties, which witnessed the last great splurge of foreign lending, many investments were ill-advised and after the onset of the depression defaults became common. Thereafter, international lending slumped; by 1939 it was evident that the traditional type of capital movement was incapable of real revival. The League of Nations loans to central European countries for currency stabilization purposes in the twenties had given an indication of the potentialities of a system of internationally sponsored loans. But this particular experiment, as it happened, was quite inconsistent with the commercial policies of the lending countries. By denying to the countries of central Europe access to their markets, the lending countries largely cancelled the effect of the loans, and made the repayment of funds virtually impossible. It can be concluded, therefore, that international investment arrangements after the war must be more compatible with the self-respect of the borrowing countries, must deal more with the governments of the borrowing countries, while provisions for repayment must be more flexible than they were in the past. It is to be doubted whether these conditions would be favourable to a large-scale revival of the old type of international lending.

On the other hand, the possibilities for the investment of outside capital in countries which are still economically undeveloped are enormous. There will, of course, be the need for assisting the countries of Europe and the Far East to meet the immediate problems of relief and elementary physical reconstruction. Such assistance, however, should not involve repayment. But looking beyond this transition period, there is enormous scope for capital assistance in China, the U.S.S.R., South America, south-eastern Europe, and elsewhere. The industrial countries of the world will have the capacity to produce the equipment and materials needed to build transportation systems, public utilities, harbours, power plants, irrigation projects, and the like in those countries which are impoverished for lack of them. Their governments would welcome such assistance so long as the terms are reasonable, while the lending countries would thereby find markets for their surplus industrial capacity.

An international investment corporation would involve joint governmental participation in planning and financing specific works; it might be necessary to set up a series of development corporations on which both the borrowing and lending countries and perhaps others who were not directly involved would be represented, to promote and supervise the specific works. It is suggested that, following the pattern of the type of public corporation (such as those of the Tennessee Valley Authority and Ontario's Hydro-Electric Power Commission) with which we are familiar in the domestic sphere, the operation of these corporations at the management level would be independent of direct government control. It is possible, too, that this kind of agency could also provide an opportunity for the investment of private funds, though allotments of governmental capital would be more typical.

It would be vain to try to blueprint the details of an international investment authority; nor is it easy to find suitable antecedents for such an agency. Some of the League of Nations loans of the twenties embodied the principle of international sponsorship but these were concerned more with relief, not with developmental investment. A League of Nations programme to promote international public works was formulated in the early thirties but the rise of Hitler shelved all such plans. The closest analogy is to be found in certain joint financial agencies set up by the United States since the outbreak of war to assist South American countries with the capital needed for projects designed to produce war materials for the United States (e.g., the Export-Import Bank). However, a wider degree of international collaboration than this would seem to be required if the difficulties sketched earlier are to be minimized. On the other hand, the necessities of the case would suggest that nations who are ready to co-operate in plans of this type should not postpone operations until every country concerned is ready and willing to join the undertaking. Scruples of this sort caused many a League Convention to be still-born.

The Foreign Exchanges

Running closely parallel to this problem is the question of exchange stabilization. At present the external transactions of almost every country are subject to a tight system of exchange control. International transfers of funds are regulated so as to prevent the movement of private capital funds, and, as a rule, to make foreign exchange available only for essential imports. Insulated in this and in other ways from the influence of foreign commodity and security prices, domestic prices in most countries at the end of the war will be out of equilibrium with "world" prices. This means that, in the absence of exchange control, the resultant flow of goods, services, and capital would diverge from the normal to a great but unpredictable extent. A new set of equilibrium prices and exchange rates might be ultimately re-established, but only after a period of great confusion and instability. In view of the difficulties to which many countries will be exposed, it would seem essential that most countries should relax their existing control over exchange transfers only gradually, and then only in collaboration with other countries.

Indeed, it is possible that certain forms of exchange control may become a more or less permanent feature of international economic relations. The events of the thirties suggest that certain speculative movements of short-term capital across the boundaries of a country may be too disturbing a force to go on uncontrolled. Alternatively, where capital transfers are permitted, compensatory measures in the exchange and financial markets, involving the stabilization of exchange rates, are usually required. The stabilization of the exchange rate, however, is a task that frequently requires external assistance. At the same time, the choice of a particular exchange value for a currency is of just as much significance to foreign countries as the height of a customs tariff. That is to say, these are problems which call for international collaboration.

As a matter of fact, some progress towards an international solution had been made when the war broke out. It will be recalled that the years 1930-35 were characterized by exchange instability, by deliberate exchange depreciation in the case of several important countries, and of course by much international recrimination on that score. The United States, the United Kingdom, and other countries set up exchange stabilization funds to counteract the effects of irregular capital movements and to maintain the foreign value of the domestic currency at the level that seemed most appropriate to national interests. In this sphere of international economic relations as in others, economic isolationism was, for a time, the rule. Ultimately, the United States and the United Kingdom, having soon exhausted the benefits of exchange independence, recognized the real advantages to both in a re-marriage under new auspices. Instead of restoring the old gold standard, they chose to make a monetary agreement (involving the U.S., the U.K., and France) requiring joint co-operation in controlling exchange rates. In effect, an international code of behaviour concerning the operation of exchange stabilization funds was agreed to; under this code unilateral decisions to depreciate the exchanges were ruled out.

This method of approach to the problem of exchange stabilization might well be extended and improved after the war. It is an arrangement which is not inconsistent with a certain degree of exchange rate flexibility. What is required is a safeguard against unpredictable and unnecessary exchange depreciation on the part of countries which might seize upon this method of snatching a competitive advantage over their neighbours. The adoption of safeguards would require, it would seem, that the choice of exchange rates—together with the principles of exchange control—should be required to pass the scrutiny of some kind of international agency set up to adjudicate on such matters.

However, the restoration of any moderately free system of international transfers which is compatible with the maintenance of stable exchange rates cannot be achieved without arrangements to give temporary assistance to countries facing a shortage of exchange. In the immediate post-war period this problem, as suggested above, will be so acute as to require the continuance of the system of "mutual aid", "lend-lease" or "pooling"—call it what you will. In the long run, the restoration of freer trade, if this can be achieved, and the revival of international investment should reduce the problem to manageable proportions. But for any country, however well established may be its fundamental international economic position, temporary shortages of exchange are bound to occur from time to time. For the creditor countries this is rarely a problem; external reserves can be drawn down to meet the deficiency. For countries without external assets, or in a debtor position, exchange shortages are the prelude to exchange control, exchange depreciation, higher tariffs, and other such exchange-conservation measures, all of which tend to undermine the foundations of the international economic order. If the world is to avoid difficulties of this kind in the future, it will be necessary to establish some kind of exchange stabilization fund under the management of an international agency. The Bank for International Settlements, set up in the early thirties as a species of world central bank embodied this principle in embryonic form but the economic and political climate of the time was hardly propitious for the growth of the plan. The necessity for machinery of this kind after the war will be even more acute. When it is recognized how small and how temporary may be the shortage of exchange required to drive a country in the direction of autarky it will be seen that the disease is out of all proportion to the costs of prevention. Alternatively, it would seem to be necessary for the principal exchange-surplus countries (which group will certainly include the United States, and in respect to some currencies Canada also) to make credits available to other countries to cover their essential current purchases.[2] It is sometimes forgotten that the basic urge behind a nation's anxiety to export is its need for essential imports. If in times of stress this need can be satisfied in part by some such alternative device the promotion of exports by methods of economic nationalism could be greatly reduced.

The Reduction of Trade Barriers

The theoretical case for free trade between nations is based upon the implicit assumptions that economic

[2]Specific proposals along these lines have been elaborated by Herbert Feis, "Restoring Trade After the War" (*Foreign Affairs*, Jan. 1942, p. 282). Suggested plans for an international clearing fund have been published by the Treasury Departments of the governments of the United Kingdom and the United States since this paper was written. [Ed.]

resources are fully employed and the economy itself is tolerably stable. Granted these assumptions, the benefits of wide international specialization are beyond dispute. If unemployment is rampant, however, the gains to be derived from lowering tariffs are not so obvious. If a condition of less-than-full employment is posited it is doubtless correct to argue that, granted no *change* in the pre-existing state of tariffs, a country with low tariffs (or free trade) would enjoy a greater degree of economic welfare than if the same country had traditionally operated under high protection. Generalization can hardly go beyond that point. If, for example, a country has suffered a severe decline in employment and income, the economist is not entitled to argue that a *reduction* of tariffs by the country in question would improve its real income. Whether it would or not depends upon a series of reactions not subsumed in the comparative cost doctrine. Of these the most significant would be the behaviour of investment expenditures in response to the new profit possibilities in the export- and import-competing industries created by the tariff adjustment.

It is possible, and highly probable, that the effect of a one-sided tariff reduction on the part of a country undergoing a shrinkage in employment would be to create more dislocation to production in the import-competing industries than could be compensated for by the encouragement given to the export industries, or by the lowered costs of imports. The net advantages, if indeed there were any, might accrue in the short run solely to the foreigner; and the business cycle is a short-run phenomenon. If the tariff reductions were reciprocated by other countries, the benefits—if any—would be shared. But there is no certainty that net benefits would emerge. That being the case, it is almost certain that a country in a condition of under-employment would serve the national welfare more effectively by taking steps to expand production and employment than by downward tariff adjustments. Hence the emphasis in this paper on the need for international planning for the maintenance of employment; logically, the search for fuller employment in collaboration with other countries has priority over plans for increased international specialization.

Notwithstanding this qualification, an early attack upon the problem of trade restrictions is essential; without this the welfare of many countries must continue to languish at a level much below the maximum possible. Concretely, there is an obligation to permit those countries which do not possess the necessary variety of economic resources to obtain access to those which they lack by the processes of exchange. If the economically rich countries of this world maintain high tariffs against imports they cannot reach optimum prosperity however diverse their resources; under the same conditions countries insufficiently supplied with certain basic resources will not be able to maintain even a tolerable standard of living. A recognition of the claims of the countries in the latter group has therefore caused the governments of the United Nations to assert their belief in the efficacy of joint measures looking towards "the elimination of all forms of discriminatory treatment in international commerce, and to the reduction of tariffs, and other trade barriers." It goes without saying, for example, that the economic welfare of Canada would suffer considerably from any recurrence of world trade restrictions comparable to those which existed in the early thirties (while admitting that the effects of world tariffs at the then existing height would have been less severe if national incomes had, conceivably, been maintained at 1929 levels). And there are many other countries equally geared to a system of specialized production via export-import trade.

An immediate problem to be faced when peace returns will probably be that of preventing an increase in the existing range of protective devices. Conditions then will be greatly different from 1939. Canada, like most other countries, will be concerned with the task of finding employment for those who are demobilized from the armed services and with the search for outlets for the products of industries now engaged in producing war materials.

The types of commodity imported from, say, the United States and the United Kingdom, will be greatly different from those which were typical in 1939. Canada, like other countries, will have learned to make for itself goods which were formerly imported. The politico-economic environment, in other words, will at least be conducive to agitation for increased protection in the secondary industries. At the same time the continued existence of some of the wartime controls will lend itself to concealed forms of protection, or at least will make tariff duties less relevant to the issue of lowering trade barriers. Moreover, in view of the uncertainties that would attend the movement of trade if the existing restrictions were removed it seems likely that governments everywhere will be reluctant to commit themselves to any wide-scale abandonment of control, including control over trade, for some time to come. This means that international economic policy must be the subject of much more detailed negotiation than was necessary in a more *laissez-faire* world and that agreements must be made between the principal trading nations to decide which of the industries brought into existence as a result of war are to be retained, and which are to be discarded in favour of imports. It seems likely that the most practicable approach to the question of promoting international trade in the transition period will be the negotiation of reciprocal trade agreements between separate pairs of countries, or among relatively small groups of countries. The alternative is impracticable; it would take too long, even if it were possible at all, to elaborate a formula for the simultaneous and multilateral reduction of tariffs everywhere. Experience indicates that this is only possible as a long-run procedure, although several such formulae have been proposed.[3]

However, there are certain impediments to the negotiation of trade agreements between two countries, or between regional blocs. First, there is the most-favoured-nations convention, according to which tariff concessions exchanged between two countries must be automatically extended to all other countries, irrespective of the degree to which the latter restrict imports.

In these circumstances, tariff reductions achieved through bi-lateral trade agreements are nowadays confined to commodities which are imported principally

[3]See, for example, J. Viner, "Objectives of Post-War International Economic Reconstruction" (in *The Economic and Business Foundation*, New Wilmington, Pa., 1942).

from the second party to the agreement. Thus, under the Canadian-American agreement of 1937 Canada selected for tariff-reduction certain steel products which were typically imported from the United States; the United States, in turn, reduced the tariff on potatoes and certain species of lumber, knowing full well that the stimulus to trade would be confined to the Canadian industries concerned, and not shared by other countries who were not making reciprocal concessions. The point is that tariff adjustment between only two countries presents a manageable problem since the net consequences are reasonably measurable. A multi-sided agreement, however feasible in theory, presents too many unpredictable and therefore unmanageable aspects for negotiation to succeed or even to be commenced. The two-country or three-country[4] arrangement, however, cannot do more than tinker with existing tariff restrictions so long as they are narrowed down to commodities in which each country is the principal supplier of the other.

There is no easy solution to this difficulty. It would be folly to abandon the most-favoured-nation clause completely since its operation serves to limit discrimination in international trading arrangements. It may be, however, that the discrimination involved in an exclusive agreement between two or more countries to lower tariffs against each other might be permitted if certain conditions are satisfied. It might be required that: (a) the agreement should not involve

[4]There was a considerable degree of unity to the three separate trade agreements concluded in 1937-38 between the United Kingdom and the United States, the United States and Canada, and Canada and the United Kingdom. See J. F. Parkinson, "External Economic Policy" (in F. H. Soward and others, *Canada in World Affairs*, Toronto, 1940).

an increase of the tariff against other countries; (b) other countries who felt that their interests would be jeopardized thereby should be given an opportunity to participate in the proposed low-tariff "club", on payment of comparable tariff concessions; (c) the sanction of some international trade authority should be required before the proposed agreement became operative.

Of these three suggested safeguards the latter is the most important. What is wanted is the maintenance of the spirit of non-discrimination in trade policy. Tariff discrimination which results from the decision of one bloc of countries to reduce the duties on goods coming from the other members of the bloc is hardly an offence against a country which insists on maintaining high tariffs against all and sundry, and is unwilling to join in exchanging concessions. But it should be for some impartial but international authority to decide whether the offence is real or not.

Aside from its interest in reciprocal trade agreements of this kind an international trade authority, which might be constituted similarly to that suggested in the field of international investment, would ideally become the ultimate arbiter in disputes concerning commercial policy between countries. If international economic security is to be preserved, the right of a sovereign state to manage its internal economic affairs without regard to the interests of other countries should logically be circumscribed. It is too much to expect that nations would be willing to grant to a new and untried international authority the power to veto proposed tariff increases. It would seem feasible, however, for the nations to agree that any such changes would be submitted for "consideration and report" to this authority. The authority would then be able to suggest alternative solutions to the particular difficulty which the proposed tariff was intended to remove, and might engage the assistance of other international agencies to this end. If the proposed import restrictions originated in a difficulty in balancing the international accounts, or in a shortage of capital, assistance in correcting these deficiencies might render the tariff revision unnecessary. For example, it might be agreed that the economic interest of the area itself, and of the rest of the world, would be best served if agriculture in the Danubian Basin were directed more towards the production of meats, vegetables, dairy products, and the like, at the expense of grain production. (There is no need to emphasize the advantages of such a shift to Canada or the Argentine.) It might be found, however, that adjustments of this type in Europe are impossible unless capital assistance from the outside is given. The countries concerned may need to export grain to acquire essential foreign exchange; stock-raising may require the provision of capital and equipment which the country is too poor to provide for itself. In these circumstances it is obvious that agreements concerning tariffs must be integrated with international arrangements concerning exchange stabilization, international investment, and the like. Agreements to submit proposals to increase tariffs to an international agency might provide a "cooling off" period to give time for other counsels to prevail;[5] at best the expansion of the prestige and power of such an agency might

[5]See Percy W. Bidwell, "Controlling Trade After the War" (*Foreign Affairs*, January 1943).

ultimately give its suggestions the force of international law.

Finally, before leaving this topic of commercial policy, mention should be made of the great importance which attaches to the attitude of the United States. It is probable that after the war the world generally will need to import an enormous amount of American materials and equipment. At the same time, the United States could probably dispense with all but a few irreplaceable imports without much difficulty. Further, if American tariffs are maintained at their pre-war levels, it seems likely that, short of exchange depreciation and other such dubious measures inviting retaliation, an insufficient volume of imports would be able to surmount the tariff wall. This is the nature of the "shortage-of-dollars" problem. It is possible for the United States to make foreign exchange available in other ways, either as an outright gift or as a gift in disguise, as was done in the twenties through international loans which were not in fact repaid, or in the thirties by the gold-purchase policy. But this solution is not a satisfactory alternative to the reduction of tariffs. Fortunately, the United States in the pre-war period had already made a substantial move towards lower tariffs through the medium of the trade-agreement programme, and the expressed intention of the present administration is to continue in this direction after the war. If Canada and the rest of the British Commonwealth also play their part, the prospects for the expansion of world trade would be decidedly encouraging.

But to regard the question of commercial policy as one to be isolated and handled *in vacuo* is to miss the point of this paper. The need for a more rational and inter-dependent organization of the world economy raises questions far beyond the scope of commercial policy alone. It is implicit in the problem of the foreign exchanges, international investment, and joint anti-depression policies, and linked with the need for international arrangements concerning world shipping, the wheat trade, and many other essentially international problems.

Chapter VIII

EXCHANGE CONTROL—DURING AND AFTER THE WAR

F. A. Knox

I

In western countries exchange control is associated in the public mind with totalitarian economic systems. When used by democratic countries, in periods of great economic pressure, the dangerous tendency for such controls to create situations that seem to call for further state interference has usually been recognized and guarded against in their administration. The quick imposition upon the outbreak of war of a considerable measure of exchange control in Canada occasioned shocked surprise amongst many businessmen. In the First World War no such controls had been imposed; and our rôle in the Second World War seemed likely to be much what it had been in the First. The fear that exchange control might be followed by other controls was strengthened when the government's intention to finance this war by methods quite different from those followed in 1914-18 was announced. The fact that that fear has proved to have been well founded has roused in large numbers of Canadians the determination to see that as soon as the war is over such controls are ended immediately. Totalitarian methods may be required in total war; but the problems of the post-war period can best be solved, they feel, by more democratic procedures. Others, on the contrary, agreeing that such controls tend to persist, welcome the prospect. They see no probability that the economic problems Canada will have to face after this war can be solved by the same economic institutions and habits of mind that failed to cope with the trade depression of the thirties. According to this view a degree of expansion in the powers of government is not only inevitable but desirable. The question in their minds is what controls should be retained and how extensive their powers should be.

It is the purpose of this paper to look briefly into Canada's exchange experience in 1914-18; to survey the reasons for the adoption of exchange control in 1939 and the part it has played in Canada's new economic policy for war; and finally to consider whether the post-war world is likely to be one in which Canada can afford to dispense with exchange control.

Governments usually interfere in the foreign exchange market only when some crisis in confidence threatens a flight of capital which would drive the price of foreign exchange to heights unwarranted by the underlying economic situation or when some drastic worsening in a country's international trading position requires the conservation of a suddenly diminished stock of foreign exchange for such essential purposes as the service of foreign debts or the purchase of goods imperatively required by the national economy. In August, 1914, neither of these conditions faced the government of Great Britain; in fact so great was the volume of short-term indebtedness owing to Great Britain that the pound sterling at first soared on the world's exchanges. The partial restoration of the

London money market and the growing volume of British and Allied buying in the United States brought the pound back to par and then threatened it with depreciation. But the British Government was able, by selling in the United States many of the United States dollar securities held by British investors, and by borrowing from New York bankers, to raise enough dollars to peg the pound at $4.76. Exchange control was not imposed. In 1917 when these sources of United States dollars were almost exhausted, resort to drastic exchange control was avoided by the American declaration of war. The United States Treasury now provided the dollars required to support the pound.

Though formal resort to exchange control by the British Government was thus avoided there was of course much indirect interference with exchange transactions through governmental control of shipping and of the import trade. There was also some patriotic pressure upon British citizens not to undertake transactions which would make the government's task more difficult. So great was the British determination to retain the forms of the gold standard, upon which it conceived much of its economic strength and financial prestige to be based, that these forms were not abandoned till the war was over. It is almost impossible to identify the moment when the interference with actual business became so serious, in any of these matters, that the British Government in fact abandoned the gold standard.

While the American Government had a lively enough appreciation of the value of stable exchange rates, especially between partners in a great war, it was quite without Britain's respect for the gold standard or her determination to maintain it. As soon as it became clear that it would be costly to maintain stable exchange rates with certain neutral countries in which Allied purchasing had expanded and whose nationals were finding a profitable market for their goods in the United States, the American Government put an end to the free export of gold and forced private dealings in foreign exchange to be conducted through the Federal Reserve Banks under governmental supervision and regulation. Gold payments were stopped and exchange control imposed without hesitation to prevent neutrals withdrawing their deposits from American banks, except as the American Government might permit, and to prevent their selling their goods freely in the American market. Exchange on neutral countries was being conserved for the purchase of commodities the American Government deemed important in the conduct of the war.

In August 1914 the Canadian Government showed a similar North American carelessness about maintaining the gold standard. Curiously enough, however, our government was not preoccupied either with the problem of keeping exchange rates stable or with conserving exchange for war purposes. Our bankers and the Minister of Finance were concerned lest Canadians, fearful of the financial future of a new country hitherto markedly dependent upon the London money market for support, might convert their bank deposits, bank notes, or Dominion notes into gold and hoard it. Should this occur on a large scale the "backing" for the government paper money would be seriously impaired and the solvency of the banks and the country brought into question. To prevent this an Order-in-Council was passed which brought gold payments abruptly to an end despite the fact that the country had the honourable record of having maintained specie payments unbroken since before Confederation.

Contrary to what might have been expected the Canadian dollar did not depreciate in New York as a consequence. Not until 1918 was there any shortage of American dollars despite a remarkable increase in our imports from the United States. For this stability of the exchange rate with the American dollar there were three main reasons: contrary to common opinion Canada continued to borrow abroad during the war as before it; our exports of food and munitions to Britain rose in value much above what was thought possible in 1914; and, most important of all, the pegging of the pound sterling in New York made it possible for us to convert into American dollars the sterling we received for those exports. Though the London market was closed to us after 1916, our securities found ready sale in the American market. In the years 1914-17 our net capital imports exceeded eight hundred and fifty million dollars, apart from dealings between the Dominion and the British Government. Such borrowing was the expected thing for a new country, even during a war. But the phenomenal scale of our production of food and munitions for the Allies was unexpected. When the war began our rôle was conceived as mainly that of food producer. We would undertake to finance, in addition, an expeditionary force; but neither the British nor the Canadian Government thought of Canada as an important producer of industrial products. Even when a group of Canadian industrialists had succeeded in getting enough orders from the British Government to convince it of our power to produce shells and guns, the Dominion Government refused either to organize that production or to assume more than a limited responsibility in financing it. It was organized by a committee of Canadians, acting directly as the agents of the British Government, by which it was mainly financed, with the aid of the Canadian Government and banks. In 1918 when the British Government was no longer able to provide dollars to finance this production and the American Government was unwilling to finance it on the scale to which this production had attained by 1917, the Canadian Government, believing apparently that it had reached the limit of the financial aid it might extend, allowed Canada's production of munitions to decline. But so great had been the increase in the national money income that there was no marked slump. Canadian industry began its re-conversion to a peacetime basis before the war had come to an end, under the stimulus of a very high level of spending by Canadians. However, in 1918, the decline of our exports and our exclusion as borrower from the New York market reduced our current supplies of foreign exchange just when civilian desire for imports from the United States had reached its maximum. Presumably because this production of munitions in Canada was not being restricted by any shortage of critical materials from the United States, the Dominion Government imposed no exchange control to conserve the supply. Consequently the price of New York funds rose in Montreal: the depreciation of the Canadian dollar had begun.

In the light of this experience and in the absence of

any announcement of a change in government policy, the imposition in 1939, within two weeks of the outbreak of war, of a drastic control over foreign exchange was, not unnaturally, an astonishing development to most Canadians. In line with the international trend in such matters some degree of interference with the freedom with which Canadians might conduct international transactions was generally expected. But few believed that the free market in foreign exchange would be brought to an end, and many expressed strenuous disapproval.

Now that the financial side of the war policy which the government had decided to follow has been fully revealed, it is clear that drastic control of international transactions was the basic element in the whole structure. Only those who cling to the belief that the methods of 1914-18 might have been adequate to 1939 still demur. So different were the various features of our economic situation in 1939, however, that it is difficult indeed to believe that reliance on the old methods of economic freedom could have ended in anything but economic confusion and the frustration of our war effort.

Even in 1939 it was clear that our contribution to the Second World War would be very different from that made in 1914-18 and that it would involve more serious problems both of foreign exchange and domestic finance. The Canadian economy being industrially more mature, a larger effort was to be expected of it. Nor would Canadians again be content to have the production of war materials in Canada organized by a British Commission for whose transactions with Canadians the Dominion Government took no direct responsibility. We would organize and finance our own war production and would not permit it to decline for lack of money to maintain it. We were still dependent, however, upon the United States for machine tools and some critical materials. Our needs for United States dollars were therefore bound to be great. Nor were they to be eked out, this time, either by selling newly-issued securities in the American market or by selling to Americans the pounds sterling which the British might find it possible to pay us for our products. American national policy prohibited the flotation of securities in the United States by countries at war; and any United States dollars put at Canada's disposal to ease our scarcity of American funds would have to come from the pool of such dollars at Great Britain's disposal—a pool already being conserved by rigorous exchange control. Clearly we would be expected to reduce our drawings on that pool to the minimum. Under such circumstances it was imperative that action should be taken at once to conserve the United States dollar balances already in the possession of the Canadian banks, corporations, and private individuals; they had become for Canada the most vital of war materials.

In 1914 the great danger feared by the Canadian banks was the loss of the country's gold stocks into domestic hoards. In 1939 there was no such danger; Canada was not on the gold standard. There was great danger, however, that our gold and United States dollar balances would be used up in a panic flight of capital from Canada seeking refuge in the security of American banks. In 1914 there was not a great deal of American money invested in Canada; most foreign money in Canada was British and it would have been impossible for private British investors to find in Canada a market for the Canadian Government and railway securities they held, had they wished to get rid of them. In the late thirties on the contrary the Canadian security market was well organized and active. Canadians had been buying back from Americans many of the securities sold in the United States during the First World War and in the twenties. There was thus every probability that American investors would attempt to sell such securities amidst the uncertainties created by the outbreak of war and that Canadians would snap up such bargains willingly enough. But the sale of large amounts of Canadian dollars for United States dollars would have made serious inroads on our war chest of American dollars. That this very thing had already begun is indicated by the fact that when Foreign Exchange Control was imposed on September 15, 1939, the price of the United States dollar had already risen sharply in Montreal. Against such a rush to buy American funds for the purpose of exporting American capital invested in Canada or of increasing the balances carried by Canadians in American banks there was but one protection. All exchange dealings had to be put in the hands of a central authority so that the use of United States dollars might be limited to the usual current transactions. As a consequence, unfortunately, the capital of some Americans was frozen in Canada for the duration of the war. But the conservation and rational use of our stocks of United States dollars, which the imposition of foreign exchange control made possible, assured the American investor that payment of the usual interest and dividends would be made. The prompt establishment of control in the movements of capital contributed powerfully to financial and economic stability in Canada in the autumn of 1939.

Having thus firmly established its control over the international economic transactions of Canadians, the Dominion Government then announced a policy for war finance which definitely raised the spectre of more such controls to follow. In all the Allied countries in the First World War governments had secured the production of munitions and war materials by offering high enough prices for them to induce individuals to make war goods rather than the usual goods desired by the consumer. Because the money paid to workers in war industries soon appeared in the market for consumer goods, profits in their manufacture rose also. The government was therefore forced to offer yet higher prices for the munitions of war. This competition between the government and the consumer caused a very serious rise in the cost of living. Those workers who were in a sound bargaining position were able to keep their wages rising fast enough so that the purchasing power of their total earnings was not much diminished. They thus were able to pass the economic burden of war—restricted consumption—on to those in the community whose incomes were relatively fixed. This method of organizing war production left huge profits in the hands of some producers. Though the government taxed some of this profit away, most of it remained in their hands. At the same time the majority of the people were unable to save much; though their earnings rose, the cost of living kept pace. The injustice of this "profiteering" so deeply impressed the public that in 1939 the government announced that the basic principle of its policy of war finance was to be the equitable sharing of its burden. Beside this principle the government placed another of equal importance; the magnitude of our war effort was not to be limited by financial difficulties. The setting up of a Department of Munitions and Supply indicated the government's desire to organize the industries of the country efficiently for war. The early establishment of a Wartime Prices and Trade Board indicated its realization that control over the behaviour of prices would become necessary in the interest both of maximum production and a just sharing of war costs.

In the autumn of 1939, however, such problems were not pressing. The initial period of disturbance having been weathered by the aid of exchange control, the main task was to get all Canadian workmen employed in the production of something. If at some future time heavy taxes and large bond subscriptions would have to be paid, then the national money income must first be raised by putting everyone to work; if "belt-tightening" faced the consumer when our war effort at last demanded a large portion of our working force, then every effort should be made to stock up on consumer goods while that might be done. To tool-up for war production would obviously take time; the ordinary business of the community should be encouraged meanwhile. In the first war budget presented on September 12, 1939, nothing was done that would cause the ordinary stream of consumer buying to shrink much. Though the "shape of things to come" was clearly outlined, increased income and corporation taxes and the new excess profits tax would not begin to divert funds to the government for some time.

Meanwhile, the Minister of Finance raised the additional money required by borrowing from the banks; and the Bank of Canada so increased its holdings of securities as to provide for the increased demand for hand-to-hand currency and to increase chartered banks cash reserves. The banks in turn bought more securities and increased their current loans.

How far the actual expansion in production which occurred in the first autumn and winter of war is to be attributed to this easy money policy and the stimulus of war buying by the government is impossible to say. Two other factors exerted a powerful influence on the Canadian economy at the same time—the buying boom in the autumn of 1939 in the United States and the effect of the depreciation of the Canadian dollar on prices in Canada. Through the phenomenal rise in exports to the United States during the first four months of war, Canadian business was powerfully stimulated. When the Foreign Exchange Control Board fixed the price of the American dollar to Canadians at a premium of eleven per cent. it put in operation forces which were bound to bring a comparable rise in the Canadian prices of most commodities by comparison with that prevailing in the United States. Under the stimulus of all these forces—war orders to the boot and shoe, the textile, and the iron and steel industry; monetary ease and rising prices caused by the pegging of the Canadian dollar below the American and by the American buying boom—Canadian production made remarkable progress and retail sales in Canada reflected the rise in the national money income which accompanied it.

In the spring of 1940 Hitler's attack on Norway and

the devastating speed of his reduction of Holland, Belgium, and France, put an end to the comparatively peaceful progress of the Canadian economy towards full employment. The revelation of the new rôle of machines and of the appalling urgency for their production galvanized the Canadian war programme into action on a scale not hitherto contemplated. During the rest of 1940 our imports of machine tools and essential war materials from the United States grew apace. As Mr. Ralston pointed out in his budget speech of June 24, 1940, there had arisen an "active competition for foreign exchange with which to purchase imports between consumers and private business on the one hand, and the government and firms supplying government orders on the other." To conserve the supply of foreign exchange there was imposed in his budget a 10 per cent. exchange tax on imports from non-Empire countries. In July, 1940, the Foreign Exchange Control Board was instructed by the government to refuse dollar exchange for purposes of pleasure travel. By the War Exchange Conservation Act of December, 1940, the importation of some goods from the United States was prohibited and that of other goods greatly restricted. Meantime Canada's supply of foreign exchange had been centralized in the hands of the Foreign Exchange Control Board by the Foreign Exchange Acquisition Order of April 30, 1940, which required all Canadians to sell their foreign exchange, except "normal working balances", to the Board and directed the Bank of Canada to transfer its gold reserve to them also. So large were our war purchases in the United States however that, despite these restrictions on the use of United States dollars for civilian purposes, the deficit in our balance of payments with the United States grew. Not only did we have to sell to the United States the whole of our own expanded gold production and a large amount of gold obtained from the United Kingdom; we also depleted very seriously our reserves of United States dollars.

Throughout 1941 this drain continued at a mounting pace as our war production programme grew and with it the imports required from the United States. Apart from the discovery of some new source of United States dollars the Canadian war production would have had to be curtailed. Even more drastic restrictions on non-war uses of United States dollars by Canadians would probably not have saved enough exchange to make much difference. Finance, in other words, was threatening to prove a real limitation on the production of war materials in Canada despite the promise of the government that this would not be allowed to occur. But this foreign exchange limitation was one that the Canadian Government was powerless to lift except by the aid of the American Government. Had the worst come to the worst the Dominion Government would undoubtedly have requested permission of the United States Treasury to float a Canadian security issue in the American market.

Fortunately the government of the United States had already assented to the use of America's great productive power on the side of Great Britain and had also determined that when Britain's power to purchase in the United States had been exhausted, further aid should be extended by the new device of Lend-Lease. At the same time it was recognized by the Americans that Canada's potential productive capacity was great and that the maximum North American output could be obtained only if production were organized on a continental scale. To permit this desirable consummation some arrangement was required to overcome the handicap to our production which the shortage of United States exchange threatened to become. So a joint declaration of the President of the United States and the Prime Minister of Canada issued in April, 1941, at Hyde Park announced the intention of the American Government to recompense the Canadian economy for materials purchased in the United States for the production of goods for Great Britain of a type which the American Government was shipping to the British without payment under the Lend-Lease arrangements. The declaration also provided that the American Government would buy directly from Canada certain of the products of its war plants which it would in turn use for its own armed forces or turn over to Britain or other belligerents under Lend-Lease. The first part of this declaration was intended to reduce somewhat our total need for United States dollars and the second was intended to provide us with the additional United States dollars we would need to keep our war production at a high level. In this fashion, arrangements which have removed the continental financial restriction on production were worked out. But, quite properly, the Hyde Park arrangements have not been used as an excuse to relax on Canada's travel or import restrictions, which had already been imposed to conserve exchange. As Mr. Ilsley pointed out in his budget speech of April 29, 1941, it was a "magnificent contribution to the success of our common struggle, not to the ease and convenience of the Canadian people".

Though our acute need for United States exchange has thus been met, the continued success of the arrangement depends upon the adequacy of the purchases of war materials which the government of the United States chooses to make in this country.

Thus far foreign exchange control in Canada has been operated so as to conserve the one currency scarce to us, the United States dollar. There has been no occasion to be careful in our purchases from Empire countries as all such purchases increase Britain's ability to pay for the vast amounts of food and munitions she has been getting from us. So large have these amounts been that the limited amount of goods the British could justifiably make for export to Canada and their services to the Canadian troops in Britain have not been sufficient to meet more than a small part of the value of food and munitions Canada has shipped to the British Isles and other parts of the Empire. Up to the end of 1940 the difference was met in part by the transfer to Canada of two hundred and fifty millions in British gold, which, incidentally, was very useful to us as an additional means of increasing our supply of United States dollars. A further part of the difference was made up by the resale to Canadians of Canadian securities which had been sold to British investors in past years. At the end of March 1942 settlement was made by a seven hundred million interest-free loan, made to the British Government by the Government of Canada. The deficiency for the following fiscal year was made up mainly by the gift of a billion Canadian dollars to the British Government. In accordance with the Mutual Aid Bill the future excess production of food and munitions is distributed amongst all the

United Nations in order best to serve the common cause. That distribution is not affected by the recipients' ability to find Canadian dollars with which to pay.

Foreign exchange control in Canada has so far been a most flexible instrument adaptable to the changing international situation and the alterations in national economic policy which have occurred. Policy has been made by the government and the Board has administered the regulations so efficiently as to secure the general approval of the business community in Canada. This experience has demonstrated that foreign exchange control can be limited to a particular objective —the conservation of United States exchange—and so administered as to form an essential part of an economy directly organized for war. We must now turn to the question: what part has foreign exchange control to play in the post-war period in Canada?

II

Consideration of the advisability of retaining some measure of exchange control in the post-war world involves two questions which should be distinguished in the discussion. Immediately peace is concluded the expediency of retaining control over foreign exchange dealings during the period of military and industrial demobilization must be decided upon. Then when the economy has been converted to a peacetime basis, the propriety of retaining exchange control, say for the rest of the first post-war decade, must be settled. The first question concerns the usefulness of exchange controls in a period which is bound to be a very unsettled one internationally; the second concerns the rôle of exchange control when the sort of international situation likely to persist for some time is known. Of these two questions the former is much easier to answer.

If Prime Minister Churchill's forecast of the probable course of events proves accurate, the world will not be confronted with a sudden "outbreak" of universal peace. If the United Nations concentrate their power on the defeat of Germany, leaving Japan to be dealt with thereafter, the present phase of maximum war production and of military enterprises rapidly expanding in extent may be succeeded by one in which war production can be curtailed somewhat and military activity will be less extensive. From an economic point of view such a situation would be easier to handle than one in which peace comes at the very peak of war production at home and military effort abroad. A large part of the working population would be retained in the armed forces, the services of supply, or war production. Yet both men, materials, and plant would be available to expand the production of ordinary consumer goods such as textiles and other clothing products and to "tool-up" the motor car industry and other industries producing durable consumer goods such as radios and electrical appliances to produce the new models which are being so liberally promised. Preparation for their production could be carried on while a considerable volume of war products still came from the same plants. Production of foods and other civilian goods would also be required in large volume for the reconstruction of Europe. Indeed already, before peace is in sight, the demands of the civil populations of occupied areas have appeared on the desks of those who control North American production. For the moment, that may mean additional restriction of consumption; but in time, as soon as any relaxation is possible, it will mean the gradual restoration of civilian production under the stimulus of government buying for gift or Lend-Lease to the peoples of the conquered and liberated countries. As soon as the major task, the defeat of Germany, has been accomplished, consumers in North America are likely to restrain themselves less in spending their money than they will do in 1944. A serious competition may well arise amongst consumers and between consumers and the government for the current output of consumer goods. If allowed to express itself without hindrance in the market-place this would tend to produce a rapid price inflation such as was experienced in 1919-20. If the war ends at about the same time on all fronts, the demand for civilian goods and equipment for Europe and Asia will be yet greater. If they are supplied as they should be, the shortage of civilian goods may be as great in North America as during the war itself.

The fear of unemployment and of inadequate market demand in the post-war years has been so widespread that many view the prospect of post-war price inflation with equanimity if not with positive enthusiasm. Rapidly rising prices for consumer goods are the forces which, they argue, will encourage businessmen to convert their war plants to peacetime production with the maximum speed. Price ceilings and materials and manpower priorities having alike disappeared, the businessman will be able to plan his own production as he wishes. The consumer goods which are, in the meantime, in short supply, will be rationed in the good old-fashioned way; he who is able to pay the price will get the goods.

In weighing the probable effects of such an abolition of wartime controls immediately the war is over, one must distinguish between the situation in the United States and Great Britain and the situation in the rest of the British Dominions and the republics of Latin-America. Presumably in western Europe the reconstruction of economic life will proceed under such close control of money, prices, and the volume of international transactions that the present argument will not apply there, since no such possible post-war boom as is here under discussion would be permitted. So far as the United States is concerned there are two strong arguments against permitting such a price inflation to take place. If rationing of consumers' goods which are in short supply is equitable in time of war it is surely still equitable as long as the shortage lasts, even though peace has come in the meantime. In the second place the continuance of the price ceiling and rationing controls for such commodities (i.e., for goods for which the demand at the current prices is much in excess of the supply) is not likely to retard the speed of the conversion of men and materials to their production. While a rise in price is normally required to induce additional production, that is not the case where the low level of production is the result of the diversion of men and materials to the production of munitions. The general price rise which a large volume of consumer demand and a general shortage of such goods is bound to produce, if uncontrolled, is not necessary to induce the resumption of civilian goods production once the men, the plant, and the materials are released from war uses. To permit a general price rise in such circumstances would be to distort the price structure to no useful purpose and thereby probably induce a reversal of these price movements when the supply of consumer goods becomes adequate once more. It would surely be wise to permit wartime price and rationing controls to continue so long as they are required. Price stability would thereby be greater and it is difficult to see in what respects the reversion to manufacture under conditions of private enterprise would be retarded.

All these arguments apply with equal or even greater strength to the British Dominions and other small countries dependent primarily upon export trade for their standards of living. In addition, to abolish wartime controls over prices and foreign exchange would, in these countries, introduce a further disrupting factor of great importance, the fluctuations of the price of foreign exchange, especially a probable rise in the price of United States dollars. It is true that if a price inflation were allowed to occur in the United States, the export industries of these countries would be stimulated. But with a few exceptions the supply of export commodities in these countries is little more elastic than that of ordinary consumer goods. The effect therefore would be to accentuate the rise in the national money income and the consequent demand for peacetime commodities which are already in short supply. In the smaller countries, where industry is less diversified, much of the post-war demand for consumer goods becomes at once a demand for American goods and so a demand for New York funds. If exchange control had been abolished the result would be a rise in the price of the United States dollar which would further stimulate a rise in the price of imports and exports. The upshot would probably be, not only a general price rise greater than that in the United States by the amount of the premium on New York funds in terms of the local currency, but in addition a serious distortion of the relations between the prices of the various domestic and imported commodities. Such price movements, in so far as they influenced production at all, would give it a wrong direction; just as soon as the world shortage of consumer goods began to disappear the price of New York funds would tend to decline, the domestic demand would relax and the price level would begin to fall. In such countries there would seem therefore to be even stronger reasons for the continuance of wartime controls till the consumer goods shortage begins to pass. Continued control of the exchanges would be particularly advisable. Consumers should be forced to confine their buying largely to the domestic market; no considerable expansion in the demand for the United States dollar should be permitted. There is no good reason to dissipate the country's stock of foreign exchange merely to permit certain individuals to satisfy their desires for foreign-produced consumer goods a few months before they become generally available. The size of our export trade after the war is uncertain: we may need that exchange to service Canadian securities held in the United States.

When consumer goods become relatively abundant once more, when the conversion of men and plants from war production has been largely accomplished and most of the men in the armed forces discharged, then the free economy of the western countries will meet its first real post-war test. Is depression to come once more? If price inflation of a type comparable to that of 1919-20 has been permitted to occur, rapid price deflation and the restriction of production and employment which follows it are very probable. But the avoidance of such price fluctuations by the continuance of wartime controls would be no guarantee that, when consumers' demand returns to a more normal percentage of current income, conditions will be such as to induce private manufacturers to provide anything like "full employment" at all times. Both economic theory and bitter experience support that conclusion. Economists now generally agree that the source of fluctuations in employment lies in the fact that at some times businessmen find it profitable to invest in new plant and equipment while at other times they do not. The multiplied effect of these changing investment decisions of businessmen is felt throughout the economic system in the form of a changing volume of employment and market demand. The prospects, after the immediate conversion of industry to peacetime production has been accomplished, will therefore depend upon the attitude which businessmen take toward the profitability of investment.

At the moment it is quite impossible to tell what the prospects of profitable investment will be two years or so after peace has come. It is easy to argue oneself into a very pessimistic frame of mind. Given the range and complexity of international political and economic problems sure to be met after the war, and assuming the continued timidity of businessmen who remember the 1930's, it would seem plausible to argue that little positive action to maintain employment can be expected from private business and to conclude that the state must be prepared therefore with a huge investment programme of its own. On the other hand, much has happened since 1939 to restore in businessmen some of the self-confidence they felt in the twenties and to awaken in them the realization that if they do not risk much to maintain the volume of investment and employment, leadership in the modern world is bound to pass from them. The necessity of their acting is reinforced by the widespread public belief that the war has provided a clear-cut demonstration of our ability to spend ourselves into prosperity, a belief which is being strengthened by those who, ignoring the essential and critical differences between government spending in war and in peace, demand that what they loosely call "full employment" be maintained at all times in the post-war world. Perhaps also the changing relations between capital, labour, and government will make possible a social policy under which labour will share with business and government not only the rewards of employment but some responsibility for its maintenance.

Whatever the upshot, these and similar considerations will be the determining factors upon which the level of employment in the United States and Great Britain will depend. If these two great powers do not succeed in maintaining employment and expanding the market in their midst for the exports of the satellite countries, the economic situation of the latter will be serious indeed. In such countries consumers tend to spend a much larger part of their incomes on imported commodities than do the consumers of large countries such as the United States. Should the money income of countries so situated be raised by governmental spending, the resulting stimulus to domestic industry is lessened by the "leakage" of purchasing power into buying abroad. Huge governmental expenditures might be required to maintain the national income if no restrictions on such foreign trade were imposed. If all countries engage in income-raising policies the "leaks" to a great extent offset each other. But no country so largely dependent upon international trade as we are in Canada could carry out such a policy alone without a progressive diminution in the volume of its international transactions imposed by exchange and similar controls. A rapid extension of state control of domestic business would probably follow.

Should the United States and Great Britain succeed in preventing serious depression, the situation of the export countries would be much more hopeful. Not only would their sales in the great consuming markets steadily expand but the consequent improvement in the domestic money income in these countries would provide a sound basis for more trade amongst themselves. Expansionist policies pursued in these smaller countries would reinforce the world-wide upward movement of business. In fact, one of the essential conditions of the success of such policies at the centre is the co-operation of the peripheral countries. Certainly this is true for Great Britain, and it is probably truer for the United States than is commonly believed.

Should such be the happy outcome, should it prove possible to avoid serious depression for say the first five or six years of peace, it would not follow, even in this the most favourable situation for the abolition of wartime controls, that exchange control should be immediately, or even ultimately, abandoned by Canada.

Further difficulties lie ahead. In time governmental spending upon war and reconstruction would become relatively unimportant; the investment boom would be mainly a private one. But, to repeat, both experience and theory warn us that long-continued investment like that of the 1920's is likely to be followed by a temporary relaxation like that of the early 1930's. Is such a decline, when it comes, to be allowed to degenerate into another international catastrophe like that of 1931-33? Assuming that peace has been effectually organized and that war expenditures are no longer required on a significant scale, such a slump may be difficult to prevent or moderate. If it is avoided it will be by the world-wide adoption of adequate economic policies prepared in advance for immediate application when the necessity arises.

There are two aspects to this problem: the working out of the proper economic policy to deal with the threatening depression, and its general adoption. We are concerned here only with the latter. Assuming that economists and civil servants have the outlines of an adequate policy in mind and assuming furthermore that general public support for it in the major countries has been obtained in advance, how is its general adoption at the right time and with the proper vigour to be assured? If left to the decision of each particular country, proper timing would seem to be improbable; but its application as a matter of common strategy would seem to imply either a very great development of institutions of international finance in the years immediately following the war or the growth of habits of international co-operation in economic matters between sovereign powers of which there is as yet not much sign. In either case there would surely be needed in each of the countries in which the common policy was to be carried out, not only an adequately organized central bank but also institutions through which control over actual international transactions might be imposed when desired. Exchange control, at least over capital movements (i.e., not necessarily their prevention but at least their regulation) would probably have been continued since the war. But on occasions such as the threatened slump now being discussed it might be deemed advisable to combat it not only by the familiar indirect monetary measures but by more direct interference with particular types of transactions till the emergency is passed.

But, it may be asked, does a fully-functioning international economic system require all this new-fangled institutional apparatus? Is there no chance of the recurrence of such circumstances as made it possible for the international economy to function successfully in the nineteenth century without all this conscious attention by governments? To ask such questions is to raise most complicated and important problems of historical interpretation and economic analysis upon which there is as yet no agreement amongst economists and economic historians. Some believe that the nineteenth century economy worked passably, under the international gold standard, only because of the overwhelming economic power and financial skill of the British. The rise of the financial power of the United States divided international leadership disastrously thus bringing the frustration and defeat of the inter-war years. Order, they imply, is only to be restored to the international system when the economic power of some one country has again become so over-riding that whatever economic policy it chooses to adopt is thereby almost automatically imposed on the smaller countries. They see the United States in that rôle in the years to come. Others think that only the combined resources and experience of the United States and Great Britain could exercise the required power successfully. Still others believe that the day is gone when any one country might exercise such control merely because of the attraction of its huge markets for the exports of smaller countries, because of their dependence for economic development upon capital investments made from the wealth and savings of the older country and by the sheer prestige of the economic policies adopted in a country so wealthy and so great. They argue that smaller countries will wish to have a voice in the determination of international economic policy, in the results of which they are so vitally concerned. Since they have equipped themselves with central banks and exchange controls, nations have become touchy on the subject of their economic sovereignty, and will never again submit their monetary policy to be determined by some other country as they did in the nineteenth century when they adopted the international gold standard, which was in fact a sterling exchange standard in disguise.

The sort of action taken by the United Nations in the immediate future will go a long way in determining how the international economic system is to be guided in the more distant future. Important questions will have to be solved shortly. Rates of exchange appropriate to the later period of the war and the early post-war years will have to be agreed upon anew; arrangements will have to be made to extend to all of the smaller countries both the long-term loans for economic development and short-term banking accommodation they may require to maintain stable exchange rates in times of temporary difficulty. The way in which such matters are handled will indicate whether we are to have a world of independent nations each pursuing its own immediate advantage, or one dominated by the United States and Great Britain, or one in which general economic co-operation will be the rule.

Should it turn out that the United States and Great Britain are able to maintain domestic prosperity; if they are willing to allow other nations to participate freely in that prosperity by selling their goods in the American and British markets; and if they are wise enough to support a new international monetary system with the necessary long- and short-term loans, as did the British in the nineteenth century, then the exporting nations may well be able to relax or to abolish their controls over dealings in foreign exchange. But if the British and American people are unprepared for the sacrifices and changes such leadership is sure to involve, particularly in the United States, then all the western nations together must attempt to compensate for that lack of leadership by deliberately organizing a common economic policy under which each government, by positive domestic action on lines generally approved, will make its contribution to the maintenance of international prosperity and to the development of the economic resources of all the nations. If required, such a programme would likely develop slowly, with some significant failures along the way. While experience is being gained and co-operation developed, each nation would be well advised to retain its institutional arrangements for exchange control and impose such controls whenever domestic stability can be promoted thereby without repercussions upsetting to other countries. If the United States refuses to exercise in a positive fashion the leadership to which her economic power and resources destine her and returns to isolationism and economic nationalism, or if the international co-operation which might be an alternative fails of achievement, then we shall assuredly have exchange controls with us for a long time—and much else beside!

Chapter IX

CANADIAN AGRICULTURE IN THE POST-WAR WORLD

W. M. Drummond

The most outstanding wartime agricultural development has been a rapid and pronounced expansion in the production of livestock and livestock products, particularly marked in the case of hogs, poultry, eggs, milk, milk products, beef cattle, and the grain and forage crops on which this production (of livestock) depends. While additional output has been the rule in all parts of the country, the most notable and continuous expansion has taken place in the prairie provinces, where the increase in feed grains, poultry, eggs, and dairy products has been quite marked and that of hogs phenomenal. A relatively greater increase in the West has been possible because of a very considerable shift from wheat-growing to more diversified types of farming. To some extent this shift, well under way when war broke out, has represented an attempt to secure a more stable farm income. For the most part, however, it has been due to the lack of sufficient markets and reasonable prices for wheat during a period when the markets for livestock and livestock products were reasonably satisfactory.

This increase in production is a direct result of the special demand that has arisen during and because of the war. The special export requirements plus the increasing effectiveness of domestic demand have made it possible to dispose of greatly enlarged supplies at considerably higher prices. The combination of increased volume of sales and increased selling prices has added appreciably to both individual and national farm income, and improved significantly the general economic position of the average farmer. It should be noted that the extra sales volume has meant extra output per farm rather than additional farms. While the improvement may not be all that could be desired most people would feel reasonably satisfied if they were assured that it would continue during the post-war years. It is generally recognized, however, that its continuance will depend largely on the possibility of retaining present markets.

In considering post-war market prospects it is necessary to distinguish between the immediate post-war years and the later period. There will probably be no lack of markets during the earlier stages of the reconstruction period. Except possibly in the case of wheat there can be little doubt that all available supplies will be needed to feed the half-starved millions in continental Europe and elsewhere. Lack of purchasing power in these areas may make necessary extensive resort to some form of Lend-Lease financing and result in unit prices being kept moderately low. Moreover, in view of the prolonged nature of the war and the serious disruption of farming land, loss of soil fertility, depletion of livestock, feed, and agricultural supplies generally, a considerable period, perhaps two to five or more years depending on the product and area being considered, will be needed to restore European agricultural production to anything like pre-war normal.

During the first part of this period also we are likely to witness a continuation of manufacturing, construction, and general business activity in Canada. While it will take time and considerable capital to adapt and re-adapt plants for civilian production, the process of doing so will go at least part way towards maintaining employment. In addition and in particular, the need for replacing worn-out equipment and capital goods generally will be acute. Moreover, it will be possible and necessary to supply the many kinds of consumer goods that will have become extremely scarce because of wartime curtailment. The satisfying of these various needs may well result, for some considerable time, in consumer purchasing power and the Canadian demand for food remaining at a high level.

Export Market Prospects

The real problem of finding markets is most likely to present itself as the immediate reconstruction period draws to a close. When that time comes the actual extent to which importing and exporting of farm products takes place will depend on the possibilities of following an economically scientific system of international production and exchange. In view of the general objectives of the United Nations as stated in the Atlantic Charter and elsewhere, and the dire consequences of following the pre-war tendency towards economic self-sufficiency, it may perhaps be reasonable to assume that, somehow or other and despite the many difficulties in the way, a fairly sensible and scientific system of international or inter-regional trading will be developed. Some clue to the probable arrangements is obtained in the terms of the wheat agreement concluded at Washington in July, 1942, by representatives of the governments of Canada, the United States, Argentina, Australia, and the United Kingdom. This agreement provides that the United States will arrange a post-war conference of all substantial wheat importing and exporting countries for the purpose of deciding whether an international wheat agreement is necessary and, if so, what its nature should be. A tentative agenda for this conference has been prepared in the form of a draft convention which begins by suggesting that any lasting solution to the wheat problem must be based on a reciprocal expansion of international trade generally, between the wheat exporting and importing countries. In the meantime and in anticipation of the full conference the four big exporting countries have agreed on a production, carry-over, and export control plan which they will follow during the first two post-war years, and which may be continued indefinitely if incorporated as part of a larger agreement which may be reached when the full post-war conference meets. This plan calls for the placing of a definite limit on production, the establishing of minimum and maximum carry-over figures, and the division of the total export business on a quota basis.

A range between minimum and maximum carry-overs was provided because of variations in yield. In the case of Canada it was agreed that carry-over stocks should not be less than 80 million nor more than 275 million bushels under peacetime conditions; that Canada should export forty per cent. of the total exported by the four countries, this percentage being in line with her share of the export trade in the period between the two wars; that the sharing of export markets on a quota basis should not begin until such time after the war as shipping facilities are freely available; that the prices ruling just prior to the end of the war should be maintained for the first six months after the armistice; and that, during this six months' period, the United Kingdom should arrange with the four exporting countries a range of prices which will be fair to exporting and importing countries alike and which will bear a reasonable relationship to the general level of prices then prevailing. The prices so arranged are to continue until the end of the second year after the armistice unless they become part of a larger agreement reached during the above-mentioned post-war conference.

Whether the total amount of wheat entering international trade will be larger after than before the war will depend mainly on the extent to which the pronounced pre-war economic nationalism is replaced by an expansion of international specialization and exchange. Any progress made in this direction is likely to be gradual. Moreover, so far as European countries are concerned, a decision to devote less acreage to wheat would hardly reduce production to the level prevailing before the trend towards self-sufficiency began. Technical progress in production since then might be expected to result in higher yields per acre on the reduced acreage. Irrespective of any increases in exports to Europe, the United Kingdom is certain to remain our chief customer. Regardless of what agricultural policy she adopts the United Kingdom will find it necessary to import a large part of her food requirements, including wheat. Several British authorities have recently estimated[1] the acreage that would be planted to wheat in Britain under any reasonable post-war farm policy. The average of these estimates is about 1,800,000 acres, which is close to that of the pre-war years. However, if the British agricultural policy places emphasis on productive efficiency, as now seems indicated, the same number of acres may yield considerably more wheat than before the war. At the same time it should be noted that the new National bread made from flour containing 85 per cent. wheat is now preferred by many British consumers. The change from the old white to the new National bread is said to have released 640,000 tons of shipping per year, which is equivalent to reducing wheat imports by over 21 million bushels. In the light of these developments one would expect that Great Britain's wheat imports will be somewhat less after than before the war. However, it is not likely that such a decrease would be sufficient to offset any possible increase in the amount going to continental Europe. On balance, the wheat imports of European countries, including Great Britain, should significantly exceed those of the pre-war period.

We may next inquire as to the prospect for exporting Canadian bacon. For bacon the only external market of any significance is the United Kingdom. Before the war Canada was only one of many countries which shared this market on a quota basis. During the war, however, Canadian exports to Britain have gone up as

[1]See J. A. Scott Watson, "British Agriculture in War Time and After War" (in *Canadian Society of Technical Agriculturists Review*, September, 1942, p. 10).

Britain's home production went down, and as it became impossible for her to secure supplies from various countries in continental Europe. In other words, Canadian exports have increased as supplies from other sources have dwindled or disappeared. A crucial question is: to what extent, if any, is this process likely to be reversed after the war?

While accurate prediction is obviously impossible, consideration of some likely developments may supply at least a partial answer. First, there will be a pronounced increase in the export requirements immediately after the armistice, or at least as soon thereafter as additional shipping space can be obtained. The replacement of the present four-ounce ration by normal consumption should make it possible to dispose of much more bacon in Great Britain. Moreover, Canada will be expected to supply a considerable part of the large special meat requirements in continental Europe. Whether exports can be increased suddenly in response to this demand is perhaps open to doubt. Much will depend on the ability to increase the number of hogs marketed just prior to the end of the war and in the months following the armistice. Since this product can be stored for only a short time and since storage space is limited, it will be necessary, for the most part, to meet increased export demands out of current production.

Once this special demand of the earlier post-war period has been satisfied, the United Kingdom may be expected to resume her rôle as the only export outlet for bacon. At the same time the several European countries which exported bacon to Great Britain before the war will be renewing their bids for a share of that market. When that time comes Canada's export prospects will depend upon Great Britain's total import requirements and the share of that total secured either in open competition or as the result of some special sharing arrangement. A British agricultural policy which refused to foster high-cost hog production and which stressed production of milk, fresh vegetables, and protective foods generally, would have the effect of raising bacon imports considerably above pre-war levels. On the other hand, a serious attempt to follow the international trading plan forecast in the Atlantic Charter would certainly prevent Canada from securing the sort of preferred treatment that resulted from the Ottawa Agreements of 1932. If it is decided to divide the market on a quota basis, Canada's wartime performance should be an important factor in determining the size of her quota. At the same time the pre-war performance of countries like Denmark would go a long way in substantiating their claims and in affecting those of Canada. A scientific setting of quotas involves consideration of each country's need for markets together with its ability to fill all of the quota set. On both counts past performance furnishes the best and, in fact, the only guide.

Should the sharing of the market be left to open competition between the exporting countries it is difficult to forecast Canada's exports. Our ability to compete on a basis of quality should be greatly enhanced as a result of the special precautions now being taken to insure that the product exported be of high and uniform quality. Moreover, the greatly increased production plus post-war retention of centralized control over storage and shipping (if that may be assumed) should make it possible for Canada to equal any other country in the matter of regularity of supply. It must be realized, however, that no matter how strong our quality and service competition may be, it will not win export customers unless accompanied by the ability to quote price terms at least as low as those offered by other countries. If Canada is to win a large share of the British market against competition like that of Denmark before the war, it will be necessary to produce and market hogs and hog products more efficiently than before. If export bacon prices fall appreciably below present levels, as may be assumed, we shall have to choose between reducing costs and reducing production. In this connection it should be remembered that the recent large expansion in hog production has resulted from pronounced advances in hog prices and the important fact that the price of grain used for hog feed has remained relatively low.

While post-war hog production on the present scale would require a large export market, that market would not require to be as large as at present. The reason is that exports are now being increased very considerably as the result of artificial curtailment of domestic consumption. When restrictions on domestic sales are removed at the end of the war, the domestic market will naturally absorb a much larger share of the total product.

Much of what has been written regarding bacon applies also to cheese, with some important differences. While the production and export of cheese has increased during the war in somewhat the same ratio as bacon, nearly all the extra production has taken place in the established cheese-producing provinces of Ontario and

Quebec whereas in hog production the major increases have occurred in the prairie provinces. On the demand side it is important to note that, whereas extra bacon exports have been needed to replace supplies no longer available elsewhere, Canada was asked to export more cheese primarily because the wartime cheese requirements exceeded those of the pre-war years. Although several European countries exported cheese to the United Kingdom before the war, the aggregate of such exports made up only a small part of the total British imports. The great bulk of the cheese was imported from Canada and New Zealand. As the war period has progressed the United Kingdom has requested steadily increasing shipments from both Canada and New Zealand. In addition Australia and, more recently, the United States, have become large cheese exporters.

To the extent that cheese exports have been increased to meet special war conditions one would expect that, once those conditions (including the losses at sea) have passed and the early post-war requirements have been satisfied, world cheese exports will decline. In that event the best that Canada can hope for is that the United States will retire from the exporting picture and that Australia will revert to something like her pre-war emphasis on butter as distinct from cheese. There is, however, another important factor which should help to preserve a large export market for Canadian cheese. Current declarations of post-war British agricultural policy indicate that all the milk produced in Britain will be needed for consumption in the fluid form. If, as seems probable, none of the milk is manufactured into cheese and butter, the equivalent of the cheese and butter made in Britain before the war will have to be imported. Since additional amounts of both cheese and butter would apparently be needed, an arrangement might be worked out whereby the extra butter might be exported by Australia and New Zealand and the extra cheese by Canada. In view of this possibility and the well-established reputation of Canadian cheese in Great Britain, one may be fairly optimistic regarding Canada's cheese export prospects. As with bacon, however, much may depend on our ability to produce and market efficiently. During the winter of 1942 when the negotiations regarding that year's cheese contract were taking place, the British Food Ministry suggested that the price of twenty cents a pound which was agreed upon was considerably higher than could be expected under post-war conditions.

It is impossible, due to lack of space, to make more than passing reference to the many other products. It is probable that export markets will be lacking or greatly reduced for products like flax and soya beans, which at present are enjoying a special war industry demand. On the other hand, where export markets have been cut off because of the special exigencies of war, as for apples, canned fruits and vegetables, tobacco, and other products, it is reasonable to expect a large measure of market restoration. In respect of this latter group of products, however, it is well to remember that Canadian producers may not have the pre-war advantage of preferred tariff treatment.

The Domestic Market

While more gradual, less spectacular, and less advertised than the developments in the export market, the wartime improvement in the domestic market has been pronounced in extent and of real economic significance to Canadian farmers. The improvement has been twofold. Not only has increased food consumption expanded the size of the domestic market but the expanded volume of products has been sold at a considerable advance in unit price. Since this improvement has resulted from the increase in employment and purchasing power, its continuance after the war will depend on the ability to maintain the present condition of full employment. It follows that any general economic policies which may be invoked to prevent a post-war depression and the accompanying unemployment will be of vital concern to Canadian farmers. Farmers need to learn (and the improvement generated during the present war should go a long way in teaching them) that an economically healthy domestic market, such as exists today, is worth much more to them than a market characterized by depression and low purchasing power. Before the war there was a tendency on the part of farm leaders to assume that urban consumers could and would pay higher prices for food products if necessary. It was also commonly assumed that the payment of such higher prices would not appreciably reduce the quantity purchased. In contrast the war experience has shown that it is possible to secure a higher price and at the same time expand the volume of sales if consumers are provided with an increased supply of purchasing power. This experience suggests that a major aim of post-war agricultural policy should be the fullest possible backing of any programme designed to assure full employment. Agricultural policy and general economic policy have a common interest and should not be separated.

This last point may perhaps be stated differently. Before the war the central problem of agriculture was that of finding markets. Lack of markets was reflected in the existence of large and, apparently, chronic surpluses. Since it was felt that very little could be done to improve the demand, those who attempted to solve farm problems tended to emphasize the possibilities of influencing supply. The central aim was to secure reasonable farm prices and income in spite of the absence of demand. The various concrete plans or suggestions included attempts to prevent foreign supplies from entering the Canadian market, plans whereby a higher average price could be secured through the subsidized export of the smaller part of a product, various marketing schemes which provided for limiting the quantity of a product that might go to market, the practice of restricting the number of producers who might cater to a given market, and a few attempts at limiting supply directly by controlling farm production. With the coming of the war the surplus problem has disappeared (except in the important case of wheat) at least temporarily, and with it the need for the various programmes restricting supply. Whether this change can be made permanent is, of course, the important question. The basic soundness, from the standpoint of agriculture and society at large, of working in the direction of expanded rather than restricted production suggests that future efforts towards improvements should place the emphasis on distribution and demand.

Assuming that everything possible is done to maintain the present effectiveness of domestic demand, the further question arises as to whether the post-war years are likely to witness any changes in either the quantity or character of domestic consumption. The answer here will depend upon the progress in human nutrition and efficient marketing and also upon immigration. The experience of war is serving to focus attention on these matters. It is forcing us to see more clearly and quickly both the need for and possibilities of improvement.

It is safe to assume that improved nutrition and the increased education of consumers that accompanies it will constitute an important national objective in the post-war years. More difficult to predict is the actual extent to which such programmes may be pushed. However, we are here concerned chiefly with stressing the fact that, in so far as progress is likely to be made on these lines, an improved demand for farm products will take place. Improved nutrition should definitely increase the demand for the so-called protective foods, such as milk, other dairy products, and fresh and canned fruits and vegetables. In addition to the extent that many consumers are even now (according to nutritional authorities) receiving an insufficient *quantity* of food nutrients, it should result in a considerable expansion in the demand for food products in general as distinct from any class of foods in particular. It will also mean that even greater attention will have to be paid to the producing and marketing of products of specified types and qualities. In any case, because of the beneficial effect on demand, if for no other reason, farmers would be well advised to foster and support programmes aimed at better nutrition whether they be thorough-going plans applicable to all consumers or merely something in the nature of a Canadian "Stamp plan" calculated to benefit the most disadvantaged groups.

While, as present experience indicates, consumers will buy more food if they have more money to pay for it, it is also a fact that they will buy more food at a low than at a high price. Although particularly applicable during periods of low purchasing power, this rule holds to a greater or lesser degree at all times. The mass of consumers have limited incomes even in prosperous times and are compelled to do with somewhat less food as the price rises. We make these statements as a basis for the claim that the market for farm products could be expanded significantly were it possible to quote lower consumer prices. To reduce consumer prices without lowering the prices received by the farmer, it is necessary to do the marketing more efficiently. Narrower marketing margins, in turn, can only be obtained by reducing the number of marketing functions or finding less wasteful methods of performing them. In this connection the somewhat revolutionary changes which are being effected under the pressure of wartime necessity may prove of lasting value. The current attempt at maintaining retail price ceilings, while paying higher farm prices in order to ensure production, is forcing the search for ways and means of narrowing the margin. It is hardly to be expected that all the innovations resulting from the work of the Controller of Transport and the Division of Simplified Practice of the Wartime Prices and Trade Board and those introduced by marketing agencies themselves will be discarded as soon as the war is over. At any rate the search for increased efficiency in marketing must and will go on. To the extent that extra efficiency can be achieved the farmer stands to receive a twofold benefit. He will be able to sell more products without necessarily having to accept a reduced selling price. In the second place, since farming has such a large element of fixed costs, an increased volume of sales would permit increased production, fuller use of the farm plant, and hence lower unit costs. Incidentally a larger volume of farm products would in itself make for more efficient marketing. Generally speaking, real marketing efficiency can only be obtained where volume of business is sufficient to permit the adoption and full use of specialized technique.

In regard to the effects of immigration on the domestic market, not much can be said at this date. The general view at present, however, is that Canada will receive a substantial body of immigrants after the war and that the newcomers will find employment in the development of natural resources generally and not merely in agriculture. It may also be stated that the principles enunciated in the Atlantic Charter call for the removal of barriers to the free flow of people. Even partial application of those principles would probably result in a very distinct movement of people to this country.

Before leaving this section mention should be made of another potential development in the realm of demand. Present indications are that the future will see a rapid expansion in the use of farm products as industrial raw materials in addition to their use as human food. Here again the necessities of wartime are doing much to speed developments and there can be little doubt that the lessons learned during the emergency will be carried forward and bear considerable fruit in the post-war era. It is much too early to agree with the more enthusiastic devotees of the science of chemurgy in their claim that the industrial demand for farm products will be the really significant demand of the future. On the other hand, it is well to recognize that experiments in the use of farm products for industrial purposes were well under way prior to the war (the war preparations of the Axis Nations involved considerable use of these developments) and that this trend will have become reasonably well established by the end of the war.

Marketing Methods

It will be evident from what has been said above that future methods of marketing are likely to bear some relation to those developed during the war and also to the requirements of export markets. If trading arrangements require that Canada export stipulated amounts of the various products at certain times and prices, it will be necessary to have a marketing system which will move the products to the markets in an orderly and organized way. It may be that a necessary condition of remaining a strong bacon exporter will be the retention of the Bacon Board or some corresponding agency. One thing is certain: we shall have to provide high and uniform quality and reasonable regularity of shipment. We can scarcely hope to comply with these requirements without the aid of an agency such as the Board to supervise inspection, standardize processing, allot the total business, undertake the necessary storing, and direct the shipping. Some kind of unified direction will apparently be essential. Although there is nothing to indicate that the actual business of marketing will pass out of private hands, it is probable that certain market functions previously considered as part of the job of the private marketing agencies will be performed under public auspices. Furthermore, the necessity of being able to offer price and quality competition in foreign markets, whether goods are sold in open competition or under the terms of special contracts, will serve as a spur to the finding of more efficient marketing methods.

While the need for orderliness may be less urgent in the case of purely domestic marketing, there can be little doubt about the need for lower marketing costs. A continuation of the present attempts at eliminating marketing wastes, such as those resulting from the supply of special services, duplication of deliveries, excessive competition in transportation, and incomplete use of facilities generally, will be most necessary. It will also call for control by the government or producer co-operatives or possibly both. Really efficient marketing requires enough volume of business to permit fairly full application of the specialization principle. In many farm communities, however, operation on such a basis is made impossible because there is not enough product to provide each of several competitors with a large volume of business. In many such cases the only way to secure the necessary volume is to have all or a large number of the farmers agree to perform the function co-operatively.

There are other cases where it is not so much a lack of volume of business as simply the fact that the activity concerned is naturally unsuited for competition. There can be no doubt, for example, that the transporting of milk from the farms to large market centres has been very inefficient and that great increases in efficiency would result if milk producers were able and willing to undertake the transportation of milk on a co-operative basis. The cost, for example, of transporting the milk in the Dayton, Ohio, milkshed has been reduced twenty-five per cent. because the producers were instrumental in replacing wasteful duplication by a carefully planned routing system. As this is being written attempts are being made to eliminate duplication and otherwise effect savings in the transportation of milk, cream, livestock, and other products. The pressing need for economy in the use of trucks, tires, gasoline, and drivers is forcing those now in the business to assist the transport controller in working out a more rational system. If suitable plans are developed, they will doubtless become a permanent part of our marketing mechanism. If not, the state will probably be compelled to undertake transportation. In any case the need for improvement is so obvious that any gains made will have to be carried forward to post-war years. In a country like Canada, where distances are great and farm production is still of the extensive sort, the cost of transportation, even when performed as efficiently as possible, makes up a large part of the total marketing margin.

Another sphere in which government action will be called for, or joint action between governments and the various agencies engaged in marketing, is in the domestic distribution of fruits and vegetables. For some years prior to the war there was an urgent and well recognized need for the construction and operation of wholesale markets in our larger cities. Several special investigations have shown that market facilities have not kept pace with the growth of urban centres, the expansion of production, and the changing needs of consumers and that, as a result, marketing margins are needlessly wide. There is waste of time, trucks, labour, produce, and much confusion and uncertainty in regard to supply, demand, and prices. There is almost general agreement that modernized market facilities are necessary, including an up-to-date market information service. Incidentally the construction of such facilities would constitute a productive type of project for a government seeking to stimulate post-war employment.

Production and Prices

The main justification for devoting so much space to the prospects for markets and marketing methods lies in the fact that post-war developments in farm production and prices will be greatly influenced by the extent and character of demand. In the post-war (as in the pre-war) years, the basic requirement and possibly the basic problem of agriculture will be the securing and maintenance of a satisfactory relationship between the prices the farmer receives and those which he has to pay. Where such a relationship does not exist it will be necessary either to lower farm purchase prices or raise the prices received for farm products. In order that farm prices be raised one of three things must happen. The price will rise if demand can be increased relative to supply. Some artificial means of reducing supply may be employed. Or, finally, government subsidies sufficient to raise prices to the desired level may be paid out of the national exchequer.

It is obvious that the most natural and economically

desirable method is an increase in demand. Such being the case, it is in the farmer's as well as the general interest that everything possible be done to maintain or, better still, to expand the demand for farm products. In spite of the desirability and also the potentialities of solving the problem in this way, however, one would need to be very optimistic to believe that progress in this direction will be other than gradual or that such efforts will prove all-sufficient. At the present time there are few who would be willing to count upon the future problem of farm price being solved by the automatic working of supply and demand.

It is largely because demand is expected to fall off after the war that so much is being heard these days about the desirability of post-war planning of farm production. If all the supplies that would result from an unplanned production could be absorbed at satisfactory prices there would be much less, if any, occasion for planning production. Most people who visualize a planned production assume that demand will be definitely limited and that the only way to assure reasonable prices and income is to control the amount produced or sent to market. Past experience has shown that the only alternative to such control is large-scale relief payments at the expense of the general taxpayer. What is being thought of, therefore, is a planned or systematic contraction of production in line with a restricted demand.

A planned programme of production presupposes an accurate knowledge of market requirements. Once market needs are known, the plan consists in allotting the production on a regional, provincial, county, and, eventually, an individual farmer basis. As this is being written[2] a detailed blueprint of what Canada expects from her farmers in 1943 is being presented at a production-planning conference in Ottawa. Known export needs have been added to known military and civilian needs and the total of each product has been set up as a goal towards which each branch of agriculture will aim. After each province has examined the requirements and made known the share it could hope to produce, provincial quotas are set up and provincial officials made responsible for further subdivision.

It is probably much easier to operate such a plan when the objective is the greatest possible expansion, as at present, than when a specific degree of contraction in production is being sought. It is one thing to ask a farmer to try to increase his hog or milk output by five or ten per cent. and quite another to get him to produce a different product, move to a different area, or cease farming altogether. Experience in the United States and our own recent experience in reducing wheat acreage indicate that farmers have to be well paid before they will switch or curtail production. Nevertheless, Canadian governments and Canadian farmers are likely to become reasonably familiar with the idea and the technique of producing according to a plan by the end of the war, and it will be surprising if the experience is not carried forward to the post-war years. It should be noted, however, that the practicability of producing according to a plan will be greatly influenced by the extent to which total demand can be calculated in advance. This, in turn, will depend upon the extent to which post-war exports are disposed of on a bulk contract basis and at fixed prices.

[2]December, 1942.

It is highly probable that, after the war, the production planning idea will be linked with farmer insistence upon guaranteed minimum prices. This is almost certain to be the case if demand proves to be limited relative to possibilities of production. Farmers will argue that if Canada was able to maintain a general price ceiling in wartime to prevent out-of-hand inflation it can just as logically establish and maintain a general price floor to prevent equally disastrous deflation. The establishment of minimum prices, however, would lead logically towards production controls. Any government which undertook to guarantee minimum prices would not only insist upon a systematic control of production but would require that farmers, on their part, maintain a high level of efficiency in production. The main fact is that not only will farmers demand a reasonable remuneration for their efforts but that farmers and government alike will be determined to achieve a real degree of market stability. The general effects of past instability have been so apparent and so costly that one can reasonably count on a special drive to prevent their recurrence. Moreover, it should be noted that many of the procedures now being followed by government agencies are exactly the kind necessary in any programme aimed at securing market stability for agriculture. These procedures include the giving of price guarantees, buying and storing in bulk, estimating future needs, and other devices employed by the Wartime Prices and Trade Board or the Agricultural Supplies Board.

Organization of Farm Production

During the last war the need for increased farm production tended to become more urgent as the supply of farm labour was reduced, with the result that mechanized farming was given a tremendous impetus. Tractor farming and the use of commercial fertilizer and fertilizer drills emerged. Improved spraying and dusting machines came into common use and several new machines were used in the production, harvesting, and processing of such crops as potatoes, apples, flax, and sugar beets.

While the period between the two wars was marked by fairly steady progress in the development, improvement, and distribution of many agricultural machines, the tempo of agricultural mechanization has been speeded up tremendously since the outbreak of the present war. There has been a great improvement in, and wider use of, tillage machinery, including ploughs, the tiller-harrow or one-way disc, the combination tiller-seeder, and light tractors with row-crop equipment. Among harvesting machines, combine harvesters, with and without windrow pick-up equipment, are meeting with wide favour on many farms across the country and for many crops. As for haying machinery, there has been a greatly increased demand for hay loaders and side delivery rakes, while the recently developed pick-up hay baler is meeting with considerable favour on large farms. Much more popular, because comparatively inexpensive, is the new buck rake which is reputed to have more than halved the time needed to save the hay. Another new machine is the ensilage harvester which is proving to be an important labour-saver where the corn acreage is sufficient to warrant its use. The development of machines used in the production of livestock and livestock products has been less spectacular but, even here, the attempt to lower costs and save labour has had its effects. Milking machines have been improved and many more of them have been installed. A more widespread use has also been made of such things as feed and litter carriers, self-feeders, feed grinders, power-operated water systems, and milk-cooling equipment. While some of these are minor items others represent a very considerable capital investment.

If war conditions and requirements have stimulated developments along mechanical lines they have also served to intensify the general search after more scientific farming methods. When, as at present, the demand for farm products is virtually unlimited and farm labour is extremely scarce and therefore expensive, it becomes especially necessary to arrange things so that the correct amounts and kinds of all the other productive agents are combined with the limited labour supply. This means that farmers must pay closer attention to the exact nature of their soil and its special plant-food requirements; that they must learn more about the various strains of livestock so as to be able to select the ones that will make the greatest gain in weight, and yield the largest amount of milk or eggs per unit of feed and labour; that they must know more about the results of animal and plant nutrition research and be able to apply new suggestions; and that they must become better students of the science of farm mechanics. Moreover, scientific scrutiny in the use of all farm productive agents has become increasingly necessary as war conditions have restricted supplies of these agents. In short, wartime conditions have been responsible for a much greater quantity and variety of scientific agricultural research together with a far more widespread application of research results.

These developments in mechanization and scientific agriculture are of notable significance in farm organization. The central fact is that it is physically and financially impossible for the average individual farmer operating on the present average scale to make anything like full use of these developments. The increasingly complicated and scientific nature of farming is making it more and more difficult for any one farmer to master all branches of his job. To be really successful a present-day farmer must be a mechanic, a carpenter, a scientist, an accountant, a salesman, as well as a man who works hard and is familiar with the ordinary arts and practices of farming. Since very few can hope to possess all these abilities in sufficient degree, there appear to be only two possible ways in which reasonably full use of the specialization principle can be obtained. Specialization by task in farming can be applied only to the extent that specialized farming is substituted for the present generalized type or to the extent that the farm production unit can be increased in size to the point where the scale of operations warrants sub-division of function between specialized people.

So far as mechanization is concerned the problem is that, while it is essential that farmers secure the gains which result from the efficient use of modern machinery, the average farmer has not sufficient volume of business to warrant purchase of many of the larger and more expensive machines. The farmer is in the awkward position where he can neither afford to own the machines, nor to do without them. Since the basic farm machinery problem is one of lowering overhead costs per unit of product, any method of dealing with it must aim at enlarging the volume of business. Various methods of achieving this end have been applied with increasing frequency in recent years, and all of them have been receiving special consideration as the war period has progressed.

One method is that whereby the farmer seeks to increase his volume of business either by farming his existing acreage more intensively or by purchasing or renting additional acreage. Application of this plan is limited for various reasons, one being the difficulty of finding enough extra land nearby and financing its purchase. A second method involves the custom use of machinery. Instead of every farmer owning his own machine, some or all of them hire machine-owners to do mechanical work for them. The machine-owners may be neighbouring farmers or non-farmers living in the community. The chief technical difficulty in the way of a wider use of this method is the need for timeliness in performing farm operations. Seeding and harvesting, in particular, have to be done at a particular time and within a limited period of time if best results are to be obtained. The result is that all farmers tend to want the machine at the same time. Despite this obstacle the custom use of machinery has expanded rapidly of late. Some idea of the technical possibilities may be obtained from the numerous reports of actual achievements. One recent report[3] states that, by equipping the tractor with lights and operating twenty-

[3]Pamphlet entitled "Community Farming" published by several farm organizations and obtainable from the Agricultural Representative, Barrie, Ontario.

four hours a day, one custom outfit in Simcoe County, Ontario, has done all the heavy tillage work on more than a dozen farms for the past two years. Further evidence of the increasing popularity of custom work is seen in recent attempts to establish scientific charges and to arrange a schedule of operations well in advance of actual performance.

The method whereby state-owned machines would do custom work under the supervision of County Agricultural Committees has not yet developed in this country. An interesting development along this line has recently taken place in Great Britain, where the County Agricultural Committees set up by the government have established tractor pools. The tractors and the trained operators are supplied by the government while the County Committees make the necessary arrangements with farmers who have tractor work to be done. In view of the fact that Agricultural Committees of County Councils already exist in many parts of Canada it would be quite possible to follow the British precedent here. The County Committees could own and operate pools of all the more expensive machines. It is interesting to note that in 1942 the Quebec Government purchased and operated a number of bull-dozers, which are very expensive machines. Farmers who wished to employ these machines made the necessary arrangements through the Agronomes of the several counties.

Quite a different method of dealing with the machinery problem is that whereby several farmers undertake to buy and use the more expensive machines co-operatively. While this method has been applied to a limited extent for many years, it is only recently that we have begun to consider seriously the potentialities of the plan or the rules of procedure that should be followed when using it. For the most part only a few types of machines such as corn binders, ensilage cutters, potato planters and diggers, and, occasionally, threshing machines, have been owned and operated co-operatively. Moreover, there have been comparatively few cases where the co-operative use of machines has been scientifically arranged. Where the plan has not worked satisfactorily the chief criticism has been that the machine was not fit to use when needed, that it wore out too fast, that it was not carefully housed, or that some farmers used it more than others. It would seem that much of the trouble could be avoided if the farmers in the group made a business-like arrangement regarding the operation, repair, and upkeep, and divided the cost in proportion to the amount of work done. Much more of the trouble could be avoided if one member of the group were given full responsibility for operating the machine and keeping it in proper condition. That there is an increased trend in the direction of more and better co-operative use of machinery is indicated by recent developments. Particularly significant is the fact that within the past year a special set of by-laws covering the Co-operative Ownership and Use of Farm Machinery[4] has been drawn up and has received considerable publicity.

Still another method of dealing with the machinery problem involves the purchase of a large number of small farms and their operation as a unit on a corporation basis. There is already some trend in this direction in Canada, the outstanding example being that of the

[4]Available from the United Farmers Co-operative Company, Toronto.

Colonization Finance Corporation in Western Canada. This plan, of course, in addition to providing for fuller use of machinery, should make it possible to obtain all the economies that accompany adoption of the specialization principle. Apart from other disadvantages, however, it is open to the serious objection that its adoption would mean the disappearance of the family farm unit and the family farm life which is based upon it. In view of the many individual and social advantages of retaining the family farm it is to be expected that corporation farming will be resorted to only if and when other methods have proved unworkable or insufficient. Expansion of any or all of the other methods suggested will go a long way in solving the farm machinery problem, and all will permit the retention of the family farm. If, however, we desire to keep the family farm and all its desirable contributions and at the same time secure anything like the full advantages which would come from a general application of the specialization principle, it would seem necessary to develop along co-operative farming lines. While this would represent a departure from traditional practice and mean a partial loss of the farmer's present independence of action, it would preserve most of the virtues of the family farm while bringing added benefits of a technical, economic, and social character. In essence it would represent the application of the partnership basis of business organization to farming. It would be a way of bringing to the small farm at least the main advantages of the larger unit.

That co-operative farming is far from unthinkable is shown by several contemporary experiments. A recent issue of *Farm Forum Facts* reports that thirty Alberta farmers are planning a co-operative farm specializing in hog production. The very considerable development of community pastures in both the United States and western Canada in recent years further indicates the trend. There can be little doubt that the future will see a speeding up of the various plans mentioned above. All of them have received at least some application, and all are receiving an impetus from wartime developments.

Other Post-War Trends

Present indications are that post-war agriculture will become even more specialized by product and by regions and more commercialized. We are also likely to witness a renewed emphasis on productive efficiency and a fairly realistic attempt to conserve agricultural resources. Sub-committees on agricultural rehabilitation and conservation have already been established as part of the Dominion Government's general reconstruction programme, and it is logical to expect that programmes aiming at soil conservation and proper use of land will constitute an important part of their recommendations. That farming will become more specialized and commercialized and that farmers will seek greater efficiency in production is indicated by several current developments. Urban centres, for example, are likely to increase in number and size, and farming always becomes increasingly specialized in areas adjacent to such centres. Also many eastern farmers may find it difficult or impossible to produce livestock and livestock products as cheaply as their new competitors in western Canada and, if so, they will be compelled to adjust themselves by producing special products in line with their comparative advantages. Moreover, new developments along nutritional lines and the trend towards industrial uses of farm products will call for more specialized production. One commercializing influence is the fact that a sizable number of city people with considerable capital and accustomed to business methods will have become engaged in farming. This fact will be especially true of areas adjacent to the larger urban centres of eastern Canada. Another is the fact that wartime needs have forced farmers to think in terms of producing for sale rather than for home use. Still another is the war-induced education in respect of farm prices. Farmers are being educated to study price levels and price information is more complete and being more widely disseminated than ever before. Again, as already indicated, the war will leave farming more mechanized and the new machinery will compel farmers to operate so as to use it more efficiently. Finally, the future will see an increase in the number of hired farm workers, who are likely to become organized and to demand higher wages and better working conditions than they had formerly. This, in turn, will force farm-owners to farm more efficiently in order to supply the increased wages and better labour conditions. It might also be mentioned that the present increased emphasis on farm income taxes is forcing more attention to farm bookkeeping. Should farmers learn to keep books during the war, they may continue the practice in the post-war years, and hence an important step towards the development of business management as distinct from technical farm management will have been taken.

While agriculture is likely to become increasingly scientific and commercialized, it does not follow that

Canadian farmers will be characterized by an unhealthy type or degree of materialism. What they will and should strive for is a standard of social and economic well-being comparable to that of other classes in the nation. The great majority have yet to secure a reasonable minimum of the recognized essentials of ordinary living. In particular there is a pressing need for improved educational and recreational facilities and health services in the rural areas. That the future will see campaigns for improvement on the part of farm organizations is clearly indicated by the recent development of interest and action programmes in these matters.

Conclusion

Much of the foregoing is necessarily speculative and conditional. Several major factors are likely to play a large part in determining the physical pattern and economic status of Canada's post-war agriculture. It is clear that post-war agriculture will be conditioned by the general nature of the agricultural set-up at the end of the war. Much will also depend on the extent to which the special experience gained and methods employed during the war are considered desirable and are actually applied in time of peace. Another important factor will be the extent to which the present universal declaration in favour of a better economic deal for the less privileged classes results in concrete action. A further influence will be the degree of success achieved in securing satisfactory international trading arrangements and the resulting export markets for farm products. Finally, much will depend upon the nature and success of national programmes designed to prevent a general post-war business depression and its accompanying unemployment.

Chapter X

A LONG-TERM POLICY FOR CANADIAN INDUSTRY

Francis Hankin

Perhaps the future historians of our times will record that the most significant outcome of the two World Wars was the death of *laissez-faire*, the passing of the belief that the capitalist, the manufacturer, or the entrepreneur could do as he liked with his own. The First World War dealt a resounding though not a knock-out blow to this belief. But enough adherents of uncontrolled individualism survived to prevent the full social regulation of misused power, whether economic or political.

The persons who stood in the way of adapting our political systems and our methods of production and distribution to the new conditions created by mass production and rapid transportation and communication were ignorant rather than malevolent. The captains of industry and finance did not see the need for maintaining the purchasing power of the citizens within their own country or of their buyers abroad. They charged prices that were too high or paid wages that were too low; they impoverished foreign buyers of their goods by refusing to purchase the products these customers had to sell. Unwilling or unable to take a long-term view of the conditions surrounding their activities, they were helpless before the advent of a depression which they themselves had brought on by thus constricting purchasing power. As a consequence, the wealth they sought to retain or enlarge withered in their hands first through depression, and then as a result of the war which followed in the train of discontent.

The Second World War is totalitarian in scope because it was begun by dictators who have absolute command over the economic systems of their nations. These systems have utilized modern techniques and controls so that they can provide the necessities for survival with the work of only one-third of the adult population. The remaining two-thirds have been commanded to fight or to produce weapons of warfare. In order to attain victory it has been necessary for the governments of the United Nations to impose compulsion on their citizens on a similar scale. Thus even in the democracies industry has had to accept the national obligation of helping to win the war. And, if its leaders are to show greater wisdom than was in evidence after the last war, post-war industry must accept the national obligation of winning the peace.

Post-War Demand for Full Employment

What duties does this obligation impose upon industrialists? Their nature and scope are becoming clearer as our war effort reaches its zenith. Broadly stated they are comprehended in the obligation to provide full employment and a decent standard of living for all. This is no nebulous generalization that can be pushed into a musty pigeon hole after the war is over. The citizens of the United Nations who have seen full employment provided for purposes of destruction in two

World Wars are not likely to accept any excuses for unemployment on any considerable scale when peace comes. If private enterprise cannot give jobs to everyone the state will be called upon to do so, and, as a consequence, will be compelled to take over and administer larger and larger areas of industry. Should the old plea be advanced, that the nation cannot afford to pursue such a course, it will be laughed to scorn, for the people will point out that any country which can afford to spend millions daily on war can equally afford to spend the same sums in peacetime in order to prevent unemployment which, through distress and discontent, leads to war.

If it is to preserve its autonomy private enterprise must make preparations now so that it may play its proper part in maintaining full employment. Each plant or industry in Canada should be prompt in making complete plans in order that, when peace comes, it may turn as soon as circumstances permit from the production of war material to the manufacture of peacetime goods. And, following the example of the General Electric Company and other large American enterprises, each plant ought to collaborate with the other units in its industry for the purpose of planning to expand production so that it may continuously employ its fair share of the Canadian working population which will include not only all the workers the plant normally employs but also a proper proportion of demobilized soldiers or disbanded munition workers.

In order to provide such full employment a third duty will fall upon the shoulders of the managers of Canadian enterprises. They must be prepared to submit to disciplines that will regulate their prices, their profits, and their demand for capital facilities in such a manner as to provide, through the payment of adequate and regular wages, a high and continuous purchasing power for consumer goods so that employment may be as full and constant as possible, and the standard of living as high as conditions will permit.

The source of such disciplines is the state. It may forego the use of its power as it did during the ascendency of *laissez-faire*; it may delegate the power to impose disciplines as it has done to many professions; or else it may exercise the power itself directly as it does when public utilities are regulated by government commissions. The managers of our Canadian enterprises must recognize that government has just as much reason to regulate industry as to assist it. Hitherto, business has asked for favours—tariffs, quotas, embargoes, "easy money", relief from taxation—but it has generally resisted any form of regulation, e.g., of prices or profits or through compulsory insurance, as being an unwarranted invasion of the rights of property. If regulation is necessary in order to get full employment, businessmen must accept it and co-operate with government so that it may be imposed in the most efficient way. Should they be unwilling to do this, they may wake up one day to find themselves compelled to submit, not to regulation that leaves them a large measure of autonomy, but to expropriation by the state which will completely destroy their independence and freedom.

Already the circumstances of war have compelled the government to make great inroads upon the autonomy of all Canadian enterprises. They must accept a considerable amount of regulation which is likely to grow greater rather than less before the war ends. Indeed, it may become so comprehensive as to make all enterprises organs of state. But when peace comes two schools of political thought will seek office. In one group will be those who will want to perpetuate the power of government over industry which war made necessary, and among them many may demand full government ownership and administration of large sections of business and finance. In another group businessmen will clamour for the abolition of regulation as soon as possible. Which side is likely to prevail?

Structure of Post-War Industry

Since we are not ready to embrace dictatorship, either Communist or Fascist, we shall probably follow the usual democratic middle-of-the-road policy no matter which party comes to power. It is not likely that wartime controls will be relaxed with the speed with which they were discarded after the last war; they will be retained to prevent inflation, to spread employment, and to assist orderly demobilization. As circumstances permit they will no doubt be progressively diminished so as to give entrepreneurs as much freedom of administration as will be conducive to efficiency and equity in production and distribution. The red tape of wartime operation will largely disappear, but we shall not revert to the socially unregulated conditions of pre-war days.

Therefore, unless victory should go to those who would hand over the administration of all productive enterprises to the state, we shall probably find that our economic system will embrace many kinds of operation, and many kinds of discipline to make operation efficient. Our system will not be one of dull and plodding uniformity. It will have the attractive diversity of a mosaic. The outstanding methods and disciplines will probably be: (1) full and fair competition, (2) government-regulated monopolies, (3) industries imposing disciplines upon themselves through self-government, and (4) enterprises administered by the state.

Competition is favoured by most businessmen who want to be free from interference by government. But if it is to be an effective method of disciplining their practices, it must be full and fair. No concern, because of its size, ought to be able to dominate a market; no industry should be unduly protected against foreign competition; and unfair competition carried on by a powerful unit for the purpose of destroying competitors should be prevented. If, instead of regulating them, it should be decided to dissolve monopolies, care must be taken to see that full competition is restored in such a manner as to become an effective self-regulating discipline which will result in reasonable prices, adequate wages, and a proper standard of products and services.

In many areas of economic life competition is intentionally set aside because, if allowed to exist, it would be wasteful. The avoidance of competition is deliberately brought about by the state when it allows only one public utility providing water or gas or light and power or other services to operate within a certain area. When the discipline of competition is removed in this way, so long as the utility is operated by private enterprise, regulation takes its place, for the rates and standards of service of the utility are subject to approval or modification by a public utility commission established by government. Regulation has not always been an effective means of assuring that public utilities will provide proper service at reasonable rates, because political interference, nepotism, or bribery and corruption may interfere with the work of the commissioners. But even when these practices were most prevalent, it was never suggested that monopoly privileges should be withdrawn and that competition should be relied on to give the public a proper service at reasonable rates. If regulated private enterprise fails, government will take over the monopoly and operate it.

Except in wartime the policy of regulation has not been applied to those monopolies which cannot be described as public utilities. They are numerous and important and figure largely among the two hundred giant corporations which control nearly fifty per cent. of the corporate wealth, nearly forty per cent. of the industrial wealth, and over twenty per cent. of the national wealth of the United States.[1] Canada also has a hundred big corporations of similar power.[2] With a more or less complete approach to monopoly they dominate such industries as heavy chemicals, cement, aluminum, primary iron and steel, etc. in Canada as well as in the other important industrial countries. Hitherto they have not been subjected to an effective discipline. Either they have been left alone as in England, or else, as in North America, government has relied on anti-trust laws, or has split them up into small

[1]See Berle and Means, *The Modern Corporation and Private Property* (New York: Macmillan, 1929).

[2]*Report of Royal Commission on Price Spreads* (Ottawa: King's Printer, 1935).

units in the hope that full competition would be restored. These measures have been inadequate and, as a consequence, the exploitation practised by "big business" contributed to the pre-war maldistribution of income. Common sense would seem to dictate that regulation of prices or profits or both must continue after the war or else the monopolies or quasi-monopolies which are in a position to exploit the public must be taken over and operated by government.

But in countries where a measure of private enterprise still exists, there are many undertakings that neither practise full and free competition nor constitute monopolies in the strict sense of the word. Their goods, such as automobiles, radios, washing machines, are sold at fixed prices over a season. There may be no definite collusion among the members of industries of this sort but nevertheless they do not engage in daily competition such as prevails on a commodity market or on a stock exchange. They practise "imperfect competition", and their prices set for a season are called "administered prices" because they are fixed by the administrations of the different undertakings and are not subject to the higgling of the market. Experience shows that these prices are too high and, therefore, are partly responsible for that malaise of our times which results from inadequacy in the distribution of goods. But it has been suggested that an adequate social control of such industries might be obtained through self-government, that is, each industry would impose measures of discipline on its members as the professions now do under the supervision of a government officer for the purpose of keeping prices low and standards high. Should an industry indulge in anti-social practices the government officer would recommend the application of such disciplinary measures as regulation of prices or profits, cancellation of patents, or reduction in tariff protection.

If none of the above disciplines should be sufficient to bring any particular private enterprise under effective social control, the state ought to expropriate and administer the delinquent undertaking. As the largest employer of labour, government has experimented with many forms of administration in order to avoid inefficiency and the evils of bureaucracy which are latent in all large enterprises. The chief forms it uses are administration by a department of government, by a semi-autonomous commission, or by a public company which is supposed to be run like any other incorporated company and to be quite free from interference by government.

In a class by themselves are the social undertakings operated by government for the purpose of providing services either without charge or at cost or less. Many of these undertakings such as education and policing must operate continuously, but others, such as public works and housing, may be timed so as to produce employment during a depression.

Most of the enterprises in the above categories are recipients of favours from government either in the form of protection against foreign competition or of stimulants used for the purpose of increasing demand when it is slack. At the same time they are subject to various forms of controls which government uses to protect the worker or the consumer.

The favour most commonly received by industry until the last depression was the protection from foreign competition provided by a customs tariff, embargoes, or quotas. When this protection was excessive it acted as a boomerang since indirectly it reduced the ability of foreign customers to purchase our goods. The newer favours which industry has received or may expect, take the form of stimulants to buying. Thus the central bank, now virtually under the control of government, may make money and credit plentiful during a depression in order to stimulate buying. Remission of taxation on expenditures for the purchase of capital goods or for capital improvement has also been used by the Dominion Government as a stimulant in a depression. New buildings and machinery are not needed when much of the existing supply is idle as in a slump. Then unemployment in the capital goods industries is great. But if manufacturers can be persuaded to build better buildings and install improved machinery in anticipation of a renewed demand, employment will increase. Low interest rates or remission of taxes may tempt them to do this.

Durable consumer goods, e.g., automobiles, radios, washing machines, form a larger proportion of the national production than capital goods. It is important to maintain the demand for them and to prevent violent fluctuations in that demand. Hitherto no stimulants have been used directly to encourage the purchase of such goods during a depression, although direct steps have been taken to discourage their purchase during war by cutting down the period of credit in instalment buying, by prohibiting manufacture, or by making it impossible through withholding raw materials. If a growth in sales is required to provide increased employment when business is bad, hesitant buyers might be induced to purchase if they were offered longer credit and possibly a special depression discount which would be withdrawn when business improved. If long-term co-operative action within the industries were possible, these discounts might be provided by the industries themselves and the sacrifice recouped during periods of prosperity. But if such co-operation proved to be impossible, the government might finance the discount and recover through luxury taxes imposed in good times. The principle would be the same as that relied on when taxation on capital expenditures was remitted.

Industry in Canada as in other countries has been progressively subjected to an increasing measure of government compulsion embracing voluminous Factory Acts to protect the health of workers, compulsory insurance against accidents and unemployment, and measures to protect the public from misrepresentation, fraud, and adulteration. During the war that compulsion has grown by leaps and bounds. Prices have been limited, excess profits taxed to the point of disappearance, workers and materials diverted from many channels to the production of war materials. How much of this compulsion will continue when peace comes? Control over workers and materials will probably remain only during the period required to bring about an orderly resumption of peacetime employment. But what about prices and profits and credit? Already the central bank tries to make the volume of money and credit in the country suit the condition of industrial activity, restricting it during booms and making it freely available during depressions. If the constitution is amended or interpreted to allow it to do so, government may enlarge or restrict facilities for instalment buying to check booms and increase buying during a depression. It should also tax the excess profits of all enterprises not subjected to full and fair competition in order to prevent exploitation, and to maintain among the mass of the people an effective purchasing power for consumer goods. If provincial authority over "property and civil rights" stands in the way of doing this, the constitution should be changed.

All the measures suggested are put forward as means of effecting a permanent improvement in our economic system and business practices so that unemployment may be removed and a high standard of living provided for all Canadians. Should it prove impossible to adopt these measures, or should they, if adopted, show themselves incapable of providing full employment, recourse must be had to employment reserves built up by private enterprise and the state. The former would arise out of the capital needs of industry for replacement and expansion. In order that these needs may afford an employment reserve available during a depression, it will be important for industry to defer or anticipate its capital requirements not merely to suit its own interests but also to assist in levelling out employment. Privately-owned utilities ought to follow the same practice, and of course the state should do so as well for its considerable requirements in public works, public utilities, roads, housing, and whatever it may decide to do for conservation.

Post-War Responsibilities of Particular Segments of Canadian Industry

Within the framework of an economic system such as that described, operating in a democracy and designed to preserve as much individual initiative as possible, what measures can be taken by particular segments of industry to ensure full employment? The problem of devising such measures falls into two parts, one concerned with the period of transition when we are returning our industries to their peacetime activities, the other concerned with the changes we shall have to make in our normal practices in order to avoid, or at least considerably diminish, the ups and downs of our business cycles so that severe unemployment and distress may not occur.

We should try to avoid the inflation that followed the last war so as to escape the disturbing effects of the short and sharp boom that accompanied it and the depression that followed. Our circumstances will be similar to those that existed in 1918. We shall have the same dammed-up desire to satisfy unfulfilled peacetime wants, and an accumulated though smaller fund of savings with which to buy the things we want. For a time there will be the same shortage of raw materials, shipping space, and labour skilled in the production of peacetime needs. No doubt we shall benefit from our previous experience and relax controls not precipitately but to suit developing circumstances.

We should not, however, put off the framing of our long-term policy, because what we intend to do in the decade following the peace will, to a large extent, govern the character of our transitional policy. And, if it is to be of any value, that long-term policy must be built from the ground up; in other words, it must consist of specific plans for each important industry and every government agency that provides employment which will fit into a general framework possibly somewhat similar to that already outlined. As mentioned earlier, some of the important American industries are already making such plans and we should follow their lead. Those plans are based upon an estimate of what the working population of the United States is likely to be after the war, the amount of national income necessary to provide each member with a decent standard of living, the proportion, judging from previous experience, which the industry and each unit within it should be responsible for, the physical amount of production represented by that proportion, and the actual things that production is likely to call for. The limitations of this chapter prevent a longer description of the plans which American private enterprise is making, a typical example of which is to be found in the recommendations of the Prince Committee of the General Electric Company.[3] But, concurrently with such planning, it is necessary, as already mentioned, to follow pricing, profit or wage policies which will provide a purchasing power adequate to permit these goods to be bought.

Planning of this sort should obviously be the responsibility of experts. Moreover, in order that the work of each industry may be correlated with that of all others, it should be co-ordinated by suitable national bodies. In Canada local efforts are stimulated and results collated by the Canadian Chamber of Commerce, the Canadian Manufacturers' Association and other na-

[3]R. P. Gustin and S. A. Holme, "An Approach to Postwar Planning", (*Harvard Business Review*, Summer 1942).

tional bodies. Furthermore, private enterprise should collaborate with government in its preparations, for the fight to end unemployment requires that all effort should be dovetailed so that the wastes of friction or overlapping can be avoided.

But even though detailed plans for particular industries cannot be put forward here, a few general observations upon the problems facing certain broad categories of Canadian enterprise may be of value.

Studies of what happened after the last war show that particular problems attach to certain large spheres of economic activity. The most important of these are concerned with the production of (1) non-durable consumer goods, represented by food and clothing, (2) durable consumer goods represented by such things as automobiles, washing machines, and radios, (3) capital goods represented by private dwellings, and machinery and the factories that house them. Further, we have the problems that arise out of the activities of government which have grown so greatly in wartime and which are concerned with (4) government war plant which will either have to be adapted to new uses or scrapped, except for that small part that will be retained for the continuous manufacture of war materials, and (5) the utilities and services commonly carried on by government.

Food Processers

Our supplies of food come mostly from agriculture which has special problems of its own, dealt with in another chapter. A large section of industry, however, is devoted to the processing of agricultural products. What plans ought food processers to make in order to play their part in bringing about full and continuous employment? Since they are more closely in touch with agricultural producers, they should be more aware than others of the need of keeping the purchasing power of these producers at as high a pitch as possible so that they may be large and continuous buyers of the products of industry. These manufacturers can help to increase the returns to their producers by improving the practices of their own normal business in two ways. On the one hand, they can make sure that their manufacturing processes are carried on in the most efficient manner, and that the prices they charge for their products include only a moderate profit so that the largest possible volume can be sold. And on the other hand, they ought to do their best, through collaboration with their competitors and with government, to eliminate the wastes of distribution that occur in some fields. Especially should duplication of delivery be eliminated in the sale of milk and bread. Probably some measure of compulsion by government will have to be used to remove this duplication. Compulsion has been used during the war, and was found necessary before the war in order to cut down the high costs of gasoline distribution due to duplication in Nova Scotia and some of the New England states.

Processing industries ought to co-operate with agricultural producers to develop industrial uses for their products. The need for such co-operation was seen before the war by the Canadian Chamber of Commerce which organized the National Chemurgic Committee for the purpose of making a survey of the possibilities of the industrial utilization of farm products. With the assistance of "the Canadian Society of Technical Agriculturists, The National Research Council, the

Canadian universities, agricultural experiment stations, the Federal and Provincial Government Departments, and the private and industrial laboratories" a report[4] was issued in 1941. It points out that new industrial processes are the result of four stages of development: (1) the idea, (2) development in the laboratory, (3) pilot plant experiment, that is, construction of a plant operating on a small commercial scale, but lacking the savings that come from large production, and (4) full commercial production. There are differences of opinion as to how far government should go in this work. Some people think it should stop at the second stage, others think it should be responsible for the third, but most are agreed that it should not embark on the fourth.

Mention is made of the work the United States has done in this field. The federal government has set up large laboratories in four different parts of the country manned with several hundred experts and assistants to study the problem of how to expand the industrial uses of agricultural products. Whilst we cannot hope to come anywhere near such an effort, it is suggested that a fully equipped laboratory be provided by the Dominion Government in Winnipeg for the purpose of developing new uses for Canadian agricultural products.

The report lists many industrial processes which could be put into commercial production within a reasonable time, those "unlikely to yield results of practical value in the near future" and "problems involving government policy". In the first group are described processes and improvements for the production

[4]*A Survey of Canadian Research on the Utilization of Farm Products*, Canadian Chamber of Commerce, 1941.

of many things including starch, plastics, briquettes, and drugs. In the last group are stated the problems involved in the production of alcohol from wheat and of linseed oil and soyabean products, in the increase of domestic consumption of fibre flax for textile purposes, and in the institution of a canned meat industry for western Canada. The National Chemurgic Committee will no doubt continue its work in co-operation with the Federal Committee dealing with Reconstruction.

The food processing industries, like all other industries, need capital goods and, therefore, by the timing of their purchases they can affect the economic life of the country advantageously or otherwise. To assist in stabilizing employment each plant should budget for its capital requirements for five or more years ahead. It should break up its capital needs into those for immediate, necessary in the near future, and remote expansion. The second of these, but more particularly the third, could be deferred during a boom and released during a depression. Such action may require managers to disregard short-term considerations, for example, as to whether the depression will last longer and prices go somewhat lower. Instead they should take into account the broader but more remote benefits that will accrue from a general revival of activity. The former attitude arises from mere opportunism whereas the latter betokens the presence of wise economic statesmanship which is so necessary if the method of individual enterprise and initiative is to survive.

Clothing

Clothing is our second necessity but our need for it is less urgent than our need for food. There is greater fluctuation in demand because we can defer the purchase of a new suit since we can be quite comfortable, even though we may not be quite happy, while wearing an old suit. When peace comes men in the armed forces will want to get back to "civvies" as soon as possible, as they did after the last war. And civilians who have watched their clothing go threadbare will want a new suit or frock. If all this demand is released at once we shall see a boom in the clothing business which will inevitably be followed by a depression as our previous post-war experience has shown. The obvious course to follow is to ration clothing, giving preference to demobilized service men. The capital needs of the textile and clothing business ought to be dealt with in the same way as that suggested for the food processing industries.

Housing

Shelter, our third indispensable need, calls for housing. It is a source of considerable employment, and, together with other construction, is a major contributor to fluctuations in employment. It is an activity carried on partly by unaided private enterprise, partly with public assistance, and partly by direct effort of government, whether central or local. In post-war England during the twenty years between the two World Wars four million new dwellings were built, one million by local authorities, half a million with some sort of public aid, and the remainder by unaided private enterprise. But even in this last category government can do much to stimulate or depress activity. Through the action of its central bank and by other means it has an influence upon the rate of interest which is the most important factor affecting the rent or the rate of return on houses. And many governments now guarantee mortgages in order to stimulate lending.

Housing, plus business and other construction, provide a substantial part of the employment of every nation. For example, in the United States during the years 1919 to 1933, the average annual expenditure for new residential and business construction was six billion dollars; add to this a further five billions for maintenance and repairs, and we have a total of eleven billions, or one third of the average capital formation and about one seventh of the average annual national income of those years. Construction occupies a place of similar importance in most countries, but what is of more significance than its size is the great fluctuation between boom and depression which occurs within the industry. Typical of such fluctuations is the expenditure of the United States for new construction. In 1925 it was over ten billion dollars but in 1933 it had dropped to two and one-third billions. Experience in Canada, though on a smaller scale, was similar. Obviously those concerned with construction must do what they can to iron out these fluctuations. The most powerful agency for doing this is government, and private enterprise should co-operate with it to the fullest extent of its ability.

Capital Goods

Factories and commercial buildings form part of the capital resources of industrial and commercial enterprises, and construction of such buildings is affected by the fluctuations in business prospects. The machinery housed within these buildings is the other important part of capital requirements. Workers engaged in providing these requirements are subjected to much fluctuation in employment if no control is exercised over capital expansion. The reason is clear. Because capital goods depreciate slowly but progressively over a period of ten to forty years, the people normally employed on the construction of factories and of machinery to be used in them, if working full time and at full speed, could furnish only a small fraction of the total capital used in any country. Therefore, a ten per cent. increase above normal demand for a commodity may result in full employment in the industry making the machinery required to fulfil that demand. Conversely, a ten per cent. drop in the normal demand for a commodity may cause a complete cessation of the production of the special machinery its manufacture requires, because the industry already has more than it can use. Thus, if fluctuation in employment in the capital goods industries is to be avoided or diminished, an attempt must be made by the concerns that need these capital goods to budget their requirements over a fairly long period, and to fill them regardless of immediate conditions and prospects. No doubt such a policy will involve co-operation between the units within an industry and the taking of some risks. But if all industries could be persuaded to take the same course in dealing with their capital requirements, the small disadvantages and risks associated with it would be more than offset by the benefits arising from the regularity of employment resulting from it. Moreover, efforts of this sort will have the blessing of government which has already helped employment in the capital goods industries by remission of taxation.

Durable Consumer Goods

A segment of industry which provides extensive employment and a considerable demand for capital goods is that concerned with the production of durable consumer goods, such as automobiles, radios, washing machines, refrigerators, percolators, electric irons, and toasters. The ability to produce and to purchase these things in considerable quantity indicates that a country enjoys a high standard of living. But it pays for this advantage by being subject to sudden unemployment because of the rapidity with which demand for these things can decline when perils threaten the economic future. It is easy to use last year's car, to put off the purchase of a new radio, and so on. When large numbers of people are seized with panic at the same time the demand for durable consumer goods diminishes very rapidly. So also does the demand for the capital goods needed to make these consumer goods with the result that much unemployment occurs.

The importance of this category of employment in North America can be seen from the figures of the annual average purchases of durable goods of all sorts in the United States during the years from 1919 to 1932. They amounted to twenty-three billions of dollars against a total for non-durable consumer goods chiefly represented by food and clothing of sixty-four billions.

For the purpose of bringing about stability in Canadian employment it is important that steps should be taken to prevent excessive purchases of durable consumer goods at the height of a boom, probably by putting restrictions on instalment buying as we have done during the war, and to try to expand purchases at the bottom of a depression by increasing facilities for instalment buying, and, if possible, by offering a depression discount as already suggested. If these measures should require government guarantee or subsidies similar to those provided for housing, the cost without question would be more than balanced by the improvement that would result in employment.

The State and Industry

Even before the war the state exerted a powerful influence on industry. Not only did it provide many of the essential services required through the public utilities and transportation systems it owned and operated, but, in its capacity as the largest employer of labour in the country, it was, through the salaries and wages it paid, the most important source of purchasing power for the goods which industry produced. And since the war, its relation to industry has become even more important because it has bought and built an enormous quantity of new capital goods capable of being turned to peacetime production when the war ends. In planning to provide full employment when peace comes the state, therefore, presents two problems. (1) What shall be done with wartime plants? (2) How can the normal activities of government help to provide full employment?

Obviously no policy can be formulated until we know what we have to deal with. A catalogue of war plants and an inventory of the contents of each should be prepared. Then experts should state to what peacetime uses the plant can be put (1) in its present state as a going concern, (2) by using the buildings alone as determined by local potentialities, (3) by dismantling and shipping the machinery and equipment elsewhere.

No doubt the best course will be to dispose of the plant as a going concern provided it is reasonably adapted to the uses to which it will be put, that its products will be in reasonable demand, and that its value will not have to be too greatly depreciated. If these conditions are found to exist two classes of plant can be disposed of without much difficulty, namely, additions to existing privately owned plants which can be sold by the government to the owners at a reasonable price, and those plants which the government decides to retain as arsenals for the production of war material necessary for future defence. But even when these two categories are deducted a large volume of plant will be left. This will include factories which can be easily adapted to peacetime production but with a capacity much greater than any conceivable domestic demand, and capable of helping to swamp foreign markets or of producing ruinous competition for them. Some of their products will be aeroplanes, merchant vessels, optical glass, aluminum, and magnesium. Since production will have to be regulated, these industries will probably be monopolies either operated by government as public companies, or if under private enterprise, strictly regulated so that exploitation may be checked. Another category will probably be plant that is found suitable for the institution of new enterprises such, for example, as those providing outlets for agricultural products. Private enterprise may be willing to take the risk accompanying such ventures and to purchase some of the plant and equipment at a fair price. But if the risk proves to be too great, it might be beneficial to Canada for the government to inaugurate the new enterprise even though a loss should occur for a few years, for it might provide considerable employment for persons producing the raw material, or else it might be the only way by which an industry, likely to be profitable when fully developed, would be started in this country. The justification for such action could be found partly in the possession by the government of buildings and plant that would otherwise be useless. Any plant that remains after all these avenues have been explored should not be scrapped until it has become obsolete. It should be kept in repair so that it will be available in case an industrial use for it should arise, and, in the meantime, it might be used for vocational training or for other social purposes.

Normal Activities of Government

Although the federal government in Canada, except in wartime, has refrained from entering the manufacturing industry, it and the provincial governments, in the discharge of the functions of government and the operation of public utilities and systems of transportation and communication, are large buyers of material and large employers of workers whose wages are spent on the products of industry. What government does in the operation of these undertakings has a considerable effect on the economic activities of the country. More than any other concern it is able to defer purchases and construction or to release them in advance of need in order to exert a stabilizing influence on employment. Hence, any national planning agency such as the National Resources Planning Board of the United States finds the main reserve, out of which employment may be provided when needed, in projects prepared ready for bidding and construction, not only for the central government but also for the state or provincial and local or municipal governments. The Reconstruction Committee at Ottawa created a sub-committee which has tried to persuade the federal and provincial Departments of Public Works and the local authorities to prepare projects similar to those mentioned, but it is doubtful whether as much progress has yet been made in Canada as in the United States. In spite of our preoccupation with the war, it is important that these preparations should be made to provide a means to prevent or diminish post-war unemployment.

As has been the case in other countries, housing ought to form an important part of such projects. Our pre-war efforts were fairly satisfactory except that they did not meet the housing needs of the persons in the lowest income brackets. Up to 1940 loans under the Home Improvement Plan totalled nearly fifty million dollars, and under the National Housing Act nearly sixty-four millions for new houses. Of the latter about forty per cent. were owned by persons with a yearly income of $1,500 or less. But very few houses were constructed out of public funds, and no subsidies were granted to allow persons in the lowest income brackets to lease houses within the scope of their purses. If the problem of housing for all income brackets is to be fully dealt with after the war ends, preparations must be begun now by all three parties to the problem. It has been suggested that "the proper division of responsibility be: *financial* to federal and provincial governments, *planning* to provincial and local governments."[5] This division is sound providing the allocation is not mutually exclusive. For example, the central government in England found it necessary to put some small financial responsibility on the local authorities; otherwise waste occurred. Likewise the federal government at Washington, through the provision to local bodies of expert advice and assistance, exercises some supervision and probably a certain amount of control over planning to ensure a reasonable chance of its reaching its social objectives. Moreover, housing of this sort is an aid to the alleviation of unemployment—a problem that can best be dealt with federally—as well as a means of providing "decent" homes.

* * * * *

Unless through apathy and ignorance we are defeated by reaction which in time will bring on another war, or unless we are so overwhelmed with the difficulties of social reconstruction that we are led to accept the easy solution of dictatorship whether fascist or communist, thus losing all personal liberty, we Canadians will follow the evolutionary method of leaving alone what is good in our political and economic structure and improving where improvement is necessary. This process will, I think, go on no matter which of the existing political parties gains office. If the Co-operative Commonwealth Federation comes into power we shall have an increase in state ownership and operation of economic enterprises, but a large field will be left for private effort which, however, will be socially regulated.

[5]Professor C. A. Curtis, "Housing in Canada" (in *Canadian Banker*, July, 1942).

If either of the other parties or a combination of them forms the government we shall have less government ownership and more government regulation. But should the government come under the control of those pre-war interests which were responsible for the depression of the thirties and the present war, the future will be bleak as we shall then face revolution and possibly another war. In my view this third course is unlikely because, if Canadians display their usual common sense and courage, if their present temper lasts and they persist in their demands for full employment after the war, those anti-social interests will be rendered impotent and will exist only as the wraiths of an unregretted past.

SELECT BIBLIOGRAPHY

This is not an exhaustive list, but simply a guide to readily accessible material on the subjects dealt with in the preceding pages. Some works have been included on non-Canadian post-war plans, where these were felt to illuminate the Canadian problems. For further reading, the student is referred to a carefully selected bibliography by Professor R. Flenley, *Post-War Problems: A Reading List*, published in April, 1943, by the Canadian Institute of International Affairs.

I. General

BOOKS, PAMPHLETS, AND REPORTS

Ashley, C. A. (ed.), *Reconstruction in Canada*. Toronto: University of Toronto Press. 1943. 145 pp.
—This book covers such topics as the general economic setting to reconstruction in Canada, international economic collaboration, democratic institutions, soil, water, and forest resources, construction projects, the social services, housing and town planning, and a recapitulation and statement of the ideals of reconstruction.

British Columbia Government; Post-War Rehabilitation Council, *Interim Report*. Jan., 1943, 201 pp. *Appendix to Interim Report*, Jan., 1943, 422 pp. Victoria: Parliament Buildings.
—The *Appendix* contains the documentation of the Council: representations of witnesses, reports, proposals, statistical data, and so on. The *Interim Report* presents an analysis of the probable post-war situation in the province, with attention to each aspect of its economy, and concludes with a "Summary of Recommendations."

CANADA, HOUSE OF COMMONS, SPECIAL COMMITTEE ON RECONSTRUCTION AND RE-ESTABLISHMENT, *Minutes of Proceedings and Evidence*. Ottawa: King's Printer.
1942, Nos. 1—13 (meetings from April to July, 1942).
1943, Nos. 1—24 (meetings from March to July, 1943).

CANADA, ROYAL COMMISSION ON DOMINION-PROVINCIAL RELATIONS, *Report:* Book 1—Canada, 1867—1939; Book 2—Recommendations; Book 3—Documentation. Ottawa: King's Printer. 1940.

DAWSON, R. MACGREGOR (ed.), *Canada in World Affairs: Two Years of War 1939-1941*. Toronto: Canadian Institute of International Affairs. 1943. 342 pp.
—Although not specifically a post-war study, this volume describes the political, economic, and social developments of Canada during the first two years of war, and is therefore useful in indicating the conditions that may prevail when the war ends.

FLENLEY, R. (compiler), *Post-War Problems: A Reading List*. Toronto: Canadian Institute of International Affairs. April, 1943. 62 pp.
—This bibliography, arranged topically and annotated, provides a useful guide to the most significant post-war material in print up to Feb., 1943. See especially sections VI ("Economic: Principles, Problems, and Proposals"), and VIII: (ii) (Canada).

LOWER, A. R. M. and PARKINSON, J. F. (eds.), *War and Reconstruction, Some Canadian Issues*. Toronto: The Ryerson Press. n.d. (1942?). 106 pp.
—Addresses given at the Lake Couchiching Conference held in August 1942 under the auspices of the Y.M.C.A.

UNITED STATES GOVERNMENT: NATIONAL RESOURCES PLANNING BOARD, *National Resources Development Report for 1943* (78th Congress, 1st Session, Document No. 128). Washington: Government Printing Office. 1943.
Part 1—Post-War Plan and Program; Part 2—Wartime Planning for War and Post-war; Part 3—Security, Work, and Relief Policies.

.........*Prepare Now: A Suggested Policy for Post-War Reconstruction.* Available from the Bureau of Information, Legislative Building, Edmonton, Alberta. n.d. (1943?) 72 pp.
—The resolutions, which form the basis of this booklet, were adopted at a public conference on Post-War Reconstruction held in Edmonton.

ARTICLES

Canadian Chartered Accountant
"The Planning of Canadian Reconstruction Policies" by F. Cyril James. Oct. 1942, pp. 250-64.

Canadian Forum
"Planning Post-War Canada", April, 1943, pp. 11-16.
"Planning Post-War Canada: What is a Planned Economy?" May, 1943, pp. 38-41.
"Planning Post-War Canada: How Can We Get a Planned Economy?" June, 1943, pp. 62-5.

Foreign Policy Reports
"What Canadians Think About Post-War Reconstruction", March, 1943.
—In the Maritime Provinces, by C. F. Fraser; in French Canada, by E. Turcotte; in Ontario, by B. K. Sandwell; in the Prairie Provinces, by G. V. Ferguson; in British Columbia, by B. Hutchison.

Public Affairs
"Canadian Post War Organization", n.d. (1943?) 124 pp.
—A special issue of this publication of the Institute of Public Affairs, Dalhousie University.

II. AGRICULTURE AND OTHER PRIMARY INDUSTRIES

BOOKS, PAMPHLETS, AND REPORTS

BOOTH, J. F., *Canadian Agriculture in the Post-War Period.* 1941. 10 pp. mimeo.
—Address at the Annual Meeting of the National Dairy Council, Oct. 28, 1941.

CANADA, DEPARTMENT OF AGRICULTURE, AGRICULTURAL SUPPLIES BOARD, *Objectives for Canadian Agriculture in 1943.* Ottawa: King's Printer. 44 pp.
—The reports, dealing with various commodities, as considered and approved by the Conference held by the Agricultural Supplies Board, with the Provincial Departments of Agriculture and the Canadian Federation of Agriculture, Dec. 7-9, 1942.

LLOYD, TREVOR, *Canada's Last Frontier.* Toronto: Canadian Institute of International Affairs. 1943. 32 pp.
—Examines the present condition and post-war possibilities of the Canadian North-West.

NESBITT, L. D., *What's Ahead for Prairie Agriculture?* Alberta Wheat Pool. 1942. 14 pp.
—Address at the Annual Convention of the Alberta Association of Municipalities, Nov. 19, 1942.

O'NEILL, J. J., *The Exploitation and Conservation of Mineral Resources in a Balanced Development of Canada* (Proceedings and Transactions of the Royal Society of Canada, 3rd Series, Ottawa, 1940, Sec. 4, pp. 1-14).

PETERSON, C. W., *The "New Order" and its Problems.* Calgary: Farm and Ranch Review. 1942. 80 pp.
—An economic study, based on the Canadian experience.

UNITED CHURCH OF CANADA, *The Farmer in the National Life: A Report of the Economic and Social Research Commission Appointed by the Board of Evangelism and Social Service.* Toronto: The United Church. 1942. 22 pp.
—A study of farm conditions in Canada, having as its object the recommendation of measures whereby the farmer's standard of living may be improved.

.... *Guelph Conference Report on Conservation and Post-War Rehabilitation.* Toronto. 1942. 15 pp.
—A brief survey of existing conditions with regard to dessication, floods, forest, wild life, etc., and demand for planning for the future.

ARTICLES

Canadian Journal of Economics and Political Science
"The Economic Problems of Canadian Agriculture in the War and Post-War Period" by J. F. Booth. Aug. 1942, pp. 446-59.

Food for Thought
"Agriculture Looks to the Future" by E. A. Corbett. Dec. 1942, pp. 7-11. (reprinted from *Round Table*, Sept. 1942).

Foreign Affairs
"Agricultural Surpluses in the Postwar World" by Leslie A. Wheeler. Oct. 1941, pp. 87-101.

Forestry Chronicle
"Post War Rehabilitation", March 1943, pp. 7-55.

Journal of Farm Economics
"Agricultural Program for the Postwar Period" by E. C. Young and J. C. Bottum. Feb. 1942, pp. 17-34.
"Canadian Agricultural Post-War Planning" by J. E. Lattimer. Feb. 1943, pp. 326-37.
"Transition to the Post-War Agricultural Economy" by John D. Black. Feb. 1942, pp. 52-74.

Pulp and Paper of Canada
"Natural Resources in the Scheme of National Planning" by J. S. Bates. April 1943, pp. 359-62.

Saturday Night
"Can Farm and Labour Interests be Reconciled?" by Paul Murphy. July 3, 1943, p. 26.

III. SECONDARY INDUSTRY

BOOKS, PAMPHLETS, AND REPORTS

CANADA, ROYAL COMMISSION ON PRICE SPREADS, *Report*. Ottawa: King's Printer. 1935. 506 pp.
—See especially Chapter IV (Industry).

CANADIAN CHAMBER OF COMMERCE, *A Program for Reconstruction.* 1943. 34 pp.
—As submitted to the Special Committee on Economic Re-Establishment and Social Security of the Senate, and the Special Committee on Reconstruction and Re-Establishment of the House of Commons.

CANADIAN NATIONAL RAILWAYS, *Brief presented to the Special Committee on Reconstruction and Re-Establishment* (*Minutes of Proceedings and Evidence*, No. 25, July 8, 1943).

CANADIAN PACIFIC RAILWAY COMPANY, *Submission of the Canadian Pacific Railway to the Special Committee of the House of Commons on Reconstruction and Re-Establishment.* Montreal: C.P.R. 1943. 11 pp.
—"Some information concerning this company's plans for post-war activities."

LEVER BROTHERS AND UNILEVER, *The Problem of Unemployment.* Toronto: Oxford University Press. 1943. 63 pp.

YENDALL, WILLIAM R., *The Common Problem.* Toronto: The Ryerson Press. 1942. 340 pp.
—The impressions and suggestions of a business man.

ARTICLES

Business Week
"Co-operative Plan under which Business and Government can Collaborate in Postwar Adjustment", June 19, 1943, p. 104f.

Canadian Business
"Industry's Share in Post-War Planning" by H. G. Cochrane. April 1943, pp. 56-7, 87.

Canadian Forum
"Wartime Controls in the Future" by H. Brockington. June, 1943, p. 66.

Continuing Study of Trends in Post-War Planning
(This is a new Canadian monthly published by the Association of Canadian Advertisers. Each issue contains a packet of Reprints from various sources, and an editorial, on some aspect of post-war planning.)

Industrial Canada
"Post-War Industrial Reconstruction" by E. S. Bates. April 9, 1943, pp. 19-20.

International Labour Review
"The Transition from War to Peace Economy: Analysis of an International Report" by E. J. Riches and L. B. Jack. July 1943, p. 1.

Plant Administration
"Must Relax Wartime Controls in Post-War Reconstruction Plan", Nov. 1942, pp. 14-15.
—A review of Dr. Cyril James's statements on the subject.

IV. Money and Finance

BOOKS, PAMPHLETS, AND REPORTS

British Exchequer, *International Clearing Union* (Keynes' Plan). New York: British Information Services. 1943. 32 pp.
—A reprint of the White Paper.

Canada, Royal Commission on Price Spreads, *Report*. Ottawa: King's Printer. 1935. 506 pp.
—See especially Chapters VI (The Primary Producer), and IX (The Problem of State Control).

Sandwell, B. K., *Post-War Finance*. Ottawa: Royal Society of Canada. 1942. 12 pp.
—A paper read at a joint session of the Royal Society in the Convocation Hall of the University of Toronto on Friday, May 29, 1942.

United States Chamber of Commerce, Foreign Commerce Department, *Summary of Various Current Proposals for Post-War International Action.* April, 1943. 78 pp.

ARTICLES

American Economic Review

"Basic Issues in Post-War International Economic Relations" by Robert Bryce. March 1942, pp. 165-81.

"Problem of Exchange Systems in the Post-War World" by H. S. Ellis. March 1942, pp. 195-205.

Bulletin of International News

"Wage Policy and Inflation in Great Britain, Canada, and the United States", May 29, 1943, p. 475.

Canadian Business

"Canada Weighs the World's Currency Schemes", May, 1943.

Canadian Finance

"International Currency?", April 7, 1943.

"Two Currency Plans", May, 1943.

Canadian Journal of Economics and Political Science

"Monetary Reconstruction" by H. Michell. Aug. 1942, pp. 339-50.

V. External Relations

BOOKS, PAMPHLETS, AND REPORTS

Canadian Institute of International Affairs, *Canada—Crossroads of the Airways.* Toronto: C.I.I.A. 1943. 24 pp.

—The implications of the world development of air transport for Canada.

Canadian Institute of International Affairs, *Canada and the United Nations.* Toronto: C.I.I.A. 1942. 62 pp.

—Report of the proceedings of the fifth annual conference of the Canadian Institute of International Affairs, held at McMaster University, Hamilton, May, 1942.

CANADIAN-UNITED STATES COMMITTEE, *Canadian-American Developments*. Canadian Chamber of Commerce. 1942. 10 pp.

—A report of the Committee, maintained by the Chambers of Commerce of Canada and the United States, summarizing major developments of the year and "indicating the directions and objectives of recent measures taken by the two nations."

CARTER, GWENDOLEN M., *Consider the Record: Canada and the League of Nations*. Toronto: Canadian Institute of International Affairs. 1942. 24 pp.

—Dr. Carter concludes her analysis of Canadian policy in the past with a summary of the lessons it teaches for the future.

SCOTT, F. R., *Canada and the United States*. Boston: World Peace Foundation. 1941. 80 pp.

STEWART, ANDREW, *Canada in a Hungry World*. Toronto: Canadian Institute of International Affairs. 1942. 20 pp.

—The repercussions on Canada of the world's post-war food problem, and alternative policies that may be adopted.

TAYLOR, GRIFFITH, *Canada's Role in Geopolitics: A Study in Situation and Status*. Toronto: The Ryerson Press. 1942. 28 pp.

ARTICLES

Canadian Historical Review

"Canada and Foreign Affairs" by Eric Harrison. June 1943, pp. 172-83.

Dalhousie Review

"Canada's Foreign Relations" by C. F. Fraser. April 1942, pp. 48-54.

Foreign Affairs

"Canada in the Western Hemisphere" by P. E. Corbett. July 1941, pp. 778-89.

Queen's Quarterly
"Canada and Foreign Policy" by A. R. M. Lower. Winter 1940, pp. 418-27.

Round Table
"Canada: What is her Future to be?", June 1943.

Saturday Night
"A Greater Canada's Place Among the Powers" by Lionel Gelber. Feb. 27, 1943.

VI. Constitution, Politics, and Social Services

BOOKS, PAMPHLETS, AND REPORTS

Beveridge, Sir William, *Social Insurance and Allied Services.* Toronto: The Macmillan Company. 1942. 229 pp.
—A reprint of the White Paper.

Canada, House of Commons, Special Committee on Social Security, *Minutes of Proceedings and Evidence.* Ottawa: King's Printer. 1943. Nos. 1—26 (meetings from March to July, 1943).

Canada, House of Commons, Special Committee on Social Security, Advisory Committee on Health Insurance, *Health Insurance: Report.* Ottawa: King's Printer. 1943. 558 pp.

Canada, Senate, Special Committee on Economic Re-Establishment and Social Security, *Proceedings.* Ottawa: King's Printer. 1943. Nos. 1—3 (March to June, 1943).

Canadian Federation of Mayors and Municipalities, *The Role of the Municipalities in Post-War Rehabilitation and Reconstruction.* Montreal: Canadian Federation of Mayors and Municipalities. 1943. 15 pp.
—A reprint of the brief as submitted to the Dominion Reconstruction Committee.

Cassidy, Harry M., *Social Security amd Reconstruction in Canada.* Toronto: The Ryerson Press. 1943. 197 pp.

DAVIDSON, GEORGE F., *The Future Development of Social Security in Canada.* Ottawa: The Canadian Welfare Council. 1943. 17 pp.
—Reprint from *Canadian Welfare,* Jan. 1943.

INTERNATIONAL LABOUR OFFICE, *Approaches to Social Security: An International Survey.* Montreal: I.L.O. 1942. 100 pp.

MARSH, LEONARD C., *Social Security for Canada.* Ottawa: King's Printer. 1943. 145 pp.

O'CONNOR, W. F., *Report Pursuant to the Resolution of the Senate to the Hon. Speaker by the Parliamentary Council Relating to the Enactment of the B.N.A. Act, 1867, Any Lack of Consonance Between its Terms, and Judicial Construction of Them and Cognate Matters.* Ottawa: King's Printer. 1939. 400 pp.

SAUNDERS, S. A., and BLACK, ELEANOR, *The Rowell-Sirois Commission*—Part 1: *A Summary of the Report;* Part 2: *A Criticism of the Report.* Toronto: The Ryerson Press. 1940. 45 and 37 pp.
—See also the Report (listed in the general section of this bibliography).

ARTICLES

Canadian Journal of Economics and Political Science
"The Party System and the New Economic Policies" by F. E. Dessauer. May, 1943, pp. 139-49.
"Judicial Review, Federalism, and the Canadian Constitution" by H. McD. Clokie. Nov. 1942, pp. 537-56.
(The issue of August 1943 contains the Papers delivered by F. H. Underhill and G. V. Ferguson before the conference of the Canadian Political Science Association of May 1943.)

Economist
"Social Security and the Canadian Constitution", June 19, 1943, p. 792.

International Labour Review
"Social Insurance and Assistance: Social Insurance Plans in Canada", April 1943, pp. 516-20.

Round Table
"Canada: The New Conservatism", March 1943, p. 168.

INDEX

ACT OF UNION, 1841, 9
Agricultural Supplies Board, 286
Agriculture:
  concurrent powers, 83-4
  domestic market, 274-80
  Europe, 140, 203, 231, 265, 268, 270-71, 273
  export market prospects, 266-74
  marketing methods, 280-83
  population, 91-2, 94, 175-77
  production and prices, 283-94
  wartime production, 264-65
Alaska, 132, 136
American Civil War, 7*n.*
Andrews, P. W. S., 166*n.*
Angell, J. W., 164*n.*
Argentina, 140, 231, 267-68
Associated Medical Services, Inc., 104
Atlantic Charter, 78, 122, 125, 131, 138, 155, 207, 211, 266, 271, 279
Attorney General for British Columbia v. Attorney General for Canada, 82*n.*
Australia:
  agriculture, 267-68, 273-74
  British Commonwealth affairs conference, 148, 151
  Labour Party, 39
  Loan Council, 84
Austria, 68

BACON, 269-72, 280, *see also* Agriculture
Balfour, Lord, cited, 50-1
Bank for International Settlements, 224
Barker, Ernest, quoted, 57
Beauharnois power development, 76
Beaverbrook, Lord, 125
Belgium, 206, 245-46
Bennett, Lord, 77, 136, 149
Bennett Employment and Social Insurance Act, 1935, 78, 98
Beveridge Report, 78, 87, 155, 194, 217
Bidwell, Percy W., 231*n.*
Bi-lateralism, 201, 206-208, 228-29
Board of Commerce Act, 1919, 71, 75
Borden, Sir Robert, 136
British Commonwealth Conference in Australia, 148, 151
British North America Act:
  amendment, 79-87, 109*n.*, 308
  constitutional bases for national controls, 73-9
  dominion authority, 74-6, 82-3
  financial relations between federal and provincial governments, 84
  militia and defence, 61-2
  provincial authority, 78, 85
  residuary clause, 62
  Section 92, 72
  termination of the war, effects of, 66-72
  treaty-making power, 72-3
  wartime centralization, 60-6
British Poor Law Commission, 1909, 102-103
Bryce, R. B., 180
Buell, R. L., 149*n.*
Bulgaria, 68
Burma, 147
Business cycle:
  control of, 20-1, 23, 26, 28, 29, 96, 165-68
  inter-war period, 12-13, 202, 235, 297-98
  Keynesian interpretation, 162*ff.*
  see also Employment and Industry
Butler, Harold, 149*n.*, 150*n.*

CAHAN, C. H., 152
Canadian Chamber of Commerce, 310, 312
Canadian Manufacturers' Association, 310
Canadian National Institute for the Blind, 101
Canadian Society of Technical Agriculturists, 312
Canadian Trades and Labour Congress, 126
Carter, Gwendolen, 127*n.*
Census of 1931, 90*n.*, 103

Census of 1941, 35, 90*n*.
Cheese, 272-74, *see also* Agriculture
China, 134, 139-40, 145, 219
Chinese Exclusion Act, 145
Churchill, Winston S., 123, 124*n*., 125, 129, 134, 139, 251
  quoted, 40, 138, 142*n*.
Civil Service Commission, 54-5
Claxton, Brooke, quoted, 46-7
Clemenceau, Georges, E. B., 122, 124
Clokie, H. McD., 80*n*.
Coats, R. H., quoted, 179
Coldwell, M. J., 45*n*., 144
Colonization Finance Corporation, 293
Combined Production and Resources Board, 134
Conservative Party:
  1867, 7, 9
  Port Hope Convention, 38, 135-36
  Quebec, and, 35-6, 156
Co-operative Commonwealth Federation, 35, 38, 39, 147, 156, 323
Corbett, P. E., 142
Cost-of-living bonus, 75-6
Cranborne, Lord, quoted, 149
Crerar, T. A., 129

DAFOE, J. W., quoted, 128
Davenport, N. E. H., 28
Dawson, R. MacG., 77*n*., 134*n*.
Defence of the Realm Acts (British), 60
Denmark, 132, 271-72
Department of Munitions and Supply Act, 64*ff*.
Doherty, C. J., quoted, 68
Dominion-Provincial Relations, Royal Commission on, 14-6, 61, 72-3, 74-5, 78-9, 83, 84
Duff Commission on the Hong-Kong expedition, 153

EDEN, ANTHONY, quoted, 151
"Education for democracy", 58-9
Emergency Powers (Defence) Act, 1939 (British), 62*n*.
Employment:
  applicability of American proposals to Canada, 178-85
  compensatory government spending funds, 185-91, 195-98
  full, 3, 24, 91, 154, 172-78, 208-209, 245, 275
  gainfully occupied, 90-5, 175-77
  international aspects, 213-17, 226
  long-term theory of, 161-62
  policy for the United States, 168-72
  private enterprise, responsibility of, 193-95, 298-301
  seasonal, 94-5, 174-75
  short-term theory of, 162-68, 256
  structural, 177-78
  see also Business cycle *and* Unemployment insurance
Employment Services Co-ordination Act, 1919, 98
Exchange Control:
  1914-18 experience, 234-39, 243
  1939 experience, 239-50
  post-war, 250-63
  see also Internationalism: foreign exchanges *and* Foreign Exchange Control Board
Export-Import Bank, 220
External Affairs, Department of, 153
External relations:
  British Commonwealth, 148-51
  Canadian-American relations, 134-36
  collective security, 126-28
  declaration of war, 122-24
  Far East, 144-46
  India, 147-48
  Pan Americanism, 142-44
  post-war world organization, 129-31, 136-42
  representation at peace conferences, 124-26
  South East Asia, 146-47

FAMILY ALLOWANCES, 107-108, *see also* Social services
Federalism:
  confederation, 7-10
  distribution of power, 24, 56, 75
  economic basis, 28-9
  effect on political parties, 34-5
  effect on public opinion, 41
  see also British North America Act *and* Dominion-Provincial Relations, Royal Commission on
Feis, Herbert, 224*n*.

Fenian raids, 7*n.*
Foreign Exchange Control Board, 65, 242-43, 245-46, 250
Fort Frances Pulp and Power Co. v. Manitoba Free Press, 68*n.*, 70-1
Fourteen Points, 122

Galt, Sir Alexander, 7
Gardiner, James, 129
General Electric Company, 299, 310
George, D. Lloyd, 122
Germany, 67, 203, 206, 251
Glazebrook, G. P. deT., 125*n.*, 126*n.*
Goering, Marshal, 140
Gold Standard, 187-88, 201, 222, 236-37, 241, 260-61
Gouin, Senator, 144
Government control of the economy, 4, 21, 23*ff.*, 31*ff.*, 300*ff.*
Graham, Gerald P., 132*n.*
Greece, 134, 140
Green, Howard, 144
Greenland, 132
Gustin, R. P., 310*n.*

Haberler, G. Van, 163*n.*
Hailey, Lord, 147
Haldane, Lord, 68, 70
Hansen, Alvin, 162*ff.*
Harriman, William A., 125
Harrison, W. E. C., quoted, 141, 151*n.*
Health insurance, 2, 33, 98, 102-107
see also Social services
Hitler, Adolf, 3, 133, 220
Hobbes, Thomas, quoted, 37, 197-98
Hodson, H. V., quoted, 148
Holland, 133-34, 206, 245-46
Holme, S. A., 310*n.*
Home Improvement Plan, 322
Hong Kong, 144, 153
Hopkins, Harry, 125
Hot Springs Conference, 125
House of Commons, *see* Parliament
Howe, C. D., 133*n.*
Hull, Cordell, 135, quoted, 137
Humphrey, John P., 130*n.*, quoted, 144
Hungary, 68
Hyde Park Declaration, 131, 248

Iceland, 132
Ilsley, J. L., quoted, 248
Immigration, 35, 83-4, 89, 277, 279
Imperial War Cabinet, 124*ff.*, 134
India, 147-48
Indo-China, 147
Industry:
capital goods, 316-18
clothing, 314-15
control by corporations, 25-6, 302, 304-305
durable consumer goods, 318-19
food processers, 311-14
full employment, 298-301
housing, 315-16
integration, 8, 9-12, 21
private enterprise, responsibility of, 309-11
rôle of the state, 300*ff.*, 319-24
structure in post-war, 301-308
see also Monopoly
Innis, H. A., cited, 135
Interest rates, 165-67
International Labour Organization, 126, 134, 143, 155
I.L.O. Conventions, 72-3, 83
Internationalism, economics, 266
collaboration, prerequisites of, 211-13
employment, 213-17
foreign exchanges, 221-24
investment, 217-20
trade barriers, 224-33
United Kingdom, 204-11

Jackson, Gilbert, 140*n.*
Jamaica, 168
Japan, 123, 132, 145-46, 205, 251

Keynesian Economics, 26, 162*ff.*
King, W. L. Mackenzie, 41, 124*n.* 127, 139, 149, 156
National Resources Mobilization Act, 64*n.*
price and wage controls, 39-40, 63
quoted re Canadian unity, 154
——— declaration of war, 123
——— isolationism, 128
——— Islands of St. Pierre and Miquelon, 153
——— post-war world, 129-31
——— war strength, 133
Knox, F. A., 183*n.*

Labour, Dominion Department of, 98

Laissez-faire, 6-7, 11, 13, 24, 213, 228, 297, 300
Latin-America, 134, 142*ff*., 219, 253
League of Nations, 127, 138, 142, 213, 218, 220
Lemieux Act, 1907, 83
Lend-lease, 125, 131, 209, 215, 223, 247-48, 252, 265
Liberal Party, 10, 14, 35, 156
Loan Council, Federal, 84
Lower, A. R. M., 144*n*.

MacDermot, T. W. L., 154*n*.
Macdonald, Sir John A., 136
Mackay, R. A., 127*n*., 134*n*.
MacKenzie, N. A. M., 154*n*.
MacKinnon, J. A., 143
Macmahon, Arthur W., 77*n*.
Malaya, 147
Maritimes, 7*ff*., 15
Marketing Act, 1935, 75
Marsh Report, 78, 155, 194
Martin, Chester, 123*n*.
Meade, J. E., 166*n*.
Mediterranean, 133
Meighen, Arthur, 66-7
Militia Act, 60
Molotoff, V. M., 125
Monopoly, 17, 19-20, 23-4, 26-8, 179, 201, 302*ff*., *see also* Industry: integration
Moore, W. H., 40*n*.
Mothers' allowances, 102, *see also* Social services
Munitions and Supply, Department of, 64-5, 244, *see also* War materials, production of
Mutual Aid bill, 249

Nash, Walter, quoted, 150-51
National Defence, Department of, 153
National Housing Act, 322
"National" policy:
common economic interest a prerequisite, 6, 10, 12, 18, 19, 21, 23, 29
1879, 7*ff*.
National Research Council, 312
National Resources Mobilization Act, 63*ff*.
National Resources Planning Board (U.S.), 78, 194, 322
National War Labour Board, 65
Nationalism, economic, 201-204
Netherlands Indies, 147
"New Deal", 13
New Zealand, 150-51, 273-74
Newfoundland, 132, 168
Nicolson, Harold, 140*n*.
North Africa, 133
Norway, 150, 245-46

Odlum, V. W., 145
Ogdensburg Agreement, 130-31, 138-39
Old age pensions, 2, 78 82, 100-101, *see also* Social services
Ontario, 7*ff*., 272-73
Ontario Hydro-Electric Power Commission, 220
Orders in Council:
Order establishing
——— priorities, 65
——— selective service, 64
——— wage freezing, 39-40, 64
replacement of, 74
wartime usage, 40, 62-3
Ottawa Agreements, 1932, 135, 271

Pacific War Council, 125, 134, 150
Pan American Union, 142*ff*.
Paris Peace Conference, 125*ff*.
Parkinson, J. F., 154*n*.
Parliament:
declaration of war, 123-24
decline in importance, 39-42, 63
delegation at peace conference, 126
Public Accounts Committee, 44-6
public service, and, 50-1
revitalization, 42-7, 151-57
special session, Sept. 1939, 60
under-secretaries, 47
Pemberton, J. S. B., 131*n*.
Permanent Joint Board on Defence, 130, 153
Poland, 134
Political parties, 34-9, 87, 156, 179-80, *see also* Conservative Party, Co-operative Commonwealth Federation, *and* Liberal Party
Prairies, 7*ff*., 264, 293-94
Price Spreads, Royal Commission on, 14, 17

Privy Council, 77-8
Public Accounts Committee, *see* Parliament
Public Service:
effect of the war on, 47-8
reform of, 39, 48-55

Quebec:
agriculture, 271-72, 291
allegiance to Liberal Party, 35-6, 156
confederation, 7*ff*.
conscription, 12
culture, 5-6, 15, 17-18
minority rights, 81-2, 86

Radio, 57-8, 155*n*.
Railway freight rates, 8, 10
Ralston, J. L., quoted, 246
Re-establishment of soldiers, 32-3, 155
Regionalism, 9, 14-18
Reid, A. N., 135*n*.
Reynolds, L. G., 179*n*.
Roosevelt, Franklin D., 122, 125, 171
Royal Canadian Air Force, 124, 141
Royal Canadian Navy, 132-33

Sayers, R. S., 166*n*.
Schlesinger, Arthur M., quoted, 141-42
Scott, F. R., 123*n*., 131*n*., 135*n*.
Security:
individual security defined, 4-5, 88-9
social security defined, 88
see also Social services
Senate, *see* Parliament
Siegfried, André, 127*n*., quoted, 138
Smoot-Hawley tariff, 135
Social services, 32, 33, 78, 155, 194-95
causes of need, 95-6
federal government, responsibility of, 83, 109-11, 116-18
gainfully occupied population, 90-95
provincial and municipal governments, responsibility of, 111-16
social assistance, 100, 107, 111-14
social insurance, 83, 96-100, 107, 109-11, 116-18
social utilities, 114-16
voluntary welfare service, 118-19
see also Family allowances, Health insurance, Mothers' allowances, Old age pensions, Unemployment insurance, Workmen's compensation
Soward, F. H., 124*n*., 154*n*.
Spooner Oils Limited v. Turner Valley Gas Conservation Board, 76*n*.
State medicine, 106-107
Sweden, 134

Tennessee Valley Authority, 220
Terborgh, George, 169*n*.
Thorson, J. T., cited, 127
Toronto Electric Commissioners v. Snider, 83*n*.
Trade Unionism, 20, 21, 56-7, 83
Treaty of Versailles, 66-7
Trinidad, 168
Trotter, R. G., quoted, 143
"Trustification," *see* Monopoly
Turkey, 68-9

Under-Secretaries, *see* Parliament
Unemployment insurance, 2, 13-14, 33, 73, 78, 97-100
Unemployment Insurance Act, 1940, 98
Union of Soviet Socialist Republics, 133, 139, 150, 156, 168, 219
United Farmers Co-operative Co., 292*n*.
United Kingdom:
agriculture, 267-71, 273-74, 291
industry, 303, 315
monetary policy, 235*ff*., 241, 249
see also External relations: British Commonwealth *and* Internationalism, economic: United Kingdom
United States:
agriculture, 267-68, 273, 285, 294
employment, 168-72
industry, 303, 310, 313, 316, 318
monetary policy, 236*ff*., 241
post-war, 253-54
see also External relations: Canadian-American relations
United States Supreme Court, 77

Viner, J., 228*n*.

WALLACE, HENRY, 122
War Exchange Conservation Act, 75*n.*, 246
War materials, production of, 200-201
1914-18, 238-39
1939— , 240-41, 245*ff*.
War Measures Act, 60*ff*.
Wartime Prices and Trade Board, 65, 244, 278, 286
Welles, Sumner, quoted, 137-38, 142
Wheat, 182-83, 266-69, 276, *see also* Agriculture
Wheat Agreement, 1942, 267-68
Whitman, Walt, quoted, 48
Wilkinson, Sir George Henry, 124*n*.
Willkie, Wendell, 137, 147
Wilson, Woodrow, 122
Woodsworth, C. J., 144*n*.
Workmen's Compensation, 101-102
World Economic Conference, 216

YUGO-SLAVIA, 134

C.I.I.A. PUBLICATIONS

The following are some of the publications of the Canadian Institute of International Affairs (230 Bloor St. W., Toronto) under whose auspices this volume has been published:

BOOKS

Canada, The Pacific and the War by William Strange, 1937, 220 pp. $1.75.
—An Introductory survey of the situation in the Far East and the way in which it affects Canada.

The Japanese Canadians by Charles H. Young, H. R. Y. Reid and W. A. Carrothers (edited by H. A. Innis) 1938, 295 pp. $2.25.
—A sympathetic account of the difficulties inherent in the problem of the Oriental—and especially the Japanese—in British Columbia.

Canada Today by F. R. Scott, 1938, 184 pp. $1.25.
—A study of the relations between Canada's internal forces and her position in the world.

The Wheat Economy by G. E. Britnell, 1939, 259 pp. $2.50.
—A study of the way in which wheat policies of other governments influence the standards of living and cultural adjustments of the population of Western Canada.

The Military Problems of Canada by C. P. Stacey, 1940, 184 pp. $2.50.
—A survey of defence policies and strategic conditions past and present.

Canada Gets the News by Carlton McNaught, 1940, 271 pp. $3.50.
—A description for the general reader of the way Canada gets her foreign news through the newspapers and the radio.

Canada and the Far East by A. R. M. Lower, 1940, 152 pp. $1.25.
—A study of Canada's relations with the Far East in trade, immigration and defence up to 1940.

The War: First Year by Edgar McInnis, 1940, 312 pp. $2.00.

—A detailed chronological history of the war, first year, with maps and documentary texts.

The War: Second Year (318 pp.) and *The War: Third Year* (347 pp.) each $2.00. Subsequent months are covered in the quarterly "Oxford Periodical History of the War". (25 cents).

Canada in Peace and War by Chester Martin, 1941, 244 pp. $1.50.

—A series of studies of Canadian national trends since 1914—Canada viewed in her federal and external relations, her economic policies, and her position in the Commonwealth.

Canada In World Affairs—The Pre-war Years (Vol. I) by F. H. Soward, J. F. Parkinson, N. A. M. MacKenzie and T. W. L. MacDermot, 1941, 343 pp. $3.00.

—A survey of Canada's international relations in the pre-war years .

Canada and the Orient by Charles J. Woodsworth, 1941, 321 pp. $3.00.

—A complete study of the Oriental problem in Canada from 1858 to 1941.

Canada In World Affairs—The First Two Years of War (Vol. 2) edited by R. MacGregor Dawson, 1942, 342pp. $3.00.

—A survey of political, economic and military aspects, and the external relations of Canada during the first two years of war.

The Inter-American System by J. P. Humphrey, 1942, 329 pp. $3.00.

—A discussion of the role of the Inter-American system in attempts at international organization with arguments for and against Canadian participation.

A History of Canadian External Relations to 1914 by G. P. de T. Glazebrook. 1942, 312 pp. $3.00.

—A study of the historical development of Canada's external relations up to 1914.

Canada at the Paris Peace Conference by G. P. de T. Glazebrook. 1942, 156 pp. $2.00.

—Canada's part in the Paris Peace Conference as part of her developing role in foreign affairs.

India Today by W. E. Duffett, A. R. Hicks, and G. R. Parkin, 1942, 110 pp. $2.00.
—A study of the background of the Indian Nationalist Movement in its social, economic and external aspects, and her role in the present war. The 1942 edition (John Day, New York) includes an account of the Cripps Mission.

Canada After the War edited by A. Brady and F. R. Scott (Publication date Nov. 1, 1943) $3.25.
—With the sub-title "Studies in Political, Social and Economic Policies for post-war Canada" this volume contains articles contributed by B. S. Keirstead, A. Brady, F. R. Scott, Charlotte Whitton, F. H. Soward, D. C. MacGregor, J. F. Parkinson, F. A. Knox, W. M. Drummond and Francis Hankin.

CONTEMPORARY AFFAIRS SERIES

No. 1 *How We Govern Ourselves* by G. V. Ferguson. (1939) 32 pp. .25.
—A description of the way democratic government works in Canada, evaluated against the totalitarian way of life.

No. 2 *The French Canadian Press and the War* by Florent Lefebvre, edited and translated by J. R. Biggar and John R. Baldwin (1940). (out of print)
—A digest of French Canadian opinions of the war as expressed in the Press.

No. 3 *War Finance in Canada* by A. F. W. Plumptre (1940) 110 pp. .75.
—A history of war finance in Canada in the years of the last war with an analysis of the principles and their application to the present war.

No. 4 *Good Neighbours* by D. Lawrence Burpee. (1940) 30 pp. (out of print)
—A description of the history, organization and powers of the International Joint Commission and its work on the boundary problems of Canada and the United States.

No. 5 *The Rowell-Sirois Commission* by S. A. Saunders and E. Black. (1940) 45 pp. .40.
—A Summary of the report, its historical background and recommendations.

No. 7 *Why War Savings?* by C. H. Herbert (1940) 14 pp. .10.
—The place of war savings in the fight against wartime inflation.

No. 8 *Canada's Trade Policy and the War* by L. B. Jack (1940) 18 pp. .20.
—Canada's trade and tariff structure with an analysis of war trends.

No. 9 *More Farmers for Western Canada* by Andrew Stewart. (1941) 32 pp. .25.
—A study of the possibilities of post-war agricultural settlements in the Prairie Provinces.

No. 10 *India Today* by Duffet, Hicks and Parkin (1941) 110 pp. (out of print) Now available in cloth bound edition—see book section.

No. 11 *Population—Canada's Problem* by Steven Cartwright (1941) 34 pp. .30.
—Canada's population studied in its relation to world population and her own economy.

No. 12 *French Canadian Opinion on the War* by Elizabeth Armstrong. (1942) 44 pp. .40.
—A study of the main lines of thought in French Canada developed through 22 months of war (up to June 1941).

No. 13 *French Canada and Britain* by Abbé Arthur Maheux (out of print).
—An historical approach to the problem of British relations with French Canada.

No. 14 *The New Western Front* by Griffith Taylor. (1942) 28 pp. .30.
—A geographical approach to probable Allied strategy in the invasion of Europe.

No. 15 *Canada and the United Nations* by W. E. C. Harrison, A. N. Reid, and an address by Hon. Walter Nash (1942) 62 pp. .50.
—A report of proceedings of the C.I.I.A. Conference, May, 1942.

No. 16 *Canada's Role In Geopolitics* by Griffith Taylor (1942) 28 pp. .30.
—A study in situation and status of Canada's position with an eye to her resources and future settlement.

No. 17 *Are Empires Doomed?* by Lionel Gelber. (1943) 32 pp. .40.
—A study of the problems of imperialism and colonial policy with emphasis upon war trends.

No. 18 *The Treatment of Post-War Germany* edited by R. Flenley. (1943) 67 pp. .50.
—Containing three articles by authorities on the economic, political and cultural aspects of this controversial question. The contributors are "Verax", R. A. MacKay and C. Lewis.

BEHIND THE HEADLINES SERIES

1942-43 Series (Vol. III)

No. 1 *Canada and the Short-Wave War* by Albert Shea and Eric Estorick.
—A resume and analysis of the part that short-wave radio has played in the war, and an examination of Canada's position in the battle of the short waves.

No. 2 *Family Allowances for Canada* by D. H. Stepler.
—The pros and cons of a system of payments of cash to parents for each dependent child.

No. 3 *Canada—Crossroads of the Airways* by the Information Service of the C.I.I.A.
—Wartime developments in Canadian civil aviation, the development of new air routes, and Canada's stake in the civil aviation of the future.

No. 4 *Canada's Last Frontier* by Trevor Lloyd.
—Actual and potential development of the Canadian Northwest.

No. 5 *Homes or Hovels?* edited by Anthony Adamson.
—A compendium of authoritative views on Canada's housing and town planning problems.

No. 6 *Security for Canadians* by Charlotte Whitton (Sept. 1, 1943).
—Proposals for social reconstruction in Canada.

No. 7 *The Unarmed Forces—Labour in Wartime* by D. M. Young. (October 1, 1943).
—A discussion of labour and trade unions in wartime.

No. 8 *Canada's Future in Test Tubes* by J. K. Robertson.
—The scientist's responsibility to the people—what has been done, and what must be done.

Next two topics planned for Behind the Headlines are *Immigration* and *Newfoundland*.

The Behind the Headlines Series is published jointly by the Canadian Institute of International Affairs, 230 Bloor St. West, Toronto and the Canadian Association for Adult Education, 198 College St., Toronto. They are priced at 10 cents for single copies and at 7 cents postpaid for bloc orders of ten or more copies.

Additional Recent Publications

Post War Problems—A Reading List compiled by Professor R. Flenley. 1943. .25.
—A selected list of the best of the books, pamphlets and periodical articles published on Post-War reconstruction up till the Spring of 1943. The material is carefully annotated, and arranged under main subject headings.

Canada—An Introduction to a Nation by the Information Service of the C.I.I.A. .05. Sept. 1, 1943.
—Brief and simply worded, this booklet was put out by the Information Service for the use of New Canadians, members of the Allied forces in training in Canada, and the general public throughout the Commonwealth and the United States.

Other publications of the Institute in the last three years include Volume I and Volume II of the Behind the Headlines Series, published in 1941 and 1942 (now out of print); The Democracy and Citizenship Series (out of print); Data Papers for the Institute of Pacific Relations Conferences, 1936 and 1939; Data Papers for the British Commonwealth Relations Conference 1938; Data Papers for the International Studies Conferences 1937 and 1939; Data Papers for the North Atlantic Relations Conference, 1941; Annual reports of conferences of the Canadian Institute of International Affairs; Bibliographies (mimeographed) on Post-War studies, the Far East, and Russia.